Christopher Columbus

ERNLE BRADFORD

Christopher Columbus

MICHAEL JOSEPH

This book was devised and produced by
Park and Roche Establishment, Schaan.
First published in Great Britain in 1973 by
Michael Joseph Ltd, 52 Bedford Square, London WC1.

Designed by Crispin Fisher

Copyright © 1973 by Ernle Bradford

Printed by Amilcare Pizzi, Milano, Italy

ISBN 0 7181 0771 3

Endpaper: *Caravels. Woodcut after Brueghel the Elder, c. 1550.*

Half-title: *Portrait of Columbus. Anonymous.*

Title-page: *Columbus lands on Hispaniola (Haiti) 6th December 1492. From Theodore de Bry, 1594 (detail).*

Opposite: *Using an astrolabe. From Pedro de Medina's* Regimiento de Navigacion, *1563.*

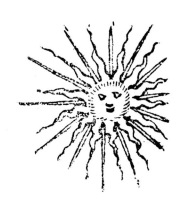

E volta nostra poppa al mattino,
dei remi facemmo ali al folle volo,
sempre acquistando dal lato mancino.

Tutte le stella già dell' altro polo
vedea la notte, e'l nostro tanto basso,
che non surgea fuor del marin suolo.

DANTE: INFERNO, XXVI, 124–129.

And turning our stern towards the morning we made wings of our oars
for our wild flight, bearing always to the south-west. By nightfall we had
raised all the stars of the other pole, while our own had so far declined
that it did not rise out of the ocean bed.

Contents

CONTENTS

List of colour plates

A Son of Genoa

In the autumn of 1451 the wife of a wool-weaver in Genoa gave birth to a boy who was destined to change the course of history. Susanna Colombo was herself the daughter of a weaver as was her husband's father. Both families came from Genoa or from the adjacent sea coast of the Genoese Republic. Their loyalties were not to Italy, for Italy as such did not exist. They were proud to call themselves citizens of Genoa, that city which was rightly known as 'The Superb'. Superb both in its wealth, its architecture, and in its pride. Susanna Fontanarossa had married master-weaver Domenico Colombo in 1445. If she had borne any previous children, they must have died in infancy, for this son, who was to be named Christopher, appears as the eldest in the records.

The name Christopher, which he was to make famous in lands hitherto unknown to Europeans, was so apposite that were one writing a work of fiction one would hesitate to bestow it upon the hero. The saint after whom the young Genoese was called was honoured in the Latin Church on July 25th, and was the patron saint of ferrymen. He was said to have been a pagan Syrian who had been converted to Christianity by a hermit and to have been martyred about 150 A.D. during the persecution that occurred in the reign of the Emperor Decius. A simple giant of a man, he was reputed to have found the austerities and spiritual exercises of a hermit's life beyond his capabilities, and to have dedicated to God the one gift that he possessed over and above those of his fellows – his strength. At the instigation of his teacher he set himself up at a ford on a bridge-less river, where he gave himself to the task of carrying travellers across from one bank to the other. On one occasion, asleep in the cabin that he had built, he heard a child's voice calling out and asking to be

Opposite: *Portrait of Columbus attributed to Sebastiano del Piombo (1485–1547).*

ferried across the river. Christopher picked up his staff, and went outside, and putting the child on his broad shoulders set out into the stream. When he was about half way across he felt his burden become almost unendurably heavy, and it needed all his strength to stop himself from falling and dropping his passenger into the waters that swirled around his knees. On reaching the far bank, panting with exhaustion, he deposited the child in safety and said in some amazement, "You have put me in great peril! Never have I known such a weight! Why, if I had had the whole world on my back I do not believe if it could have weighed more than thou!" "Marvel not!" the child replied, "for thou hast borne upon thy back the whole world and Him who created it!" As proof of his words the child told Christopher to plant his staff next to his cabin, telling him that by next day it would give him both shade and food. The ferryman did as he was ordered and on the following morning found that a spreading date-palm had grown in place of his old staff.

Christopher (meaning 'the Christ-Bearer') thus became the patron saint not only of ferrymen, but of all the world's travellers. No name could have been more applicable to the boy who began his life in a lower middle class household in Genoa, and who was to raise islands and a whole continent out of the depths of the Atlantic Ocean. The earliest known chart of the 'New World', which was dedicated to Christopher Columbus by his friend and shipmate Juan de la Cosa, has a drawing on it of Saint Christopher carrying the Child Jesus on his shoulders. And it was in his capacity as 'the Christ-Bearer' that Columbus saw himself in later years when he introduced to the pagan 'Indians' the religion of the crucified Jesus. That his faith was distorted by ignorant priests or twisted for their own ends by cynical speculators does not detract from the achievement of the Genoese mariner. Of one thing one can be sure in any analysis of the character of Christopher Columbus – his patent sincerity and his dedicated Christianity.

The world in which the young Columbus grew up was overshadowed by the massive advance of Islam into Europe. Spearheaded by the martial vigour and hardiness of the Ottoman Turks the Crescent was almost everywhere triumphant over the Cross. In 1453, when Columbus was a child of two, the greatest disaster of all happened: the city of Constantinople – for so many centuries, the bastion of Christianity in

Opposite: *Genoa in 1481 by Christoforo Grassi (detail)*.

Overleaf: *St Christopher, the patron saint of travellers, by Sano di Pietro (1406–1481)*.

MARCOCEANUM

AFRICA

ASIA

EVROPA

the East – fell before the all-conquering sword of Mahomet II, so soon
to be designated by obsequious and terrified Europe as 'Mahomet the
Magnificent'. Remote though Genoa was from the great city on the
Golden Horn, the effects of the fall of Constantinople (that ancient
Byzantium which the Emperor Constantine had made the first Christian
capital of the Roman world) were very soon felt by the merchants and
seamen – including the wool-weavers – of a city which, like its hated
rival Venice, depended upon trade with the East for its livelihood.
Genoa, again like Venice, was a great industrial and commercial centre.
It was against this background of keen mercantile rivalry and activity,
in a Europe constantly threatened by the ever-increasing power of the
Ottoman, that Christopher Columbus grew up.

His father Domenico was a master weaver and a member of the local
guild of clothiers. He was, it would seem, a respected citizen since, at a
later date when Columbus was nineteen, Domenico was appointed to
serve on a committee designed to investigate the conditions and regula-
tions adopted by the clothiers of Savona, with a view to incorporating
them into the Genoese industry. Christopher's birth was followed a year
or so later by that of his brother Bartholomew who was destined to play
a large part in his elder brother's life. There was also a sister, Bianchetta,
another brother who died while young and, finally, the youngest of all,
Giacomo who was born about seventeen years after Christopher. The
latter, who was also to accompany him on one of his voyages, is better
known by his later Spanish name of Diego. While little is known about
Susanna Colombo her husband Domenico emerges from the records as
a likeable but unbusinesslike figure; given to buying goods in excess of
his ability to pay, and of venturing out into activities that had little or no
connection with his real trade. In 1470, for instance, after the family had
moved to Savona, Domenico is described as a 'tavern keeper' and his
nineteen year old son Christopher signed a bill in acknowledgement of a
debt for wine delivered to the tavern. It is clear that even at this age that
quality of dependability which was part of his character had shown itself
to the world in general. Christopher's signature was regarded as more
reliable than his father's.

In appearance, as we know from the descriptions of those who met
him in later years, Christopher Columbus was singularly un-Latin. No
doubt, in the waves of invaders that had beaten upon the Italian coastline
over the centuries since the fall of Rome, some Germanic or other

Opposite: *The earliest known chart of the New World, dedicated to
Columbus by his friend and shipmate Juan de la Cosa, c. 1500.*

Nordic stock had become mingled with many of the families of the Ligurian coast. True, his nose was aquiline and his face long, but his hair was carroty red, his complexion ruddy rather than olive, and his eyes were blue. Despite the later claims by his brother and others that he had a good formal education there is nothing whatsoever to substantiate it. His Latin, as scholars have pointed out, was clearly learned after he had become a Spanish speaker, and there is hardly any Italian to be found in any of the writings that he left behind him. This is hardly surprising for Genoese was a spoken, not a written, dialect of Italian; it was a far call from the elegances of the language that Dante had forged in Florence.

It seems more than likely that Christopher had only a very rudimentary education, and that his subsequent proficiency in Portuguese and Spanish, as well as his acquisition of sufficient mathematics and astronomy to make him a navigator, were all the products of a self-taught man. The years that he spent in Portugal, coupled with the fact that his wife was Portuguese, made this his native language far more than Genoese. It has been pointed out that even the Castilian Spanish which he wrote was spelled in the Portuguese way. Yet if Christopher Columbus was to garner most of his maritime and navigational knowledge through his Portuguese connections – and later to deploy them in the service of Spain – he never forgot his initial debt to his birthplace. Despite some of

Venice in 1486. From Von Breydenbach's Journey to the Holy Land.

the unnecessary disputes which have arisen between chauvinistic scholars about Columbus's origins there can be no doubt that he regarded himself as a Genoese to the end. In the entail on his estate which he executed before his third voyage to 'The Indies' he directed that his heirs should always work for the honour, welfare and improvement of Genoa, "where I was born". They were also instructed to establish a fund in the great mercantile bank of San Giorgio in Genoa, which he went on to describe with evident pride as "that noble and powerful city by the sea".

It was in fact more than natural that one of the world's greatest sailors should come from Genoa. Although born into a weaving family and apprenticed to his father's trade, Columbus, no more than any other Genoese, could ever ignore the sight and the sound of the sea. It was both his city's bastion and her road to greatness. Sited at the foot of the Appennines, which provide its defence against attack from inland, Genoa gazes southward from the head of the gulf that bears the city's name. The range of hills that back the city were capped with forts and bastions. At sunset, when the light died behind the peaks, they sprang into grim prominence: a reminder of the city's power as well as of the dangers that constantly threatened her from her enemies in France and Milan. The great semicircular harbour that lay at the foot of the city bristled with masts and spars. Beyond its sheltering arms the sea would

nearly always be swaggering with the sails of merchantships homeward or outward bound, as well as dotted with the small triangles of lateen-rigged boats engaged in fishing or in the local coastal trade. It is more than probable that Columbus's first experience of the sea was in one of these as a boy, possibly on a run connected with his father's trade between Genoa and Savona.

Strikingly grand when viewed rising from the sea, the city was enriched by fine churches, some of them dating from the Middle Ages and others, which were to be built in Columbus's lifetime, showing the influence of the great Renaissance architects and artists. Politically, however, the city had long been unstable and by the 15th century it was on the decline. Its long conflict with Venice had ended in the latter's triumph and Venice was now the greatest European trading city in the East. So, with the eastern basin of the Mediterranean increasingly closed to them by the Venetians and by the Ottoman Turks, it was natural that the Genoese of this period should have looked increasingly in the other direction, towards Spain and to the newly emergent maritime power of Portugal. Force of circumstances, almost as much as natural inclination, was to cause the young Columbus, when he had put the weaver's trade behind him and taken to the sea, to look westwards towards the Pillars of Hercules – and beyond them to the long Atlantic swell.

Engraving of Columbus. From Caoriolo's Ritratti, *1596.*

Mahomet II. Woodcut from Nuremberg Chronicle, *1493.*

Apprenticed to the Sea

Because of its geographical position at the head of the gulf opening onto the Ligurian Sea and ringed by mountains at the back, the city of Genoa was destined by nature to become one of the earliest homes of sail in the Mediterranean. A large percentage of its winds came from the north and north-east, bustling down the slopes to broom the sea beyond the harbour. These gave the Genoese mariners a favourable opportunity for departure. The next highest percentage of winds were from the south and south-east – admirable again for speeding ships homeward. Quite apart from these two aspects of the wind system, the area was also blessed with the *Brise Soleil*, the solar wind. This occurs particularly during the long calm weather from June to September when more regular winds tend to be absent and most of the Mediterranean is misted with calm.

Genoa then was particularly well favoured for the development of a trade based mainly on sail, rather than – as throughout most of the Mediterranean – being heavily dependent on the oared galley. It is true that the galley remained the principal warship in these seas until the late 16th century, when it was ousted by the sailing ship that could carry a greater weight of cannon. But the Genoese had early begun to turn to canvas as their principal motive power for trading vessels. Quite apart from the climatic and meteorological circumstances of the city there was another reason for this. The Genoese dealt very largely in bulk cargoes, grain and hides from the Black Sea for instance, and they therefore required a large hold-space in their merchantmen. This was something which the lean, shallow-draught galley could not provide. The Venetians, on the other hand, whose trade was mostly with the East, in spices, gems and other articles which were highly valuable but relatively small in bulk, stuck to the galley for trading. It gave them greater consistent speed and a more regular pattern of trading voyages; as well as being highly manoeuvrable and well able to defend itself if attacked by Moslem corsairs.

21

Years later, when he was fifty, Columbus was to say in a letter to Ferdinand and Isabella that he had first gone to sea at the age of ten. There is nothing inherently implausible in this statement, for many a boy of similar age has done just that. Drake, for instance, was a ship's boy on an east coast of England trader at twelve or thirteen, while centuries later Horatio Nelson entered the navy at the age of twelve. Who, that has followed the sea, can remember years afterwards at exactly what age he first set foot aboard a boat? Columbus, according to his son Ferdinand, said to him on one occasion that he had first become a seaman when he was fourteen. There is nothing to establish at exactly what time he became a sailor in the true professional sense. To go on a coasting voyage with an uncle, or a friend of his father, between Genoa and Savona, to go out lining in a fishing boat with a harbour acquaintance – these are the beginnings of things. They can hardly be said to constitute the day when Columbus signed on in his profession. But there can be no doubt that the weaver's son must have had innumerable opportunities to get a day's sailing, or even a passage down to Corsica – where Genoa had such large interests – from the age of ten onwards.

It is unlikely that it will ever be known at what time Columbus definitely abandoned the weaver's trade and took permanently to the sea. The first record of his sea career dates from a letter, now lost, which Columbus wrote to Spain in 1495 in which he was elucidating for the benefit of his Sovereigns the difficulties of navigation. The letter is quoted by his son Ferdinand. Its date can be substantiated, because the King to whom he refers, René of Anjou, is known to have been chartering Genoese ships to support a rebellion against Juan II of Aragon, the father of the Ferdinand to whom Columbus was writing. The event to which Columbus refers could have taken place more or less any time between the autumn of 1470 and the summer of 1473.

"It happened," he writes, "that King René, now with God, sent me to Tunis to seize the galleass *Fernandina*. Now when I was off the island of San Pietro near Sardinia I was informed that the galleass was accompanied by two other ships and a carrack. My crew were disturbed by the news and refused to carry on unless I returned to Marseilles and picked up another ship and some more men. Seeing that I could not force their hand without some ruse or artifice, I agreed to what they asked me. But then, having changed the pull of the magnetic needle, I made sail at nightfall and next morning at dawn we were off Cape Carthage – whereas all aboard had been quite certain we were making for Marseilles."

Columbus does not go on to say whether his mission was successful or not, but what excites our interest is his statement that in some way or

Left: *René of Anjou. Painting by Nicolas Froment, 1475–76.* Right:
Juan II of Aragon, father of Ferdinand V of Aragon and Castile.

other he 'fixed' the magnetic needle so that the ignorant crew thought
they were heading north-west by north when in fact they were on a
reciprocal course, south-east by east. Two questions must be asked –
Could the story Columbus was telling his royal employers be a hoax, or
could it be one that he himself had heard told about another ship's captain of the time? Secondly, if the story is true, is it likely that Columbus
aged twenty or at most twenty-two could have been a ship's captain. To
'fix' the compass was certainly well within his capabilities. At that time
the compass card had the needle fastened below it, the whole being
balanced on a pivot. It was a 'dry' compass, that is to say not immersed
in liquid as in later centuries, and it was therefore easily accessible. It
would not be too difficult, either, to reverse the needle or, taking the
magnetic lodestone to it, to have changed the polarity and magnetised
the other end. In both cases the helmsman would unknowingly have
been steering the exact reciprocal of the course that he thought he was.
Columbus, then, could have played such a trick upon his seamen if he
were the captain.

It is this latter assertion that has bothered a number of historians. If
he had spent most of his life up to twenty-one working for his father or

acting as his agent, would he have had sufficient sea experience to have been master of a vessel? All depends on whether one assumes, in view of the scanty documentation of his early years, that he did spend most of them at the weaver's trade. But there is little enough to prove it – only some documentary evidence relating to various times that he was in Genoa. This does not at all mean that he spent most of his time there. Every sailor goes ashore between voyages. Antonio Gallo, a Genoese chronicler who knew the family, says that Christopher and his brother Bartholomew went to sea "while they were still youths". And a youth in those days might be anything from twelve years upwards. If Columbus had been at sea from ten (as he told Ferdinand and Isabella), twelve or even fourteen (as he told his son), it is possible that he might have become master of his own vessel by twenty or twenty-one. Drake was captain of his own coaster at twenty.

Columbus's explicit reference to his service with King René dates the episode and there is no reason to doubt that, like a number of other Genoese at that time, he was in the King's pay. The trick with the compass needle was quite feasible – furthermore it is prophetic of a trick he later played on his first Atlantic crossing, when he kept one fake log book to reassure his mariners, and another real one for himself. (He may well have learned the habit of keeping one set of books for official inspection and another for the family from Domenico the weaver.)

In the final analysis, however, the story is implausible – an anecdote contrived by Spain's great 'Admiral of the Ocean Sea' to show Ferdinand and Isabella how clever he had been even as a young man. For one thing, whether Columbus was the captain or not, the ship in which he was sailing must have been of some size if it was being despatched to capture a galleass; one of the largest types of vessel of the time. To put a ship through a change of course of 180 degrees could not have been done without the knowledge of the helmsman, and without crew members – even if asleep below – becoming aware of the slatting of the sails as she altered, and the different feel and pull of the ship on her new course. Even if Columbus had relieved the helmsman, and all the crew were below, it is more than doubtful that he could single-handed have put the ship about. Furthermore his statement that at dawn next morning they were off Cape Carthage destroys his credibility. The distance from San Pietro island to Punta Farina at the head of the Gulf of Tunis is over 130 nautical miles. Even allowing for the period of 'night' to be as much as twelve hours this would argue a speed of more than 10 knots – something quite impossible for a vessel of that period. No, one is forced to the conclusion that Columbus – not for the first, nor for the last time in his life –

is spinning a yarn to show himself to the best advantage as being a great deal smarter than his fellows.

One certain clue to the early sailing years of Christopher Columbus is provided by a reference on his first voyage to finding across the Atlantic in the new islands shrubs or small trees which he identified as the mastic or lentisk, "which I have seen myself in the island of Chios". Columbus was in fact mistaken, for the gumbo plant of the West Indies, although slightly similar in appearance, is no relation at all to the lentisk which produces mastic resin. Perhaps Columbus, here as elsewhere, was doing no more than trying to arouse his Sovereigns' hope and belief that these new islands would produce many of the herbs and spices that were so rare and valuable in Europe. Mastic, which is still obtained from the island of Chios, was particularly esteemed in the Middle Ages for use in medicine. Chios was one of the few places where the lentisk grew and the island had acquired for this reason a considerable importance. It had passed into the hands of Genoese privateers in the mid-fourteenth century, principal among them being the Giustiniani family who obtained a monopoly of the mastic trade for nearly two hundred years. There was a steady trade between the island and Genoa, and there can be little doubt that at some time between 1470 and 1478 Columbus made one or probably more voyages to this beautiful and fertile island, famous not only for the *Pistacia Lentiscus* with its tear-like drops of mastic oozing through the cuts in its bark, but for having the best claim of all places in the

Chios. Map from Thevet's Cosmographie, *1575.*

Aegean to have been the birth-place of Homer, "the blind old man of rocky Chios". The young Genoese sailor was almost certainly quite unaware of this aspect of the island, and would have been almost equally indifferent had he done so. His voyage, or voyages to Chios will have been important only that in them he saw new waters, new aspects of sky and land, and beheld for the first time unknown islands rising from the sea at dawn. He will have learned about the violent squalls that can descend on a vessel when she is on the lee side of high land, and how the wind-impelled currents can drive at 2 or 3 knots through the narrow channels separating one Aegean island from another. He will have known, too, the scent that rises off fertile islands like Chios at dawn, when all the land is soaked in dew and a combined blend of rosemary, mastic, pine and lemon makes a 'squeeze' so individual that the nostrils of an Aegean seaman can distinguish the characteristics of one island from another.

Ships were not big in those days. Indeed, they were so small that the work aboard them could hardly be divided into separate trades; there could be no mystery between one department and another. For an inquiring young man there can have been few secrets, and no doubt his seniors were happy to give the youth a little free instruction in those 'mysteries of navigation' wherewith they baffled the landsman. Columbus, who would certainly seem to have learned in the school of experience rather than in university, can hardly have failed to pick up some of the rudiments of navigation.

Genoa in the 15th century. Woodcut from The Nuremberg Chronicle.

The Navigator's Ocean

The turning point in the life of Christopher Columbus occurred in the summer of 1476. He was embarked (almost certainly as a crew member, for his name is not recorded in the list of officers aboard) in a Flemish merchant ship sailing in a convoy of Genoese ships destined for Portugal, England and Flanders. The vessels were loaded among other things with the famous Chian mastic. The reason they were in convoy was that at that time most of the nations bordering on the Mediterranean were either in a state of open or undeclared war with one another, and any single merchantman tended to be looked on as a fair prize. The convoy had passed through the Strait of Gibraltar and had headed out into the Atlantic for its first port of call, Lisbon. As far as is known, this was the first time that Columbus now aged twenty-five, saw the great ocean which he was destined to conquer.

Disaster struck the convoy when it was off Lagos in southern Portugal, not far from Cape St. Vincent and hard by the promontory of Sagres. It was at this point that the merchantships were attacked by a French naval force and in a day-long battle, in which the armed Genoese galleasses and merchantmen fought with great gallantry, three of the convoy and four of the enemy went to the bottom. Among the ships which were sunk was the one in which Columbus was embarked. He had been wounded in the fight and now, like the others, had to leap overboard to avoid going down with the vessel. Seizing an oar, and alternately swimming and resting upon it, Columbus managed to reach the shore near Lagos, some six miles away. Rested after being well looked after by the local inhabitants, Columbus, presumably with his fellow survivors, made his way north to Lisbon. This was the obvious place for him to go, since his ship had been destined for Lisbon; it was the foremost port in the world at that time and there was a large Genoese colony living in the city.

It was a strange turn of fate that Christopher Columbus, should have been cast ashore in Portugal near the beetling rock of Sagres where the lonely scholar-prince had made his home. For it was Prince Henry of Portugal, Henry the Navigator as he was to become universally known, who had first set in train the systematic exploration of the coast of West Africa and the regions of the Atlantic that lay off that coast. Henry was in many ways of similar cast of character to the shipwrecked young Genoese. He was medieval in his thinking, a militant Christian whose main aim was to drive the Moors out of Morocco and such parts of the North African coast that threatened the Mediterranean sea-routes, and an ascetic who on his death bed was found to be wearing a hair shirt next to his skin. Yet at the same time, if his intellectual background was largely that of the Middle Ages, Henry was a forerunner of the Renaissance: a man of ever-inquiring mind who employed the best savants, astronomers, chart-makers and master mariners of his day, to push back the darkness that overshadowed the continent of Africa and the Atlantic Ocean.

Prince Henry's biographer, Azurara, wrote of him that "he desired to know what lands there were beyond the Canary Islands and a cape called Bojador. For at that time there was no knowledge, either in writing or in the memory of any man, of what might lie beyond this cape." Prince Henry's approach to these problems was scientific, he did not go on any of the voyages that he initiated, but he provided at Sagres the command headquarters where all available information was cross-checked and correlated, and where the discoveries of his captains were noted and added to the new charts which his cartographers were engaged in producing. He himself had financed these first Portuguese voyages of discovery because, as Azurara again puts it, "no sailor or merchant would undertake it, for it is very sure that such men do not dream of navigating other than to places where they already know they can make a profit."

It was Prince Henry who had sown the seeds of Portugal's greatness, had laid the foundations of her overseas empire, and had initiated the great age of exploration which was to change the whole pattern of world history. By 1420 the islands of Porto Santo and Madeira had been explored by Portuguese mariners, who believed at the time that they were the first ever to have seen them. This Portuguese 'discovery' became part

Opposite: *Our Lady of Fair Winds. Tapestry from a painting by Alejo Fernandez.*

Overleaf: *Ships similar to those sailed by Columbus in Carpaccio's painting of the legend of St Ursula.*

STRENVI HISPANIAE NAVIGANTES REGINA MARIS
ARDENTISSIME FLVCTVVM VENTORVMQVE
PERICVLA SVSTINVERVNT

IN PERICVLIS MARIS
ESTO NOBIS PROTECTIO

VICTORIS
CARPATIO
VENETI·
·OPVS·
MCCCCLXXXXV

of the history of navigation until an Italian map dated 1351 revealed that the Genoese had come across the Madeira group some time early in the 14th century. An unusual factor that was to link the lives of Christopher Columbus and the dead prince was that Columbus was later to marry the daughter of Bartholomew Perestrello, a minor nobleman who had been on the first voyages to Porto Santo and Madeira, and who was later made governor of Porto Santo. Thus, when fate drove Columbus to shipwreck on the shore near Sagres, it led him also to the country where he would find a wife descended from one of the first Portuguese Atlantic explorers.

Another curious link between the two men, and between their thinking, was that one of the driving motives behind Prince Henry's desire to find out what happened beyond Morocco was the hope of finding a great Christian prince, Prester John, who was said to be immensely rich and powerful and to live somewhere south of the Arabic world. Whether he lived in Africa or in Asia – reports varied – it was always the dream of European monarchs, after the Turkish incursions into the continent, to establish communications with this great king, reputedly said to be always at war with the heathen and the infidel. Most historians now equate this rumour with the fact that in Abyssinia there was indeed a Christian kingdom, unknown and forgotten at the time. Another school of thought suggests that his real provenence was in Asia, where there had once been a powerful Khan, who had been converted by Nestorian missionaries, and who was known as the "Presbyter Khan", the Priest King. Towards the end of the 12th century, however, this Christian Khanate in Asia was attacked and overthrown by the great Mongol warlord Genghis Khan. Marco Polo, whose history of his travels in Asia and China was to have so profound an effect upon Columbus, placed Prester John as ruler of a kingdom somewhere near the Great Wall of China, while a 14th century Franciscan friar wrote that "the Patriarch of Abyssinia and Nubia is Prester Juan who rules over many lands and cities of Christians". Whatever the truth behind the legends, both Henry the Navigator and Christopher Columbus always had hopes of establishing contact with this Christian monarch in order to bring him onto their side to redress the balance against the Turk. While Prince Henry looked for him in south-west Africa, Columbus misinterpreting some native words, was later to believe that he was somewhere to be found in the West Indies.

Opposite: *King Alfonso V kneeling. Behind him young Prince John, and next to him Prince Henry the Navigator. Painting by Nuno Concalves, c. 1465–67.*

LIBRO SEGVN

DO DE LA MAR, Y SVS MOVI
MIENTOS. Y COMO FVE
INVENTADA LA NA
VEGACION .:.

A Sailor out of Lisbon

Columbus's first visit to Lisbon was necessarily a short one. Young ship-wrecked sailors do not have the time or money for hanging about the beach or enjoying the pleasures of dockyard, doxy or tavern – pleasures which in any case were unattractive to Columbus's somewhat austere, if not puritanical, temperament. Shortly after reaching the city he was embarked again, possibly in one of the survivors from the convoy. The little that we know about this voyage comes on the authority of Ferdi-nand, quoting from a now lost memorandum from his father. "In the month of February 1477 I sailed one hundred leagues beyond the island of Tile. Its southern part is 73° North and not 63° as some say. Further-more it does not lie on the meridian where Ptolemy says the west begins, but a great deal further west. To this island, which is as big as England, the English merchants go, especially those from Bristol. And at the time when I was there the sea was not frozen, but there were vast tides, so great that they rose and fell as much as 26 *braccia* [about 50 foot] twice a day."

Tile is clearly Thule, Ultima Thule as it was called, or Iceland. There was a regular trade at that time between Lisbon, Bristol and Iceland, and the Bristol merchants were in constant relations with the Icelanders, exporting their manufactured goods largely in return for fish. The ship on which Columbus sailed from Lisbon may even have been an English merchantman out of Bristol. There is nothing at all improbable in this voyage, indeed it is entirely likely that Columbus would have shipped aboard the first vessel that needed a hand. The two things which are in error are his categorical statement that the southern coastline of Iceland is 70° North when it is in fact on a latitude of 63° 30′ :

Opposite: *Ships of early 16th century. From title page of Pedro de Medina's* Arte de Navegar, *1545.*

almost exactly the figure that he challenges. His second error lies in the height of the tides, for the maximum range at Reykjavik is less than 15 foot. On the other hand Columbus, recalling his voyage many years afterwards, may well have been remembering the violence of the tidal streams in these waters; the crest of the tidal wave around Iceland moving at nearly 80 miles an hour, and the resultant tidal streams running in places at as much as 7 knots – something which would certainly have made a deep impression on a young sailor fresh out of the almost tideless Mediterranean. On the question of latitude, if, as some sceptics have maintained, this proves that he never went to Iceland at all, the answer is surely that if he was spinning a yarn Columbus could at the time of writing have checked his facts from many a chart. Clearly the figure 73° had stuck firmly in his memory, and one can only presume that the captain or the navigator of the vessel in which Columbus shipped was as dogmatic and as inaccurate about his latitudes as Columbus was later to show himself.

Some confirmation that he did indeed go to Iceland is given by the fact in a note in his own handwriting to his copy of the 'History of Memorable Things that have happened in my time' by the author-Pope Aeneas Silvius (Pius II) which reads as follows: "Men have come hither from Cathay in the Orient. Many remarkable things have we seen, particularly at Galway in Ireland, a man and a woman of most unusual appearance adrift into two boats [from a wreck]." Columbus's assumption that the two bodies he saw came from the Orient suggest that so early in his life he was all ready obsessed with the idea of Marco Polo's Cathay. The identity of the bodies has been convincingly suggested by Madariaga, Morison and others as Lapps or Finns, who, with their Mongol-type features, would undoubtedly resemble Orientals. There can of course have been no Chinese sailing around Irish waters at that moment in history. Columbus is indeed very likely to have visited Galway if, as he says, he had been on a voyage to Iceland. It is the natural intermediate port of call between Iceland and Bristol.

It would seem almost certain that Columbus went on a trading voyage as a seaman to Iceland, from Lisbon, calling at Galway on his way back to Bristol. But the evidence above is all that we have to go on. It has nevertheless provided a bone of contention between scholars, those of

Opposite: *Prince Henry of Portugal, 1395–1460, known as Henry the Navigator. Fourth son of King John I he encouraged the first Portuguese explorations and founded an Academy of geography and navigation. Detail from the Veneration of St Vincent.*

the 'Nordic School' maintaining – without a shred of evidence – that
Columbus heard from the Icelanders about the lands to the West, known
to their Viking forefathers. The 'Latin School' derides the whole idea,
maintaining among other things that Columbus would not have been
able to talk to anyone in Iceland since he did not know the language.
This in itself is not a stumbling block, for two countries such as England
and Iceland could hardly have carried on, as they did, a regular trade for
centuries without having some interpreters. Since Lisbon also played a
large part in this trade the interpreters would naturally have also spoken
Portuguese. If Columbus was already obsessed with the idea of reaching

Above: *Aeneas Sylvius, Pope Sylvester II, author of* History of Memorable Things that have Happened in my Time, *which Columbus took with
him on his voyages. From Thevet's* Portraits, *1584.*

Opposite: *Annotations in the handwriting of Columbus on the margins of
his copy of Aeneas Sylvius' History.*

Cathay across the Atlantic it would have been quite natural for him to have made some enquiries while in Iceland, just as we know that he took careful note of what appeared to be shipwrecked 'Orientals' when he was in Galway.

The story that Columbus might well have heard in Iceland was a part of the Saga of Erik the Red. It describes among other things how one of Erik's two sons, Leif, sailed direct from Norway for Greenland in the year 1000, instead of going by way of Iceland as was the usual custom. Whether driven south and westerly by gales, or through a navigational error, Leif missed Cape Farewell, the southernmost point of Greenland,

phrygiarum urbium maximę fuerunt. Sed in cęlenorum iugis quę ad lycaoniā ptinet urbs fuit noīe cęlenis :qua deſtructa antiochus ſother homines tranſtulit in eam quae poſtea apamia dicta eſt:et urbē appellauit de nomine matris apamię Artabazi filię quę ſeleuco nicanori nupta fuit. Vrbs ī hoſtiis marſię ſita fuit q amnis mediam urbem percurrebat: ab ipſa ortum habēs: Sed uehementi ac prono flumine in ſuburbanum delatus in meandrum exonerabatur. Inſigne hic emporiū fuit ſecundas poſt epheſum ferens laudes: et commune italicorum et gręcorū hoſpitium habuit. Non procul hinc lacus extat qui calamum gignit ad tibiarū linguas idoneum:hinc fabula conficta eſt de cōtentōne:quā cum apolline marſias habuit:et ſunt qui putant ab eolacu marſię ac meandri fontes emanare: laodicea cum prius eſſet:poſtea maximū cepit augumētum: quanuis ab obſidione mithridatis plurimū labefacta fuerit. nā loci uirtus et ciues qdā fortunati eam ualde magnificarunt. Primum hiero qui hęreditatem populo dimiſit ſupra duo millia talentorum & multis donis ciuitatem exornauit. poſtea Zeno orator & polemo eius filius qui ob res fortiter geſtas prius ab Antonio: poſtea ab auguſto ad regię dignitatis faſtigium euect9 eſt :loca laodicę p xima oues optimas ferunt:nō modo lanę mollitie qua myleſis pręſtāt ſed etiam colore:unde magnos prouentus aſſequuntur. In hoc tractu caper & Lycus influunt in meandrum & laodiceā a lyco dicta putant. Vrbi mons īminet nomine cadm9 ex quo lycus fluit & alter eodem nomine quo mons appellatur hic plurimum ſub terram delapſus :poſtea erumpens in idem influit : in quo alia flumina:eſtque regio ualde cauernoſa & quaſſabilis Nam & laodicea & proxima ei regio plurimum terręmotibus concuſſa eſt: Apamia quoque ante mithridaticum bellum ſępe terręmotibus afflicta fuit. Rex uero cum urbem euerſam uideret ut repararetur centum talenta exibuit. Dicunt & Alexandri tempore ſimilia contigiſſe quibus ex rebus maxima apud eos in ueneratione neptunus fuit : putantque a caeleno neptuni filio ex caeleno una Danaidum procreato urbem appellatam

and landed up either in Nova Scotia or Newfoundland. The saga describes how Leif and his men "were a long time at sea, finally striking upon a land they had not expected. It had fields of natural [self-sown] wheat and wine berries. Among the trees were maples . . ." This new land they called Vinland, or Wineland, after the grapes. Now the first medieval account to tell Europeans about the mainland of North America was the 'History of the Church of Hamburg'. This was completed about 1070 by its author Adam of Bremen, who had spent some time in the Danish court, where he had heard about Iceland and Greenland – and Vinland as well. Adam of Bremen recounts how the Danish King, Svein Estridsson, knew all the history of the sea-explorations by heart and that "he mentioned yet another island [apart from Iceland and Greenland] which many had discovered in that ocean, and which is called 'Vinland' because vines grow of themselves and produce excellent wine. There too is an abundance of unsown corn. This we know not from fables or supposition but from reliable information from the Danes."

In conclusion, considering Columbus's early voyage to the North and to Ireland, one can say no more than that he may possibly have heard while in Iceland of the lands to the north and west. Almost certainly he will have heard of Greenland, for it was only within recent years that the Norse colony there had lost touch with Iceland. There must have been many who remembered – or had even sailed to – the remote land to the north. In Ireland, it is equally tempting to suppose, he had heard of St. Brendan, that 6th century Irish saint and hero of a legendary voyage into the Atlantic where he had found the fabulous "Promised Land of the Saints". The earliest extant version of this legend – or, as Irish patriots would have it, this true expedition to North America – is to be found in the 11th century 'Navigatio Brendani'. In any case, whether in Iceland or in Ireland, Columbus could indeed have heard of mysterious lands lying to the west across the sullen and apparently empty Atlantic

Opposite (top): *Map by Henricus Martellus showing the world as imagined before Columbus's voyages, c. 1489.*

Opposite (below): *The imaginary Prester John. Detail from a Portolan chart by Diego Homem, 1558.*

Overleaf: *Portuguese carracks of Columbus's day. Painting attributed to Cornelius Anthoniszoon, c. 1521.*

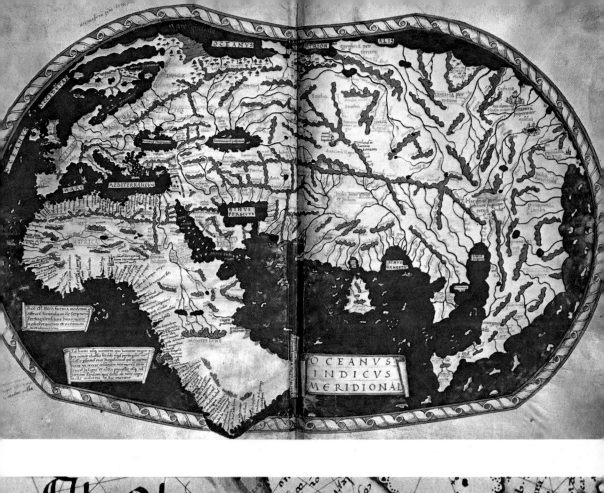

Ocean. That in his later years, when he did set out on his great voyage of exploration, he took the southern route is easily explainable. Living in Portugal he had ample time to hear about islands beyond islands in the ocean, and he was in daily communication with men who had opened up West Africa, used the Canaries as a regular port of call, and were familiar with the Azores, all of which had been recorded between 1439 and 1452, as well as the Cape Verde islands which the Venetian Cadamosto had discovered in 1456. Portuguese colonies, planted by Prince Henry, were already thriving on these new lands far out in the Atlantic.

These were realities. To a Mediterranean man like Columbus they must also have sounded far more attractive, with their warm climates, blue seas, and semi-tropical vegetation, than the harsh North which seemed to produce little except furs and fish. He was on the track of the Orient and Cathay.

The Lisbon to which Columbus returned, after his voyage to the North and to the edge of the Arctic Circle, was the most exciting port and city in the world. It was the Cape Kennedy of its day (and a great deal more). It was the place from which men were gradually pushing back the barriers of darkness and extending the boundaries of knowledge. It was also vital, rich, amusing – and intellectually and aesthetically stimulating. Here on the Tagus waterfront were the ships and the men who sailed regularly to Africa and drove the prows of their caravels night after night into an unknown darkness, while the navigator's friend, the North Star, steadily declined above their phosphorescent wake.

The eight years and more that Columbus spent either in Portugal or under the Portuguese flag as a sailor are almost completely undocumented. It is a tragedy that this – which must have been the most formative period of his life – is like one of these blanks on ancient maps marked 'Terra Incognita'. Only occasionally does one catch a glimpse of him, once through the same Antonio Gallo of Genoa, who knew the family. He recorded that Columbus's younger brother, Bartholomew, was in Lisbon before him and had established himself there as a mapmaker. Columbus, according to Gallo, was taken into partnership by his brother, something which seems to be confirmed by a chaplain who knew him well in later years, Andrés Bernáldez.

Bernáldez wrote in his 'Historia de los Reyes Catolicos' that Columbus was a traveller or agent for the sale of books in Andalusia. He went on to say that, although he had little formal education, he was a man of keen intelligence, "being very skilled in cosmography and in making maps of

Opposite: *Caravels in port (detail). From Theodore de Bry, 1594.*

the world." One thing is certain: it was during these years that he learned the rudiments of Latin and became a fluent Portuguese speaker. Castilian Spanish was probably a somewhat later acquirement, although it would not have been surprising if Columbus had learned it at much the same time as his Portuguese. Castilian was the preferred language of the upper classes in Portugal – and Columbus was soon to marry into a noble Portuguese family. The Spanish philologist, Ramón Menéndez Pidal, who made an intensive study of the writings of Columbus proved conclusively that they were written by a man to whom Portuguese was his first language, and that many of the spellings used are Portuguese and not pure Castilian. This would be natural enough, since quite apart from his everyday conversations with his wife after his marriage, the language of his trade in Lisbon and elsewhere was Portuguese. Some historians have made great play with the fact that Columbus did not write in Italian. But, as has been seen, the Genoese dialect with which he grew up was unwritten and, from the age of 25 onwards, his whole life was cast among Portuguese and Spanish speakers. Even had he been able to write formal Italian it would have been no use to him in his daily life.

The consideration of Columbus's self-taught linguistic abilities leads on at once to that of the change of his name from Colombo (as he had been born) into Colón. Colombo means 'a dove', and Columbus, as he is generally known to English speaking people, is no more than a Latinised form of his Italian name. To this day only the Italians refer to him by the real names with which he was born, Cristoforo Colombo.

St Brendan, the 6th century Irish saint and hero of a legendary voyage into the Atlantic. Landing from his ship carried on a whale's back. From Philopono, 1621.

Columbus himself changed his name into the Spanish equivalent, Colón or Colóm – an abbreviation and a simplification which was more readily pronounceable in the Portuguese or Castilian tongues. While treatises and complicated and ingenious theories have been built upon this change of name – much as the variant spellings of Shakespeare have been used to 'prove' that a man who did not spell his name consecutively the same could never have written a play. The simplest explanation of this name change can be found in the nomenclature to be found in any country, such as England or, even more, the United States, where immigrants from non-English speaking countries have anglicised their names in order to make them either easier to pronounce, or socially more acceptable.

During all these years it is more than probable that Columbus filled in some of his time by going to sea. It is possible that, like many sailors in other centuries, he worked at two trades: map-maker and book-seller in the winter months, and seaman (when he could get a ship) at other times. There is, however, only one record of Columbus at sea during these early years in Portugal, and that concerns a voyage he made to Madeira for a Genoese merchant to purchase a quantity of sugar for sale in Genoa. Some confusion took place between Columbus's employer and the suppliers in Madeira about the payment of the money and Columbus was forced to sail to Genoa with far less than the required consignment. A subsequent investigation in court showed that Columbus was blameless in the matter and he returned to Lisbon. It was shortly after this,

Iceland. Detail from the Carta Marina of Olaus Magnus, 1539. Columbus claimed that in 1477 he visited Iceland and sailed a hundred leagues beyond.

probably in 1479, that the twenty-eight year old Genoese took a decisive
step in his private life, and one that was to prove equally important in his
future career. He married Felipa Moniz Perestrello, the daughter of
Bartholomew Perestrello who had been made first governor of Porto
Santo in the Madeiras. She was also the granddaughter of Gil Moniz,
who came from one of the oldest families in Portugal and who had been a
close companion of the great Prince Henry.

How did a middle-class Genoese, part seaman and part dealer in books
and maps, come to meet with, woo, and marry – in those days of strict
class distinction – a young woman, noble on both sides of her family,
who must certainly have been living under the strictest chaperonage?
They met, according to his son, at the Convent of the Saints in Lisbon
where Columbus used to go to attend Mass. Out of the dozens of
churches and chapels with which pious Lisbon was thronged, it is not
insignificant that Columbus should have chosen this one as the site for
his devotions. It was remarkable for being the convent belonging to the
nuns of the Military Order of St. James, the purpose of which was to
provide a home for the wives and daughters of this famous order of
knights militant while the knights themselves were away fighting the
heathen in the Holy Land or elsewhere. For an ambitious young man,
anxious to become acquainted with a potential wife from upper class
society, there could have been no better place to choose for his church-
going. Young women were scrupulously chaperoned and there was no
social life in those days where a man like Columbus could meet a
suitable bride from a completely different stratum of society. Only in a
church was it possible for the two sexes to see one another – however
fleetingly – and churches as we know from innumerable accounts, were
regularly used for just this purpose, and even (in later days and laxer
societies than that of Lisbon) for the arrangement of assignations.

We know nothing about the appearance of Dona Felipa, but whether
she was prepossessing or not she was an undoubted 'catch'. As for the
lady herself, it is hardly surprising that she was taken by the appearance
of this 'extranjero', this foreigner with a romantic background. He was,
wrote Oviedo who first saw him fourteen years later in Barcelona, "a man
of fine appearance, well built, taller than most and with strong limbs.
His eyes were lively and his features in good proportion. His hair was
very red, and his face ruddy and freckled. He spoke well, was tactful in
his manner and was extremely talented. He was a good latinist and a very
learned cosmographer, gracious when he wished, but hot tempered if he
was crossed." No doubt the years had put more polish upon Columbus
when this was written, and had also endowed him with an air of authority.

48

But the promise was already there in the young Columbus, and the appearance – so dissimilar from the small, dark-skinned men of Portugal – was clearly irresistible to Dona Felipa. Under the strict eye of her mother, she "held such conversation with him and enjoyed such friendship that she became his wife."

There were practical reasons why Felipa's mother may well have been pleased to see her eldest daughter married to a young man who was clearly ambitious, of good character, and likely to make his way in the world. The family, although well born, were far from well off. She had a second daughter to support and raise, as well as having to maintain her own status in Lisbon. Her husband, Bartholomew Perestrello, had died in Porto Santo and she had been compelled for financial reasons to sell her rights in the governorship of the island. (These were later reclaimed by her son, also called Bartholomew, but at no advantage to the widow.) All in all, the red-headed, handsome Genoese who was eager to marry her daughter – and without a dowry – must have seemed a very suitable answer to the widow's problems. As far as Columbus was concerned, whether he was deeply attracted to Felipa or not, the advantages of the match were immense. She was to prove the key that was to open the way for his acceptance into a world where power and influence could be courted and obtained.

Some known and some imaginary islands in the Atlantic which may have been visited by Columbus. Map from a 1513 edition of Claudius Ptolemy's Geographia.

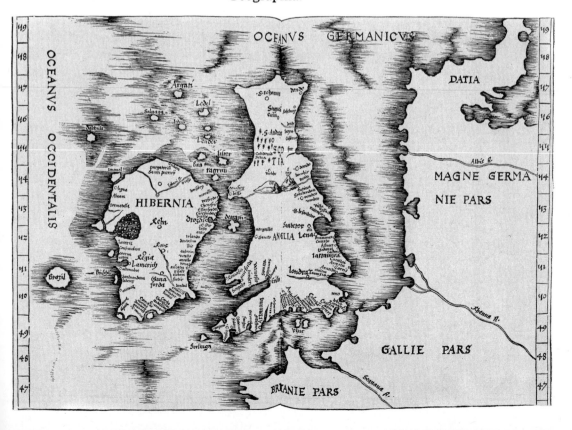

Islands in the Ocean

Southwest of Cape St. Vincent, some five hundred miles out into the Atlantic from Portugal, lies the island of Porto Santo. Just over six miles long by three wide it is hilly at either end, soaring up to over 1,500 feet at one point. This was the island of which Dona Felipa's father had been made governor after its discovery by the Portuguese in 1419. In fact, as is now known from the Italian map (the Laurentian portolano), the island and its larger brother, Madeira, had been recorded as early as 1351, and it is possible that the Madeira group was known to the Genoese even before this. But it was the Portuguese, at the direction of Henry the Navigator, who had settled and colonised the islands, Madeira having been discovered by a further expedition sent out to Porto Santo in 1420. It was at Prince Henry's instigation that, within a few years of their settlement, the hardy malvasia grape-vine was imported from Crete and the sugar cane from Sicily. Both of these were in due course to play their part in making Madeira a great wine exporter.

But Porto Santo, the island which Bartholomew Perestrello had governed, and where his son now followed in his father's footsteps, never prospered like Madeira. It was in fact almost completely ruined by Bartholomew Perestrello who, in an understandable desire to have some food available in Porto Santo, introduced the rabbit. Within two years the rabbits had grown to be such a plague that the settlers began to hate everything to do with Porto Santo . . .

This was the island to which Columbus and his wife moved from Lisbon and where their one and only child, Diego, was born. But before this transference to the remote Atlantic island it seems that Columbus and Felipa lived in her mother's house in Lisbon where, according to Ferdinand Columbus in his biography, Christopher Columbus's mother-in-law, seeing how interested he was in everything to do with the sea and with discovery, told him what she could remember of her husband's experiences. She also gave him "the charts and writings which he had left her. The Admiral was greatly excited by these and he made himself well acquainted with the voyages of exploration upon which the Portuguese were engaged." It was inevitable in any case that Columbus should know both from his own activities, as well as those in his brother's chart and map-making business, of the navigational progress that was every year being made on the African coast and in the Atlantic. It was the common talk of the city and waterfront. He could see with his own eyes the slaves brought back from Africa and the gold dust, strange fruits and spices, that were being unloaded yearly when the caravels returned. But the fact that his dead father-in-law had been a protegé of Henry the Navigator gave him an added incitement to find out more about the unknown world. It was natural then that, with his brother-in-law established in Porto Santo, he should in due course leave Lisbon and, taking his wife with him, make for the island which, coupled with Madeira, was at that time the advance headquarters, as it were, of man's invasion of the Atlantic.

For the next two or three years, from 1480 to 1483, Columbus had his home first in Porto Santo and then at Funchal, the small but thriving capital of Madeira. In both islands the modern inhabitants point authoritatively to the houses where he and Dona Felipa are said to have lived but, as with most such ascriptions, the visitor must allow for foreign demand being met by local supply. What is certain is that, while Columbus probably engaged in trade – and certainly went on a number of voyages during these years – his curiosity was constantly being whetted by meeting with sailors and ships' captains who had been to the edge of the unknown, and by the fact that he himself was living on the frontiers of the Atlantic.

"He learned," wrote Ferdinand, "from pilots who were experienced in the voyages to Madeira and the Azores facts and signs which convinced him that an unknown land lay to the west. Martin Vicente, a pilot of the King of Portugal, told him how he had taken from the water an artistically carved piece of wood, four hundred and fifty leagues from Cape St. Vincent. This wood had been driven across [the ocean] by the west wind – a fact which led the sailors to believe that there were certainly other islands in that direction which had not yet been discovered."

Both in Madeira and in the Azores further evidence came to light from time to time suggesting that there was indeed some unknown land lying far out in the western Atlantic. Large canes, pines of unknown species, and even pieces of carved wood had been picked up on the westernmost

51

beaches of the islands. In the case of the Azores it is quite likely that natural objects and even Carib artefacts were occasionally washed up, for a branch of the Gulf Stream known as the Azores current flows steadily across the Atlantic from the Gulf of Mexico in the direction of these islands. It was reported from Flores, westernmost of the Azores, that the bodies of two men had been washed ashore and the Portuguese colonists declared that their broad faces showed they were not Europeans. It is just conceivable that two Carib Indians might have been carried out to sea in a canoe and, after finally dying of starvation and exposure, have been cast up on Flores.

Some years before Columbus's residence in Porto Santo and Madeira we know that Prince Henry had come to the conclusion that there were other lands to the west. The chronicle of Diogo Gomes, one of the Prince's captains and close associates, tells how "The Prince wished to know about the western ocean, and whether there were islands or continents beyond those that Ptolemy described. [The 'Guide to Geography' of the great 2nd century A.D. Alexandrian astronomer and mathematician was a standard reference book of the period.] For this reason the Prince sent out caravels to search for lands." But Henry the Navigator's interest in the Atlantic and Africa seems to have been primarily determined by his desire to find a sea route *round* the continent, so as to make contact with India and the East. It was for this reason that all his efforts were directed southwards and down the African coast. Columbus, on the other hand, looked westward. As Ferdinand Columbus wrote, "It was in Portugal that the Admiral [his father] began to surmise that, if the Portuguese sailed so far to the south, it might equally be possible to sail westward and find lands in that direction."

Some of Prince Henry's ships did in fact sail to the west. They narrowly missed discovering Newfoundland nearly fifty years before John Cabot. (Cabot sailed from Bristol in 1497, landed at Bonavista and claimed the land for Henry VII of England.) It is just possible that Portuguese fishermen had been going to the Newfoundland banks from the Azores before Columbus settled in Madeira. Fishermen are notoriously secretive about fishing grounds. At any rate, early in the 1450's, Diogo de Teive, one of Prince Henry's captains, set out into the Atlantic northwest from the Azores islands of Corvo and Flores. They were working along the southern edge of the Azores current where the winds often blow from a southwesterly direction, and where the warm water is dense in places with Sargasso weed. With a southwest wind Diogo de Teive had it on the beam of his caravel, 'a soldier's wind' as it is known,

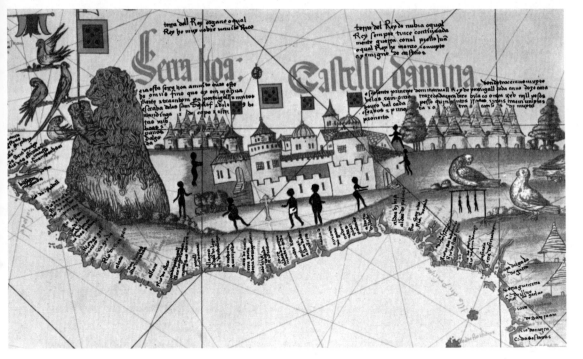

The Portuguese fort of Sao Jorge da Mina, on the Guinea coast, once visited by Columbus. From the Cantino map, 1502.

since it requires little skill to trim the sails or steer the ship. For day after day the Portuguese kept standing to the northwest, and then to their great surprise they found that they had suddenly run into an area of cold. Strong winds from the west now began to head them and the air had the taste of ice. Diogo de Teive, as this account more or less conclusively proves, had sailed right across the Gulf Stream and come out where the cold Newfoundland current runs down from the north. They were probably in the region of 50° North, off the Newfoundland Bank, and they soon realised that they were sailing into shoal water. Unequipped for the cold weather, and unprepared for so long a voyage, they turned back to Portugal where Diogo de Teive put it on record that he was convinced that there was land to the north-west. It is quite likely that Columbus heard about this voyage, but, even if he did so, he might well have connected it with nothing more than the general knowledge of the Icelanders that Greenland existed, and that there was land well to the north and west of their own island.

Antilia, the mysterious island that appears on a number of charts drawn after 1462 – and always west of the Azores – has sometimes been claimed as a Portuguese discovery of the West Indies in advance of Columbus. Its latitude is variable but it is generally situated on the parallel of Lisbon or Cape St. Vincent, and sometimes even where the West Indies were to be found. There is no evidence that any seamen had discovered new lands in the west, although it must always remain a possibility that some caravel, driving before the northeast trade winds, did sight one of the Windward Islands of the West Indies. One last puzzling feature is the "Authentic Island", depicted on a map drawn by Andrea Bianco in 1448, when the latter, who had previously been in Lisbon, was working in London. This depicts a stretch of coastline 1,500 miles west of Africa – almost the position of the Brazilian coastline. Yet Brazil, according to known records, was not sighted until 1499.

The fact is that all these speculations were in the air when Columbus was living at Porto Santo and Madeira, but they were only speculations.

During these years Columbus certainly sailed once, if not more, to the west coast of Africa, where the Portuguese were busily engaged in trade and were building a fortified trading post at São Jorge de Mina on the Gold Coast. On his copy of Aeneas Sylvius Columbus has a note against a passage concerning the climate at the equator that "Directly below the equator is the castle of Mina of the most serene King of Portugal, which I have seen." From other evidence in his notes, and in the journal of his first voyage to America, it seems likely that he made several visits to West Africa and the Gold Coast. It is clear that it was on these voyages – if not before – he became a practised, if not a proficient, navigator.

The Portuguese were at this time the foremost navigators in the world, but the whole science was still in its infancy. A misconception, at one time popular but now rightly discredited, is that one of the great achievements of Columbus was to set out into the unknown, towards the edge of a 'flat' world. Such a notion had long been rejected among the educated. Students at universities as well as self-taught men like Columbus were familiar with the work of John Holywood, or Sacrobosco as he was latinised, who had taught in Paris and whose textbook on elementary arithmetic was widely known. It was common knowledge among men and women of any culture who had read Jehan de Mandeville's 'travels' that, however much many of the stories might only be taken for their amusement value, the circumnavigation of the globe was quite feasible.

Madeira, the island where Columbus's son Diego was born. Map from Bordone's Isolario, *1534.*

In Search of a Patron

No one can say for certain at what moment Columbus conceived the idea of sailing westward across the Atlantic to find the Indies. It must have certainly been engaging his attention even before he went to live in Porto Santo and Madeira. The best evidence of this is to be found in the correspondence he is known to have had with a Florentine physician, mathematician and astronomer, Paolo Toscanelli. Toscanelli had originally been writing to a friend of his, canon of Lisbon Cathedral, Fernão Martins, who had been eager to convince the then King of Portugal, Afonso V, that there was a quicker way to the Indies than round the southernmost point of Africa. Toscanelli, who took the writings of Marco Polo as gospel, was of the opinion that the world was a great deal smaller than in fact it was. He believed for instance that the distance between the Canary islands and Japan (Cipangu) was about 3,000 miles. Columbus clearly heard of this correspondence, which took place in 1474, and wrote at a later date to Toscanelli expressing his own wish to open communications with the East by a direct voyage across the Atlantic. Toscanelli died in 1482, so the letters between him and Columbus most probably passed before he had left Lisbon for Porto Santo.

Toscanelli replied courteously to this new inquirer from Portugal, sent him a chart based on his conception of the earth, largely derived from Marco Polo's account of the Far East, and enclosed with it a copy of the letter that he had earlier sent to Fernão Martins. In his original letter Toscanelli had maintained that a course west out of Lisbon would bring the navigator to the Chinese province of Mangi after about 5,000 miles [nearer 11,000 as the crow flies] and that "passing by the Island of Antilia, which you know" he would, after only 2,000 miles, reach Cipangu.

It was Cipangu as Marco Polo had described it with its temples and palaces of gold, an island rich in all precious metals and precious stones, which stirred Columbus's imagination. With his map, and the copy of his earlier letter, Toscanelli added a cover letter to his unknown correspondent, whom he clearly presumed to be Portuguese, saying that he was "interested in your noble ambition to sail to where the spices grow." It is worth remarking that this correspondence – in a sense, the kernel of the whole project which Columbus was in due course to lay before the King of Portugal – took place between two Italians.

King John II who succeeded his father Afonso V in 1481 was undoubtedly the right man for Columbus to approach with this project of a great voyage to the west. Known in the history of his people as John the Perfect, he was as ambitious for his country overseas as he was determined to ensure Portugal's stability by curbing the power of the nobles at home. Unfortunately the state of the kingdom of Portugal was such that John was far too preoccupied at this moment with potential civil war, and disputes with Spain, to devote much time to the extension of Portuguese sea exploration. But it is evidence enough of his eagerness to promote such adventures that he agreed in 1484 to consider the plan of this importunate Genoese. Columbus must clearly have been pulling every string he could to secure an audience with King John, for without the backing of the king there could be no hope of Columbus's securing the ships and the men he needed for the voyage.

Columbus and his wife and son returned to Lisbon in 1484. It was towards the close of this year that King John, having crushed a conspiracy at home by killing the young Duke of Viseu, was able to turn his attention to foreign affairs. Columbus, armed with all the information that he had been collecting over years, was granted an audience. He was now thirty three years old.

Although the cast of his thought was essentially medieval – for he paid as much attention to the Bible and to prophecies as he did to the new field of scientific discoveries – yet he foreshadowed in many ways the Universal Man of the Renaissance. In his nature the Virgilian longing, *rerum cognoscere causas*, was as omnipresent – although without the element of genius – as it was in Leonardo da Vinci. But Columbus could certainly never have echoed the great Florentine's saying, "Poor is the

Opposite: *The "fabulous east", 15th century impression derived from the reports of Marco Polo. A map by Fra Mauro, a monk of Murano, c. 1459. Intrigued and stimulated by the tales of gold, spices and "other marvels" of the east, the Portuguese were anxious to get more information and Fra Mauro received payments on behalf of the king of Portugal for his work on this map.*

Jxola de
cmpagu

abi

man of many wants." Columbus was a Genoese to his fingertips, and as greedy as a schoolboy for the imagined gold, spices and gems of the Orient – an Orient that he was at the same time capable of envisaging as resembling the Garden of Eden, of being a foreshadowing of the Celestial Paradise. He was clearly of above average intelligence and far above average in ambition, but an ambition which, though it was flecked with cupidity, was ennobled by dreams. In later centuries detractors have been busy like sharks around a dead whale tearing at the giant body of his reputation. Little men are envious of big men. As Voltaire wrote, "When he promised a new hemisphere, people maintained that it could not exist, and when he had discovered it, that it had been known a long time." The one thing, however, that Columbus did not promise King John of Portugal was "a new hemisphere". To quote Las Casas, Columbus later told Ferdinand and Isabella, "who were hesitating on this enterprise, that he was going to seek and find the Indies by the Western route . . ."

This was exactly what he now proposed to John II: an expedition to sail west into the Atlantic, rather than following the current Portuguese practice of attempting the circumnavigation of Africa. He would thus come, by the direct route, to the desired lands and "the kingdoms of the Great Khan." Columbus's manner does not seem to have impressed the king very favourably for, as Barros relates, "he noted that this Christopher Columbus was boastful about his accomplishments and a great talker. He was full of ideas and fancies about his island of Cipangu but had no real proofs. The King accordingly did not put much trust in him." Las Casas gives the following account of this momentous meeting: "He proposed the project to the king, which was as follows: That going by way of the west towards the south he would discover great lands, island and *terra firma*, all very prosperous, rich in gold and silver, pearls and precious stones, and an infinite number of people . . ."

Columbus's own demands in return for the vast fortune that he was offering King John were in keeping with the grandiosity of his project. First of all, he should be "Ennobled and armed as a knight with golden spurs," and secondly that he should be granted the title of Grand Admiral of the Ocean Sea. Nor was this all. At that time the Admiral of Castille was the most important dignitary afloat. Columbus asked for himself that he should have all the same honours, privileges, rights and

Opposite: *Cipangu (Japan) placed to the north of Java, a small island over whose riches Marco Polo rhapsodized and a goal for which Columbus strove so persistently.*

dues enjoyed by the Admiral of Castille. He was, furthermore, to be the "Perpetual Viceroy and Governor of all the islands and lands which he might discover or which might be discovered by anyone else under his command." By now King John must have felt that this comparatively unknown foreigner was suffering from a touch of sun. Columbus was not yet finished, however, for he went on to demand "a tenth of all the income accruing to the King from all the gold, silver, pearls, precious stones, metals, spices and other valuable things, and from every kind of goods bought, exchanged, discovered or acquired within the region of his Admiralty." He concluded by stipulating that in any future expeditions he should have the right to put up one eighth of the expenses in return for receiving one eighth of the profit.

His demands and his whole manner were so high-flown that the King had his doubts about having anything further to do with him. However there must have been something impressive in this apparent megalomania, for King John appointed a commission to investigate Columbus's claims and theories. Their report, when finally concluded, was adverse. They said that Cipangu only existed in the mind of Columbus – or rather, in that of Marco Polo. Nevertheless the King remained interested in the project and determined to put it to the test on his own account. At the suggestion of the Bishop of Ceuta (who had been foremost in the opposition to Columbus in the investigating committee) the King secretly chartered two caravels. He ordered their masters to set out from the Azores and sail westward to see if they could find the great Island of the Seven Cities, legendary Antillia. The caravels returned, having been heavily buffeted by head winds, and the project was abandoned. This lack of success probably convinced the King and his advisers that they had been right to be sceptical about Columbus's plan.

In 1485, with his great enterprise rejected by King John's committee, Columbus suffered a further blow in the loss of his wife Dona Felipa who died at Lisbon. The two events coming so close together undoubtedly

contributed towards his feelings of disillusionment with Portugal. Although he remained on friendly terms with the king – returning later to the court at the latter's invitation – Columbus was already looking elsewhere for a patron. It is just possible, although there is no direct evidence for it, that he approached his native city of Genoa with the project. Certainly we know that to the end of his life Columbus's regard for Genoa remained undiminished. If he did do so, however, it is certain that he must once again have been rebuffed for we next find him in the summer of 1485 embarking for Spain.

While his brother Bartholomew remained behind in Lisbon looking after the family chart-making business, Columbus and his five year-old son Diego took a coaster bound for the small port of Palos in Andalusia. It is clear from his later correspondence with King John that one of his reasons for leaving Portugal was the fact that he was in debt, and probably pursued by his creditors. With his dreams of financial success in ruins, and with his even greater dream of discovering the Indies dismissed by the King's advisors, with his wife dead and a young son to support, Columbus enters Spain at the age of thirty-four a poverty-stricken refugee.

His first concern must have been to secure board and lodging for Diego, and he was fortunate that near the mouth of the Rio Tinto there was a Franciscan Friary, La Rábida. Since friaries at that time provided food and shelter for travellers it was natural for Columbus and his son to make their way to the gates. Here he was fortunate once again. The friar who interviewed them, Antonio de Marchena, was himself interested in astronomy and cosmography. He quickly learned in conversations with Columbus of the latter's passionate interest in these subjects. It was arranged for Diego to be taken in as a lodger in the monastery, where he

The Franciscan Friary of La Rábida where Columbus found lodging and education for his son Diego.

would also begin his education, while Columbus, with an introduction from the friar, went on to see the Count of Medina Celi. The latter was one of the most important Grandees in Spain and was also the owner of a large merchant fleet.

The Count of Medina Celi was more taken with Columbus's project than had been King John. Indeed, he was so optimistic that he proposed to underwrite the expedition himself. But, on considering the matter more carefully, he realised that anything involving the discovery of new territories must automatically involve the Crown. Accordingly he sent Columbus to the Court of Ferdinand and Isabella, with a letter commending him to the Queen. It was an inauspicious moment, for the Sovereigns' whole attention was given to the war against the Moors and to their determination to expel them from Spain forever. Nevertheless the Queen still found time to interview Columbus who, if Las Casas's account is correct, asked for no more than three or four caravels with which to attempt the passage of the Ocean. It is not exactly clear at what date Columbus had his first audience, but what is certain is that, although his reception was not unfavourable, nothing could be done at that moment. Columbus was courteously dismissed, to bide his time and await the Royal pleasure.

Bust of Columbus in the Capitoline, Rome.

Patience

The following five years of Columbus's life would have broken the spirit of any lesser man. It was now that those qualities of patience and endurance, so necessary for a seaman, were to be tested almost to breaking point. He was to learn the cold and contemptuous neglect of little men in positions of authority, the mockery of arm-chair savants, and an intimate acquaintanceship with poverty. In his dusty, threadbare cloak, pursuing the Court from one town to another as it moved around embattled Spain, Columbus is a tragic figure. Las Casas compared Columbus's long suit to a battle, "a terrible, continuous, painful, complex battle." A man who could survive the tortuous intrigue and petty-fogging delays of procrastinating officials, all the interminable discussions and passing back and forth of messages and documents – so dear to the Spanish heart to this very day – was never to falter when the chance finally came to prove his dream.

In one respect Columbus was fortunate during these long years of waiting. He found a woman to love. While he was in Cordova he met Beatriz Enriques, a cousin of the Harana family, Genoese who had settled in the city. In 1488 Beatriz bore him a son, Ferdinand, who was later to write his father's life. Both Oviedo and Las Casas say that Ferdinand was illegitimate, and there is no reason to suppose that Columbus ever married Beatriz. Although some sentimental, or moralistic, biographers have invented a secret wedding, it would have been quite out of character for Columbus – and for the standards of his time – to have given Beatriz his name. The Haranas were a country family of peasant farmers, whereas Columbus by his marriage to Dona Felipa Perestrello had elevated himself into the sphere of the nobility. It was this connection that still enabled him, poor though he was, to have access to the Court of Ferdinand and Isabella in Spain and King John in Portugal. With Columbus's high aspirations to become "a Knight with golden spurs" and Admiral of the Ocean Sea, it would have been unthinkable to have had a wife who came from common stock. It was quite usual at that time for noblemen to take mistresses among the lower classes and, indeed, to make sure that their illegitimate children were treated as well as any legitimate children they might have. For the woman concerned, and for her family, the situation offered every means for prosperity and advancement, and it is quite clear that the Harana family were pleased with the connection. Beatriz's brother and a cousin later served with Columbus at sea, and Ferdinand was to become a close friend and work diligently for the interests of his half-brother, the legitimate Diego.

The first occasion that we know for certain that Columbus met Ferdinand and Isabella was in the spring of 1486, probably early in May when the Court had moved to Cordova. The contemporary chronicler Bernáldez gives the following report: "Colón came to the Court of King Don Fernando and of Queen Dona Isabel, and he told them of his dream to which they did not give much credit . . . And he talked to them, assuring them that what he said was true, and showed them a map of the world. The result was that he instilled in them the desire to know about those lands . . ."

"The Catholic Sovereigns" as they were generally called, Ferdinand of Aragon and Isabella of Castille were a remarkable couple by any standards. Their driving desire was to expel the Moors from the kingdom of Granada, something which they did indeed finally succeed in doing. This action, which seemed justifiable and sensible at the time, was unfortunately in later centuries to rebound upon the kingdom of Spain and most of the Mediterranean. The Moors who were forced to live upon the African coast turned themselves into the most implacable pirates who, in their determination one day to regain Granada, ceaselessly harried all Christian shipping. But the greatest error committed by Ferdinand and Isabella in their passionate Catholic zeal was the expulsion of the Jews, which resulted in the loss to Spain of many of the finest intellects in science, commerce and industry. At the time of this first meeting the three leading persons in what was ultimately to be one of the greatest dramas of history were all much the same age. Ferdinand and Columbus were thirty four, and Isabella a little over thirty five.

If the King, whose interest lay primarily on the land, was to be of comparatively little use to Columbus, the same could not be said of Queen Isabella. Somewhat similar to her future Admiral in appearance, a handsome woman with auburn hair, she had considerable brilliance and – except for her religious intolerance – was more statesmanlike than her husband. This lively autocratic queen was able to discern, beneath

(Left): *King Ferdinand V of Aragon. From Capriolo's* Ritratti, *1596.*
(Right): *Queen Isabella of Castile. Portrait attributed to Bartolome Bermejo, c. 1490.*

the cloak of poverty, the character of the man who presented himself at her Court in Cordova. Because of the nature of the times, and the royal involvement in what Isabella regarded as a Holy War, Columbus would have to wait for years, but in the end the Queen would see that his project materialised.

A special commission was set up to investigate the claims and theories of Columbus, under the overall jurisdiction of Hernando de Talavera who was the Queen's Confessor, and destined in due course to become the Archbishop of Granada. It is evidence of the Queen's interest in the ideas of this strange Genoese that she appointed her own confessor to head the committee, and that its first meeting took place only a few months after she had first met Columbus. In the winter of 1486 the members adjourned to Salamanca along with the court "in order that they should hear Cristobal Colón in more detail," as Las Casas writes, "and that they should investigate the quality of his proposal and the proofs that he gave of its possibility. They were to confer and to discuss it, and were then to make a full report to the Majesties."

There is no evidence whatever of any great confrontation between the scholars and savants of the University of Salamanca and Christopher Columbus (popular though it has been with romantic writers). The lone determined figure saying that the earth is a sphere, while the aged professors and priests maintained that it is flat, is a myth. The true fact is that, as Rodrigo Maldonado, the Governor of Salamanca and himself a member of the commission, wrote, "in the presence of the Prior of Prado, who was to become the Archbishop of Granada, together with other wise and educated mariners, a discussion took place with the said Admiral about his voyage to the islands he talked about. All present were agreed that what the Admiral said was impossible. But contrary to the opinions of them all the said Admiral persisted in his intention of going there." Salvador de Madariaga commented in his life of Columbus, "Spain was then one of the best centres of cosmographical learning in Europe, and Salamanca University, far from being a nest of bigoted obscurantists, had among its staff one of the greatest Jewish astronomers of the day – Abraham Zacuto – and was one of the first homes of learning in all Christendom to adopt the Copernic system in its teaching."

There seems little doubt that at this juncture Columbus did not lay all his cards on the table. Las Casas describes him as "giving reasons and authorities to induce them to consider it [his project] as feasible, but keeping silent about his most important ones in case the same thing befell him as had happened with the King of Portugal." This seems to suggest that his correspondence with Toscanelli and the famous map were not produced. Columbus was in the usual unenviable position of most 'inventors' who have no capital themselves, but are trying to enlist it from others. If he showed them everything they could later act on their own part, and he would be left with nothing. King John had tried to circumvent him by organising a private expedition, and there was absolutely no reason why the Spanish monarchs should not do the same. But the commissioners who havered over Columbus's Enterprise of the Indies for month after month, and finally dismissed it, were not the ignorant simpletons such as tradition has made them out to be. Their contention was that the world was a great deal larger than Columbus accounted it, and that no caravel or fleet of caravels could stay at sea long enough to reach the Indies by the direct route across the Atlantic. In this they were completely correct, and Columbus was wrong. Indeed, had there been no American continent standing in the way, Columbus, when

Opposite: *The Virgin of the Catholic sovereigns. Ferdinand and Isabella are shown with Prince John and Princess Isabel. Standing (left), St Thomas Aquinas and (right) St Dominic.*

he did finally set sail, would have vanished into the immense expanses of the Atlantic/Pacific and never been heard of again.

Columbus was fortunate in having one member of the commission, Diego de Deza, a Dominican friar, on his side. It is also possible that Hernando de Talavera was not completely satisfied by the opposition to the foreigner's projects. At any rate, in the spring of 1487, the name of "Cristóbal Colómo, a foreigner" appears in the records of the Royal treasury as being paid 3,000 maravedis, and further payments over the next twelve months show that Columbus received something like twelve thousand maravedis. Since a million maravedis was only equivalent to about three hundred English pounds of that period, it can be seen that Columbus was only receiving a pittance. It was in fact roughly the same as a working man's wage – sufficient to keep body and soul together, but little more.

Despairing of receiving a favourable report from the Talavera commission Columbus once more got in touch with King John of Portugal. With Ferdinand and Isabella totally occupied with the war (Malaga fell to their arms in 1487) Columbus probably felt that King John, who had by now broken the power of the nobles in Portugal, would be in a more receptive mood. He was right in this, and the King replied courteously, inviting Columbus to visit him in Lisbon. At the same time he granted him a safe conduct against his creditors in the city.

There seems little doubt that the credit of discovering America would have gone to the Portuguese – who deserved this distinction more than any other seafaring nation – but for the fact that King John, disappointed by the earlier failure of his expedition from the Azores, had already sent another one on the African route. This was led by Bartholomew Diaz, one of the greatest seamen of all time, who had been despatched from Lisbon with three caravels to continue the southward exploration of Africa beyond the limits which had already been advanced by that other great Portuguese navigator Diogo Cão. Passing Cão's furthest limit south, Diaz had erected a pillar on what is now known as Diaz Point, in 26° 38′ South (fragments of which still exist). Proceeding even further, Diaz had reached Cape Voltas, 'Cape of the Turns' as he called it after the frequent tacks he had to make against head winds, the south point of the Orange River. At the time that King John was in correspondence with Columbus, Diaz had been away for many months and it was probably assumed that he was lost. He had however rounded the Cape and

Opposite: *Ferdinand and Isabella riding in the captured city of Grenada in 1492. 16th century altarpiece in Grenada cathedral.*

had gone as far up the east coast of Africa as Algoa Bay and the Great Fish River, halfway between Port Elizabeth and East London. From here the north-easterly trend of the coast was unmistakable. Diaz had found that dream of Henry the Navigator – the sea route to the Indies. He named the southernmost Cape 'Cabo Tormentoso', Stormy Cape, on account of the terrible weather he experienced off it. On his return to Lisbon in December 1488 King John, realising the immense importance of this discovery, gave it the enduring name of the Cape of Good Hope.

It was the end of any chance that Columbus might have had of interesting the King in his own project. He was later to record in his copy of Pierre d'Ailly's *Imago Mundi*, how he himself had been in Lisbon when Diaz arrived back. He noted that Diaz "plotted out his voyage league by league on a chart before the King", adding, "I myself was present on the occasion." It must have been a moment of almost intolerable bitterness for Columbus, a moment when many lesser men would have resigned their dreams and turned back to the simple bread-and-butter of everyday life.

Columbus never gave up. Even at this moment, when it seemed that Ferdinand and Isabella would never have any time for him and when John II of Portugal clearly no longer needed him, he was still determined to promote his dream. He would enter into negotiations with any monarch in the world who would agree to lend him a few ships – and who was capable of seeing that the quickest way from the West to the East was to sail due West.

The Road to Cordova

The Italian poet Chiabrera, who was born at Savona where Columbus had worked as a weaver, described his great compatriot as being at this time in his life "nudo nocchier, promettitor di regni" – "a pauper pilot, promising kingdoms". Such indeed he was, and it is evidence of the eagerness of monarchs at this time in history to embark on Atlantic ventures that his theories ever received a hearing in any kingdom.

At some time or other, probably in 1489, his brother Bartholomew is said to have made his way to the court of Henry VII of England, that wily and parsimonious descendant of John of Gaunt (who was the grandfather of Henry the Navigator). According to Oviedo, as well as Ferdinand Columbus, Bartholomew had an audience with the king to whom he is said to have presented a world map. Beyond this point the two chroniclers differ, Ferdinand saying that the King was interested and that discussions were still going on when the news of Columbus's epoch-making voyage reached England. This seems unlikely, for we know that Bartholomew subsequently went to the French Court where the elder sister of King Charles VIII, Anne de Beaujeu, became his patron and that he was working at Fontainebleau as map maker for her in 1492. Oviedo's report is probably more accurate. He says that "the King's advisors derided the words of Columbus and said that he was talking nonsense". Francis Bacon, who presumably had access to the records, says in his 'History of Henry VII' that Bartholomew was captured by pirates on his voyage to England, and that by the time he had been freed and "before he had obtained a capitulation with the king for his brother, the enterprise by him was achieved." An interesting footnote to this whole episode is provided by a letter from the Spanish ambassador to England written to his sovereigns in July 1498. In it he says that "Merchants of Bristol have for the last seven years annually sent out ships in search of the island of Brazil and the Seven Cities." This means that, a year before Columbus actually discovered America, ships from Bristol had been searching in that direction. Their endeavours were of course crowned in 1497, when the two Venetians, John and Sebastian Cabot, acting under the patronage of Henry VII, had reached Newfoundland and Nova Scotia.

From June 1488, when it seems that Columbus's small 'retaining fee' was no longer paid him by the exchequer, his movements are practically unknown. He was presumably part of the time at Cordova with Beatriz and his young son, and again one can be sure that he visited the monastery at La Rábida from time to time to see his elder son Diego, and to pass the hours talking about cosmography and other matters with Antonio de Marchena. With his small income cut off at source it would seem most likely that he paid his way by turning back to his old profession of map and chart maker. In 1489, according to Zuñiga, Columbus was at the siege of Baza, where Isabella herself was present dressed in full armour. One thing is certain: Columbus must have spent a large part of these years following the Court as it moved with the Sovereigns in their relentless determination to regain what the Moors had called their "delicious Andalus". Ferdinand and Isabella naturally felt that they were pursuing something tangible, whereas Columbus seemed to be offering them a mere chimera.

The final report of the commission appointed by the Queen under her confessor Talavera did not appear until late in 1490. It merely confirmed the opinions that had been expressed some four years before. The pro-

Columbus with his two sons, Diego and Ferdinand. Origin unknown.

ject was unfeasible, Columbus's conception of the globe was inaccurate, and no ships of the time could make the voyage from the West direct to the East. Columbus, for his part, had not abated one iota of the demands which he made for himself in return for this service he intended to render their Majesties. It seems incredible that he held out intractably for all the honours, titles, percentages – and all in perpetuity for his family – when he had hardly a cloak to his back. It is difficult not to be moved by the spectacle of this shabby dreamer confronting the proud rulers of one of the proudest peoples in the world, and refusing to back down in the face of their power – or in the face of the most informed opinion of the time. Columbus was courteously dismissed, but not, according to Las Casas, without being given to hope that at a more suitable time his proposition might yet again be considered.

One of the things that provides a leading clue to the whole character of Columbus is his intense religiosity. To himself he undoubtedly was what his name implied, "the Christ Bearer". It was his sacred duty to bring the Faith to the unwitting heathen of the world. He did, for instance, at one time dream that the wealth of the Indies might be used to promote a new crusade in Palestine, and to recover Jerusalem. In this respect he was akin to Prince Henry the Navigator, whose dream of making contact with Prester John through the sea route round Africa were largely determined by his passionate desire to recover the Holy Places from the infidel.

At this moment of his life Columbus seems to have come to the reasonable conclusion that he must abandon all idea of interesting the Spanish monarchs. He must have hoped that his brother might have sufficiently aroused the interest of Henry VII of England or Charles VIII of France. He returned in 1491 to the monastery of La Rábida, apparently with the intention of collecting his son Diego and leaving him with relatives before going on to join his brother in France. At long last the endless procrastination which had confronted him on every side during his years in Spain seems to have woken his temper. It certainly had not broken his spirit. He remained as indomitable in defeat as he had been when first, with some high confidence, he laid his original proposition before Ferdinand and Isabella.

At this moment in his life, when he was at the nadir of his fortunes, it is worth taking a closer look at the man and at his character, as he was described after he had become one of the most famous men in the western world. That he was tall and red-haired, we know, but "his beard and hair very early turned to grey due to his exertions. In private conversation he was cheerful and open spoken, but in his public dealings he was not only a great talker but inclined to boastfulness. Cheerful with strangers, he was of a serious disposition. With his own family and household he was good-natured and gentle, discreet and modest. It was easy for those who met him to love him. In his clothing and appearance he was modest and sober, and moderate also in food and drink."

Ferdinand Columbus confirms this aspect of his character, adding that "in religious matters he was extremely strict and in fasting and in all the offices of the Church he was so devout that he might have been taken for a member of a religious Order". Las Casas goes on to say that "in ordinary conversation he was light hearted, but when angry or rebuking someone he would say 'May God take you! Don't you agree?' In matters of religion he was so devout a Catholic that before beginning any enterprise he would always interject the words: 'I will do this in the name of

Charles VIII of France. From Capriolo's Ritratti, *1596.*

the Holy Trinity . . .' At the head of any letter or anything else that he wrote he would always put *Jesus cum Maria sit nobis in via* [Jesus and Mary be with us on the way] and I have a number of writings in his own hand to prove this. If he wanted to affirm anything of real importance, such as something upon an oath, he would say 'I swear by San Fernando!' In writing to his Sovereigns he would add 'I swear this to be true' . . . Blasphemy and profane language he hated. He had a special devotion to Our Lady and to the blessed St. Francis. He was very grateful to God for any benefits that he received, and he regularly admitted that God had showered upon him great mercies – just as He had upon David. If ever any gold or precious things were brought to him he would go into his cabin, kneel down, call to those around and say to them, 'Let us give thanks to God that He has found us worthy to discover so many wonderful things'."

"Being so exceptionally devout he was always most eager for the conversion of these people [the Caribbean Indians] and desirous that the whole world should become full of the Faith of Jesus Christ . . . He was above all a gentleman, forceful and full of high aspirations, and by nature inclined (as one can judge from his life, his conversation, his actions and his writings) to undertake exceptional enterprises and noble deeds. He was forbearing and patient (as will soon be evident), a man who forgave injuries done to him and only wanted those who worked against him to recognise their errors and to be reconciled with him. In hardship and adversity he was enduring and long suffering. Indeed, he well needed to be for he had to endure so many difficulties and tribulations that sometimes seemed unending, yet he never lost faith in the mercy of God." This was the man who now, as he made his way to La Rábida, undoubtedly swore 'By San Fernando!' that he was going to shake the dust of Spain from his cloak and shoes for ever.

Columbus was fortunate in his friends, fortunate too in something about his single-minded dedication which convinced them that whatever he said he could accomplish. It was probably this very quality that had originally impressed the Queen. The impression cannot have faded, for when it was put to her by other men that Columbus might well be right, she finally acquiesced. One of these was Luis de Santangel, the Keeper of the Privy Purse. He had observed Columbus closely and had come to the conclusion that the risk was worth taking. After all, if this adventurer failed, no more than two or three small ships would be lost. If, on the other hand, he triumphed, the honours, titles, and percentages would be little compared to what would accrue to the Throne and to the Spanish Treasury. The moment was opportune. In January 1492

Granada had fallen to Ferdinand and Isabella and the atmosphere was heady with triumph. Although Columbus had been given what seemed to be his final 'No' and had already left the Court, he was still in Spain.

While Columbus was on his way to collect his son, and to offer his services to the King of France, Santangel was pleading his cause. He went so far as to say that he would even finance the project himself if his Sovereigns did not consider it worthy of their attention. Like Medina Celi, so many years before, he was willing to underwrite the expedition – given their Majesties' permission. Meanwhile it is said that Fra Juan Perez, Prior of La Rábida, deeply concerned at hearing about Columbus's determination to take his project elsewhere, had already written to the Court urging Columbus's suit. There were others too who were prepared to invest their own money in the Enterprise of the Indies, among them his original backer Medina Celi, as well as a Florentine banker, Berardi, who was resident in Seville. In the end his long years of waiting were to be rewarded.

Columbus was less than ten miles from Granada when a messenger came spurring after him down the dusty road, bearing a royal summons for the wanderer to come to the Court at Santa Fé. He must have hesitated. He had wasted so many years. He had just been told that the Spanish Crown was not at this moment prepared to invest in his venture. He had made up his mind – his stubborn mind – to have no more to do with the endless haverings and petty animosities of small officials and smaller minds. But a royal command in those days was very much a command – and certainly not to be ignored when one was still on the territory of the sovereign concerned. Besides this, Christopher Columbus was a man not only obsessed with a dream, but a devout believer in 'The Book' – the Bible. It meant as much and more to him than Marco Polo or Pierre d'Ailly or the works of Aeneas Sylvius. The sweat-stained messenger was the agent of God, despatched to summon 'the Christ-Bearer' to his high destiny.

For Columbus the road to Cordova was his secular equivalent to Saul's road to Damascus. It was not that here, as he halted at the small village of Pinos, he had the revelation of his mission. He had had that for many years. It was here, though, that he realised that the means were going to be put into his hands to carry it out. Nothing else, at this stage of what had seemed to be a final rejection, could have prompted the Queen to send after him. He turned his mule about and, in doing so, he unknowingly set his face towards America.

The Instruments of Victory

From the moment that he arrived back in Sante Fé Columbus was no longer the humble suitor, but the courted. His obstinacy and perseverance, coupled with his patently sincere belief in the feasibility of his mission, had finally won the day.

On April 17 1492 the contract between Columbus and the Spanish Sovereigns were finally signed. The fact that Juan de Coloma, the secretary for Aragon, signed on behalf of the Sovereigns is a clear indication that Ferdinand did not withhold his approval. In any case, Luis de Santangel, who had been so largely instrumental in securing the royal acquiescence in the venture, was Ferdinand's official, not Isabella's. The story that the King and the Queen disagreed and that she pawned her crown jewels in order to back Columbus is a later invention. The financial support (about 2,000,000 maravedis according to the best authorities), was raised partly by a loan from a fund of which Santangel was one of the treasurers, and partly by private subscribers, the Duke of Medina Celi most probably being one of the main investors.

The contract is generally known as the Capitulations of Santa Fé. Juan de Coloma who signed for the sovereigns was the same who, little more than a fortnight before, had countersigned the edict for the expulsion of the Jews from Spain. Coloma therefore put his name to the two most important documents in Spanish history. The agreement between their Catholic Majesties and Christopher Columbus, who is called 'Don Cristóbal Colón' – for so he has already decided to style himself – opens with the preamble: – "The things requested and which Your Highnesses give and grant Don Cristóbal Colón as some satisfaction for what he has discovered in the ocean seas and of the voyage which he is now, with the help of God, to undertake thereon in Your Highnesses' service . . ."

The high tone of the document – "as some satisfaction" coupled with the words "ha descubierto", "has discovered" – is remarkable. This

Genoese map maker and pilot, who only a short time before was riding penniless out of Spain on a mule, is already assuming the trappings of nobility. Even more astonishing, he is asserting that he has *already* accomplished what he has not yet even set out to do. Naturally enough there has been considerable controversy over the years about the words "has discovered", some maintaining that it is proof that on a voyage of which there is no record Columbus had already reached America. The answer to this is that the document of April 17 was clearly drafted by Columbus himself. It is no more than evidence of his almost paranoiac self-confidence.

The five basic points which are incorporated in the Capitulations are that:

1. Columbus is to be made Admiral of the Ocean Sea and of the countries which he is to discover. He shall hold this dignity throughout his life and it shall descend to his heirs.

2. He is to be Viceroy and Governor-General of all the continents and islands that he shall discover.

3. He shall have a tenth share of all gold, silver, pearls, jewels and other merchandise that shall be found, bought, gained or otherwise produced in the countries which he is to discover.

4. He, as Admiral, or a deputy appointed by him, shall be sole judge in any dispute regarding mercantile matters that shall occur in the countries which he is to discover.

5. He has the option of investing an eighth part in any ships which may sail to these new countries, and in return he may take an eighth part of the profits.

It is an incredible document by any standards. Even the revised version of April 30, which has a certain legalistic caution inserted into it, reads today like some fantasy concocted by a writer who has a poor grasp of his facts. Who is this man – with far less experience of navigation and the sea than many a Portuguese caravel-captain – asserting that he is going to discover and colonise new lands? Of one thing we can be sure: he had the faith that moves mountains. It was this unswerving belief in his own ability that had finally convinced Ferdinand and Isabella, as well as hard-headed bankers and merchants, to invest in the Enterprise of the Indies.

But there is another curious feature of the document: there is no mention of the Indies. The answer is that, as there was absolutely no conception of any land mass in existence except Europe, Africa, and Asia, there was no need to specify what lands Columbus was going to colonise and

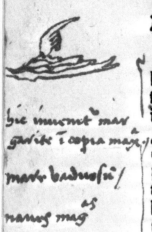

De regno maabar   Capitulū xxiij.

Ltra insulā seylā ao miliaria xl iueniī maabar q ma-
ioz inoia nūcupat Nō aūt e insula k terra firma. In
hac puincia quicz reges sūt Prouicia e nobilissiā et ditis
sima sup mooū In pmo hui puicie rex e noie Seuoeba
i quo regno sūt margarite i copia maxiā In mari eni hui
puincie e maris bzacbiū seu sinus inī firmā terrā et insulā
φoā vbi nō est aquaz pfūoitas vltra oecem vel ouooeci
passus et alicubi vltra ouos Ibi inueniūt margarite sup
oce Mercatozes eni oiuersi societates aoinuice faciunt τ
bīt naues magnas et puas boiesqz cōoucuut qui oescen-
oūt ao pfunoū aquarū et capiunt cōcbilia in quibus sunt

Marginal notes made by Columbus in his copy of Marco Polo's travels, a book he carried with him throughout his voyages. Edition of 1485.

exploit. The Kingdom of Portugal had more or less acquired a monopoly to the coast of West Africa (something which was to be confirmed by Pope Alexander VI in 1502). Clearly Columbus was not sailing off into the blue to discover some new part of Africa unknown to the Portuguese. He was going to the Indies – by the direct route. The *terra firma* and the islands "of the Ocean" that he was going to take over in the name of the Most Catholic Sovereigns were the mainland of China and other adjacent territories, including Cipangu (Japan) which, to judge from Columbus's notes in his Marco Polo, his favourite book, was the place that had fired his imagination more than anywhere else.

Almost equally incredible is the idea that a few European ships could descend upon the mighty Orient, and that the monarchs and potentates and people would automatically accede to their demands and dominion. But the limited European knowledge of the 15th century about foreign peoples was sufficient to give the impression that all of them would indeed yield at the first sight of a caravel and a handful of sailors. After all, that was exactly what had happened in Africa where – except for a few minor skirmishes – the Portuguese sailors had found very little trouble in establishing a slave trade and planting a large fort and trading depots. The confidence of the European at this moment in history – reinforced as it was for Ferdinand and Isabella by their recent triumph over the Moors – was almost boundless. The Church told them that the whole world was destined to come under the dominion of the true faith. Columbus, perhaps even more than the Spanish Sovereigns, had an implicit belief in the Bible – and in his own mission in the world. It did not seem at all incredible that a devout and faithful Christian should sail out of the wide Ocean into foreign lands and convert the natives to the one and only religion. It was indeed a duty, and one which we know Columbus believed to be his destiny. (If 20th century missionaries in the Pacific can believe that it is their duty to bring Christianity to Polynesia, why should one doubt that in 1492 the rulers of Spain and a good Christian from Genoa would have any qualms about taking over vast realms in the name of Christ?)

In any case, it is quite clear that Columbus thought that he was heading for Cathay and Cipangu. A further document with which he was furnished by Ferdinand and Isabella confirms this. It is a commendatory letter designed to be presented to the Great Khan or Prester John or whatever oriental ruler Columbus might find in the territories where he was going.

"Ferdinand and Isabella, King and Queen of Castile, Aragon and Leon etc., to the Great King –. We have heard with pleasure of the great esteem and love that you and your subjects have for us and our nation. We are also informed that you wish to have news of our country. We therefore send you our admiral Christopherus Colon bearing the news that we are in good health and excellent prosperity."

This is signed "I the King" and I the Queen" and was done in triplicate at Granada on April 30 1492. This passport was for Columbus to show to whatever rulers he met, filling in the blank space with the necessary name. The naivety of the document is proof in itself of the simple conceptions of the times, and there is absolutely no reason to believe that Columbus was any more sophisticated than his Sovereigns. He had sold them his dream and they were reinforcing it, just as they might have done had they been sending him as a delegate to some European court.

Armed with his documents Columbus was quickly on his way to Palos, the small port where he had entered Spain, where his son Diego had been cared for, and where his friends had for so long promoted his interests in the face of official contempt and disregard. We know nothing of his provisions for Beatriz, always a shadowy figure in his life, but one can only presume that she stayed with her relatives and her son Ferdinand, by now four years old, at Cordova. Diego, his legitimate son, by appointment of Isabella, was made a page to the heir-apparent Prince Juan. There seemed nothing left to detain him – except the inevitable lethargy of Spain.

Anyone who has ever fitted out a vessel in any country knows that it is

rare indeed for an expedition to get under way on time. The Enterprise
of the Indies was to prove no exception to the rule. Columbus arrived in
Palos on May 12 bearing with him the royal document that authorised
him to recruit crews and demand ships – and all this to be done within
ten days. The request was of course an absurdity. It was to be nearly
three months before Columbus actually got under way: three months of
hot summer during which he endured all the irritations and confusions
of planning, preparing, and of endeavouring to get sailors, small town
officials and others to bestir themselves. First of all there was the question of the ships themselves. In this Columbus was lucky – as were his
sovereigns. The town of Palos had at some unspecified time committed
an "offence" against the Crown. It "had been condemned and ordered"
by the Royal Council to provide, should it be required, two caravels fully
equipped and prepared for a whole year's service. That moment was
now, and this meant that Ferdinand and Isabella had saved themselves a
considerable amount of expense.

The news can hardly have been welcome to the authorities of the
town, when in the Church of St. George (formerly a mosque), Their
Majesties' commission was read out to the congregation. The citizens of
Palos were informed that Columbus had been appointed as captain of
three caravels, which were to set out "to certain areas of the Ocean Sea"
to work in the royal service, and that two of the caravels would come
from Palos. The two ships destined to make their names in history which
were provided by the reluctant citizens of Palos were *Niñã* and *Pinta*.
The third, which was chartered by Columbus, was *Santa Maria*. In
these three vessels, the largest of which, *Santa Maria*, was little over 100
tons, Columbus was to make history.

The Church of St George in Palos.

Under Way

On Friday August 3 1492 three ships sailed from Palos de la Frontera in southern Spain bound for an unknown destination. Early in the morning Columbus had made his communion in the church of St. George. He had then boarded *Santa Maria* and given the order for the crews to weigh anchor and proceed 'In the name of Jesus'. As he was to write in the foreword to his Journal of the First Voyage: "I left the said harbour well furnished with provisions and seamen on the third day of the month of August of the said year, on a Friday, half an hour after sunrise. I shaped course for the Canary Islands of Your Highnesses, which are in the Ocean, with the intention of making my departure from them and proceeding until I should reach the Indies, there to give the letters of Your Highnesses to the princes of those lands as you had instructed me to do . . ."

It is not difficult to imagine with what relief Columbus looked around his little fleet as they crossed the bar of the Saltés river some three miles downstream from Palos. Earlier, as they had passed the friary buildings of La Rábida they had heard the brothers celebrating Prime, the first canonical hour of the Divine Office. Their voices had come out over the still water as the ships slipped down on the ebbing tide:

Deo Patris sit gloria,
eiusque soli Filio,
cum Spiritu Paraclito
et nunc et in perpetuum.

'Now and Forever!' Columbus had stood with his head bared, committing his Enterprise to God. It is more than likely that he had chosen to leave at this hour quite deliberately; possible also that he had equally deliberately chosen Friday, the day of mankind's Redemption, for his departure. Symbol, gesture, these are both characteristic of Columbus,

Columbus taking leave of Ferdinand and Isabella at the port of Palos in 1492. From Theodore de Bry, 1594.

just as much as the first words that head the record of his voyage: 'In the Name of Our Lord Jesus Christ.'

Everything for him had started at La Rábida, his first encouragement on the long road that had now brought him to this dawn departure. And the last months in Palos had been as hard and trying as anything that he had endured during the years of waiting. The immediate – and very natural – reaction to the proclamation that Palos was to furnish ships and men for a voyage under a foreigner into unknown areas of the Ocean had been one of rejection. Fishermen and sailors are by the nature of their calling among the most conservative of men. Their lives are lived in narrow communities, communities which almost automatically disassociate themselves from local landsman, let alone foreign strangers.

That he had got under way at all and had managed to get the ships and recruit the sailors was due more than anything else to the influence of the Pinzón family. The Sovereigns' decree that Palos should provide two ships could not be denied – even though it had to be reinforced by the despatch of an officer of the royal household. But ships are useless without men, and they have to be overhauled, refitted, and victualled. The reluctance, the obduracy even, of anyone in Palos to have anything to do with the project was only overcome when Martín Alonso Pinzón, together with his brothers Francisco and Vicente, combined to support Columbus. They were a prosperous shipowning family, born and bred in Palos, and men whom the locals would take on trust, knowing that they would not engage in some foolhardy enterprise which showed no hope of profit. At a later date the connection between Columbus and the Pinzóns would result in one of history's most famous lawsuits between the descendants of Columbus on the one hand and the Crown on the other; the first determined to maintain that it was Columbus who had set the whole Enterprise going, and the latter that it was only the energies and abilities of Martín Pinzón that had brought the whole matter to a successful conclusion.

Columbus must certainly have met and known the Pinzóns during his earlier visits to Palos. There can be little doubt that they had long known about his project, for he never at any time made a secret of it. Whether he did in fact conclude some agreement with them for a share in the profits is unlikely ever to be known. Certainly no documents have come to light. But it does seem somewhat doubtful that a hard-headed family of local shipowners would have agreed to put themselves behind his cause unless they had seen something more in it for themselves than just the pay that would be forthcoming for their services from the Crown. One of the many witnesses in the subsequent lawsuit reported Martín Alonso as exhorting the townsfolk of Palos and others from nearby towns with the words: "Come away with us, friends. You are living here in misery. But come away with us on this voyage and, according to certain knowledge, we shall find houses roofed with gold and all of you will return prosperous and happy." Another witness reported that, "Martín Alonso applied as much energy to enlisting crews and inspiring them with courage as if the discovery were to be for him and his children . . . Some he assured that they would find houses whose very tiles were of gold, to others he offered certain prosperity, and for all he had good cheer and money. It was because of this, and the general trust in him, that so many people followed him out of the towns." Not, in fact, so very many. The whole complement of the expedition would be less than one hundred. But that was quite enough to man the small ships whose sails were already lifting with the sea breeze as they coasted under their commander's eye along the tawny shores of southern Spain.

The names of the ships can hardly have appealed to Columbus's somewhat puritanical taste and it is almost certain that it was at his instigation that his flagship had her name changed to *Santa Maria*, Holy Mary. She started out in life as *La Gallega*, The Woman of Galicia, and at some time or other seems to have been renamed by her master or crew *Marigalante*, Naughty Mary. Columbus undoubtedly frowned at either, or both, of these names – totally unsuitable for the flagship of the Admiral of the Ocean Sea. Equally undoubtedly her crew continued to call her Naughty Mary. The other two were no better, *La Pinta*, The Painted One (sailor's euphemism for a whore), and *La Niña*, The Girl.

There can be little doubt that *Santa Maria* (to use the name which Columbus preferred to call her) was, although the largest, the least suitable vessel for the Atlantic crossing. Although we have no exact details of any of the ships that went on this first epoch-making voyage and – tragically enough – no authentic contemporary paintings or even drawings of them, we know enough of the basic types to hazard a reasonably accurate guess. A number of models and reconstructions have been made from time to time of all three vessels, one of the best being in the Marine Museum, Genoa. *Santa Maria* was chartered by Columbus from her owner Juan de la Cosa, who came from Galicia, then the foremost Spanish province for ship-building. Columbus described her as *nao*, a ship, in distinction to *Niña* and *Pinta* which he calls *carabelas*, caravels. The term *nao* usually refers to the largest ships of the time, but one can be certain that *Santa Maria*, because of the smallness of her crew alone and the fact that she is referred to as of 100 tons (holding 100 tuns of wine), was only a little larger than the caravels.

As a small cargo-carrying vessel, she is almost certain to have had the typical rounded hull-shape of the period. She will have had a high triangular fore-castle and the usual traditional square-shaped after-castle for the officers' quarters. Beamy, rather heavy, and a slower sailer than the two caravels, *Santa Maria* was never to satisfy the Admiral. She will have stepped a bowsprit at an angle of about $45°$ to the foredeck and abaft this, on the foredeck itself, was the foremast which set a small squaresail. About two thirds down the centre-line of the hull from the bow rose the lofty, square-rigged, mainmast. Behind this again came the mizzen mast, the only one to set a high-peaked lateen sail. We know what a full sail plan looked like from Columbus's journal, when he describes how, on October 2, ten days before landfall, he set "all the sails of the ship". These were the spritsail, forecourse, the maincourse with two bonnets, the topsail and the mizzen. The spritsail was a rather useless little sail set under the bowsprit, which meant that in anything like a tumble of sea it had to be reefed. The bonnets to which Columbus refers were narrow rectangular sails secured by toggles or a lace-line below the mainsail to increase its area. In reefing, the main yard was lowered and one bonnet at a time was removed. The topsail of this period was a very small squaresail with little pulling power. (It was, in fact, rather less efficient than the *Siparum*, or triangular topsail of the Roman era.) It was later to evolve, in combination with a considerably lengthened topsail-yard, into one of the most efficient driving sails of the square rig era.

The two caravels would have been similar to those vessels which had been operating since Henry the Navigator's time on the Portuguese voyages to Africa. The *Niña*, we know from the record of Michele de Cuneo, who sailed in her on another voyage two years later, was about 60 tons, and *Pinta* – within a ton or two – probably identical. It is doubtful whether even the flagship drew more than 7 foot. By modern standards all three could be large yachts, and their simple gear, sturdy build, and comparatively uncomplicated sail-plan would not discourage a modern yachtsman from making an ocean-crossing in them. (But then – he *knows* that America is there!) The only real difference between the caravels would seem to have been in their sail plan and rig, *Pinta* being square-rigged on the fore and main, with a lateen on the mizzen, while *Niña* was lateen-rigged on all three. On each sail in Columbus's little fleet was painted the red Cross of Christ which, as Madariaga writes, "spread its arms in a pathetic, ever unanswered, gesture of universal peace".

All three ships were armed with light cannon, four-inch *bombardas* which fired a stone cannon ball. Small arms were also carried and Columbus refers to cross-bows and *espingardas*. The cross-bow threw a short stout shaft known as a 'quarrel' which had a metal point to it, while some types which had a rudimentary barrel discharged a lead ball.

They were efficient sea-going vessels but they could hardly have been called comfortable, and there can have been no room, even in the comparatively large aftercastle of *Santa Maria*, for more than a few of the officers, including Columbus, to have enjoyed the luxury of a bunk. The crew slept on deck, some of them under the forecastle and others on the main hatch, one of the few flat areas on the steeply cambered decks of that period. None of the men, officers included, was used to a soft life. (The luxurious interior of a modern yacht, half the size of *Niña*, would have been quite incomprehensible to them.) Their diet was as simple as their lives, but a healthy one. Water and wine were carried in casks and the basic ration consisted of about one pound a day of hard biscuit, as well as olive oil, salt meat, and salt fish. Much as today in Spain and in Portugal lentils, chickpeas, and other dried beans formed a large part of the diet. A later letter from Columbus to Ferdinand and Isabella on the subject of provisioning vessels refers to almonds, raisins and rice. The sailors could of course always catch fresh fish, and fishing hooks and lines are among other things itemised.

Columbus was in overall command as well as captain of the flagship, while Juan de la Cosa, *Santa Maria*'s owner, came on the voyage as the sailing master. Peralonso Niño, brother of the owner of *Niña*, was the flagship's pilot. Juan Niño acted as master of his own vessel under

Model of the Santa Maria constructed by Anderson in the Addison Gallery of American Art, Andover, Massachusetts.

Vicente Yánez Pinzón. The elder Pinzón, Martín Alonso, commanded *Pinta*, his brother Francisco acting as master. There were a number of specialists; a pilot for each vessel, who was in charge of navigational duties, a barber-surgeon, and a Jew, Luis de Torres, whose knowledge of Arabic it was thought would help them communicate with the inhabitants of the Indies. This was not so absurd as some commentators have made out, for Europeans of that time knew only of the various European tongues. Everywhere else that they went the language seemed to be Arabic.

The Royal Comptroller, Rodrigo de Escobedo, formed part of the company – natural enough, since his sovereigns would require their share of the fabulous treasures that they were going to find in the Indies. The cousin of Columbus's Beatriz, Diego de Harana, had also shipped aboard – proof enough that no resentment was felt at Beatriz being his mistress and not his wife. An unusual figure among the complement was Pedro Gutiérrez, the Royal Butler, acting as chief steward, an office one feels that cannot have really called for his specialist skills. But perhaps he was hoping that the Great Khan or Prester John could use his services. All in all, officers, pilots, able seamen, and ships' boys, the total of men who were embarked on the Enterprise of the Indies was about 90. If this seems a small figure by modern reckoning one must allow for the relatively small population of the time, and for the fact that the Portuguese had opened up trading posts all down the African coast with caravels similarly manned. The expedition was not, as has sometimes been made out, a hastily contrived or ill-conceived affair. It was by 15th century standards well planned and equipped, with good seaworthy ships manned by first-class sailors.

Shortly after sunset, on the evening of Friday August 3, 1492, the wind, which had been onshore all day, swung round into the north. It was this dominant wind from the north that had boosted the pioneer caravels of Prince Henry southward down the coast of Africa. A signal was made from the flagship (probably by igniting a pitch-pine torch). Martín Alonso Pinzón in *Pinta* and his brother Vicente Yánez in *Niña* knew what it meant. The Captain-General – for Columbus had not yet earned his title 'Admiral of the Ocean Sea' – was altering to the pre-arranged course. Throughout the night, reducing sail when necessary to allow for the slower speed of *Santa Maria*, they would follow the glow of the brazier which hung over the flagship's stern. South by west for the Canaries.

To the Canaries

Columbus had decided to take his departure from the Canary Islands for obvious and practical reasons. He had observed on previous voyages to West Africa that the winds in this area blew predominantly from the north-east – ideal for running down his latitude in a westerly direction. He, and the Portuguese who had preceded him, had discovered that phenomenon, the North-East Trade Winds, upon which the economy of Europe was to depend for centuries to come. It was these winds that were to boost the East Indiamen (and later the Clippers) away from European shores to all the quarters of the globe.

The northerly wind sat squarely in the shoulders of their sails as the three ships ran down the sea-lane to the Canaries. These islands had been known to Europeans since classical times, and had almost certainly been visited by the Carthaginians. Lying a few score miles off the African coast, they are probably what Herodotus referred to as "the lands beyond Libya, where the world ends and the sea is no longer navigable, the gardens of the Hesperides, where Atlas supports the sky on a mountain as conical as a cylinder." Quite apart from their harbours, the islands were valued at that time for what was called 'dragon's blood' extracted, from the dragon trees. This was a red-coloured resin highly prized as an astringent medicine, and one of the few substances known to 15th century surgeons for arresting bleeding and healing wounds. "In the islands," says Azurara, "they have many fig trees and dragon trees and dates, also a great number of sheep, goats, and swine. They shave themselves with stones and they believe it a great wrong to slaughter and flay cattle." Although the Guanches were meat-eaters, they considered the butcher's trade a loathsome one and would either hire a Christian, or appoint one of the island's criminals, as their butcher.

"On Grand Canary," we learn, "it is the custom for the ruling knights (of whom there are about two hundred) to take the virginity of all young maidens. Only after he has done with her may her father, or the knight himself, marry her off to whom he pleases. But, before they lie with them, they fatten them with milk until their skin is as plump as that of a ripe fig – for they maintain that thin maidens are not as good as fat ones. Their belief is that in this way the bellies of the fat maidens are enlarged so that they can bear great sons. When the maiden has been fattened she is shown naked to the knight who is to take her, and he tells her father when he considers she is fat enough. After that, the mother and father make her go into the sea for a length of time every day, until all the surplus fat is lost. She is then brought to the knight and, after he has taken her virginity, her parents receive her back again into their house."

Columbus made the run from Palos to the Canaries in under a week, good sailing and proof enough that his ships were suitable for the great enterprise. Only one accident marred this first leg of the voyage, and that was on August 6 when *Pinta*'s rudder gave trouble. Martín Alonso Pinzón told Columbus that he thought the caravel's owner, Cristóbal Quintero, had deliberately sabotaged the vessel. This seems highly unlikely for, after all, Quintero himself was aboard and the sea between Spain and the Canaries is a rough part of the Atlantic. It is improbable that anyone would deliberately hazard his life in such a way. This area was known to Spaniards at that time as "the Sea of the Mares", because so many mares being shipped down to the Canaries died on passage. It was from the descendants of these brood mares that there derived the stock of horses with which the Spaniards conquered the New World. From them, and from others embarked in Spain itself, the wild mustang came to inhabit the plains of America.

Pinzón managed to do a temporary repair on *Pinta*'s rudder, but when it gave trouble yet again the Captain-General detached *Pinta* into the harbour of Las Palmas in Grand Canary. After their fair wind from Spain they ran into a calm that lasted for nearly three days. Columbus, in company with *Niña,* carried on to Gomera which he had settled on as being his point of departure. Gomera, lying west-south-west from Tenerife is a beautiful island some sixteen miles long by thirteen wide. It is almost circular, with a precipitous coast, and a good small harbour on the west coast where the island's capital, San Sebastian, is situated. Rich and fertile, with a river flowing through a deep gorge into the harbour, it was one of the first of the Canary islands to have been conquered by the Spaniards. At the time that Columbus visited it its ruler was an attractive widow, Dona Beatriz de Peraza y Bobadilla.

When Columbus arrived on August 12 Dona Beatriz was away in the easternmost island of the Canaries, Lanzarote. She was daily expected back in a caravel – which Columbus anticipated might replace *Pinta* if the latter's rudder and hull troubles (for *Pinta* had also begun to leak badly) proved insurmountable. While waiting for the arrival of Dona Beatriz, he set the crews of *Santa Maria* and *Niña* to provisioning and watering their ships. After nine days in Gomera he decided to put back for Las Palmas in order to see how Martín Alonzo Pinzón was getting on with the necessary repairs.

Las Palmas had already become the main port and industrial centre of the islands and, while the blacksmiths and carpenters were working on *Pinta*'s rudder, Columbus decided to change her sail-plan and make her square-rigged like *Niña*. It had already become apparent on the run down to the Canaries that the lofty gaff on a lateen was unwieldly, and liable to cause a dangerous gybe with a following wind. Although the rig was eminently suitable for coastal work along the African shores – enabling a vessel to beat back happily to Portugal or Spain – it was clear that in the conditions of the steady north-west trade-winds it was a dangerous one. Had all the vessels been lateen-rigged they might pos-

An 18th century impression of a Dragon tree, which Columbus saw when he visited the Canaries.

sibly have tacked down wind – as modern yachts sometimes do on an Atlantic crossing – and made faster time. But the all important thing was that the small fleet keep constantly together; so to alter *Pinta*'s rig was the only solution: as Columbus put it, "so that she might keep in company with the other ships without danger and with more security".

With all repairs effected and ships stored, Columbus left Las Palmas in Grand Canary on September 1 and sailed back to Gomera. There seems no real reason why he should not have made his departure from Las Palmas but possibly, like many a sailor before and since, the thought of a night or two ashore with 'a merry widow', before taking to the high seas, was at the back of his mind. In any case, when the ships dropped anchor at San Sebastian on the following day Columbus was delighted to find that Dona Beatriz was in residence in her castle (part of which, a stone tower, is still standing). Here, according to report, he was suitably entertained by the lady, finding her eminently desirable, and she finding in this tall Genoese seafarer a handsome and ardent lover. Apart from this brief affair Columbus discovered other things to interest him in the island. He heard for instance from the inhabitants of Ferro, the western-most of the Canaries, similar stories to those which he had heard years ago in Madeira and Porto Santo of "Land to the West". This, of course, was almost certainly the mythical island of Saint Brendan which Columbus thought that he was going to find somewhere on his way between the Canaries and Cipangu.

It is a curious thought that had he not been fairly confident of finding this island, where he could water and victual on his passage across the ocean, he would probably have never set out. Among other curiosities Columbus may have remarked during his four day stay with Dona Beatriz was the way in which the native Guanche inhabitants of the island communicated with one another. As late as 1922 Samler Brown in his "Madeira, Canary Islands and Azores" records that: "A custom of the former inhabitants still survives, namely, talking by means of whistling. Not only can a peasant make himself heard at a distance of three or four miles, but a sufficiently rich language has been developed to enable conversation to be carried on.

"The town people can rarely do this, but in the country, and especially in the neighbourhood of the Montana de Chipude, where the best whistlers are said to reside, all messages are sent in this way.

"For instance, a landed proprietor from San Sebastian with farms in the south, secretly took lessons. The next time he visited his tenants he heard his approach heralded from hill to hill, instructions being given to hide a cow here or a pig there and soon, in order that he should not claim his 'medias' or share in the same.

"The same gentleman, when entertaining a foreign tourist in another part of the island, whistled across to his *medianero* to get them a partridge, these birds being so plentiful as to be almost looked upon as vermin. Some little time after, the tourist objected that it was out of season and that, in any case, only a cock should be shot. The next whistle found the *medianero* stealthily creeping towards his prey, but he understood what was said and picked out a male bird.

"The best whistlers do not use the fingers at all, and convey their meaning apparently by intonations and variations of intensity on two or three notes. It is said that there is a tribe in the Atlas Mountains which talks in the same way."

While Columbus's sailors got on with all the last-minute preparations for sea, – preparations which never seemed to be completed – he heard that three caravels belonging to the King of Portugal were lying off the island "out of envy", waiting to seize him. It is quite probable that the Portuguese were indeed keeping an eye on this expedition, to make sure that the increasingly powerful Kingdom of Spain did not encroach on their African preserves. It is equally possible that Columbus invented this story out of a desire to convince Ferdinand and Isabella that he no longer had any affiliations with his former patron, or out of some sense of guilt. After all, he had learned practically everything he knew about navigation from the Portuguese; it was the Portuguese who had opened up the Atlantic; and it was to King John II of Portugal that he had first suggested his project of the Enterprise of the Indies.

Whatever his feelings about Dona Beatriz, and however much he must have been moved by the beauty of the Canary islands – so much more lovely than the Bahamas where he was to make his landfall – Columbus was eager to be gone. He had had no desertions from his crews: evidence perhaps of the great hold that the Pinzón family had upon them. He knew well enough, however, that nothing rots ships and men more than lying in harbour. As the British Admiral Edward Boscawen was to write centuries later in a letter to his wife: "To be sure I lose the fruits of the earth, but then I am gathering the flowers of the sea." On Thursday September 6, not even waiting for the propitious Friday, Columbus gave the order for his three ships to weigh anchor. No doubt Dona Beatriz watched from her castle walls as the white sails grew on the masts and bellied in a light early morning breeze. They rounded away from the island, and Columbus sent the expected signal to the other Captains: "West – due west. Nothing to the north and nothing to the south."

"The Taste of the Mornings!"

The winds were light and variable, and for two days the ships were more or less becalmed between Gomera and Tenerife. Even on an ordinary voyage, when one knows one's destination, there can be few things more infuriating than to hang idle in sight of the land while the sails slat and bang, the blocks and tackles creak, and the ship rolls awkwardly in a sea that seems to be composed of viscous paint. For Columbus, and indeed for all those embarked, gazing at well-wooded Gomera and mindful of its streams, its women, and its human familiarity, the delay must have been intolerable. Then, on Saturday September 8, the wind came out of the north-east and the ships were able to lay their course. They left the westernmost of the Canaries, the small island of Ferro, to port and headed out into the ocean.

On Sunday they dropped the last of the land behind them. It was now that Columbus began to practise his famous piece of deception, keeping a true log (or so he thought) for himself, and a falsified one for the benefit of the crews. The object of this was quite plain. If, in the log which was available to the other officers – for it is doubtful whether many of the sailors could read – each day's run was underestimated, the men would not be alarmed at the great distances they were covering away from the land. In the log that he kept for himself, however, Columbus put down what he estimated to be the true distance run. For instance, on Monday September 10 his own log made out that they had run sixty leagues, whereas that available to the crew showed forty-eight leagues. His league was equivalent to about three nautical miles.

There was at that time no mechanical device for measuring distance at sea. All that could be done was for the captain to make his own reckoning of the distance covered. He was, after all, supposed to know his own ship backwards, and to have checked her sailing capacity when working off-shore, where he could judge his distances by known landmarks. In fact,

94

Columbus with an astrolabe. From Thevet's Portraits, *1584.*

as Admiral Morison has pointed out in his careful reconstruction of the voyage, Columbus consistently overestimated the distance in his own log. The falsified one that he made for the crew came nearer to the real distance covered. It is evidence of how much had been lost to the western world by the collapse of the Roman empire that there was no method of recording a ship's speed through the water. The Romans, for instance, had used a mechanical log on their large grain-carriers. This consisted of a small paddle-wheel on the side of the vessel which, after every so many revolutions, operated a device inside the hull that dropped a stone into a box for every mile covered. The log and line was a later 16th century English contribution to the nautical art. In this case a thin line was attached to a chip of wood, the line being divided into knots, and the speed of the vessel being measured by the number of knots paid out over the stern against a half-minute sand glass. Columbus had no such device, he could only guess.

For his calculation of time Columbus followed the Portuguese practice and used a half-hour glass. These were delicate (a number of spares always being carried) and were one of the products of the glass blowers of Venice, the Venetians having long been among the foremost Mediterranean navigators. It was the duty of the ship's boy on watch to call out when the last of the sand fell into the bottom of the glass, reversing it promptly, while the officer in charge of the watch recorded it on a slate. Naturally, such a time-keeping method was hardly accurate. If, for instance, the vessel was pounding or rolling in a heavy sea the flow of the sand would become uneven, while in hot weather the glass would have expanded causing a faster flow through the neck. (A punishable offence was 'warming the glass', whereby a ship's boy, anxious to shorten his watch, would take the glass between his hands.) The only way in which the glass could be corrected to local noon was by noting against the compass the moment when the sun lay due to the south. Since Columbus was now sailing west he was losing time, while on his eastward voyage of return he would be gaining it. The day was divided into four-hour watches, eight glasses marking one watch. The ship's company aboard *Santa Maria* worked watch and watch about, that is to say they were divided into two parts. Possibly, although we do not know for sure, the afternoon or early evening watch was divided into two 'dog' watches of two hours apiece, so that the crew did not constantly find themselves always with the same watches. The middle watch, from midnight to four in the morning, is one that all seamen find depressing, hence its nickname of the 'graveyard watch'.

All ships of course had a compass – almost certainly more than one, in case of accident, and most probably in the larger *Santa Maria* the helmsman will have had a compass to himself as well as the officer above his head on the poop. In the smaller caravels it is probable that only one

Opposite: *Martin Alonso Pinzón by an unknown artist. He sailed with Columbus on his first voyage in command of the Pinta. He tried to keep ahead of the other ships in the hope of being the first to sight the "Indies".*

compass was mounted, and the helmsman steered on the instructions of the officer of the watch. In a sailing ship this is not as difficult as it sounds, for a good helmsman soon gets the feel of the wind on his cheek or the nape of the neck, and of the way the ship is reacting to whatever sea is running. He needs only an occasional glance at the compass card. In the steady trade winds that were boosting Columbus's small fleet across the Atlantic the wind and swell are almost monotonously regular. Once the swing and scent of the sea have become (hour after hour and day after day) a part of one's life, it is easier – especially on a square-rigged vessel – to steer a straight course than a crooked one. It is noticeable that the only reference in Columbus's journal to his having to reproach his helmsman, "for letting the ship run up to west by north and even west-north-west", occurs on September 9. That is to say, they were only three days out. The man had not yet got used to the feel of the ship in a trade-wind sea.

Until he had put the Canary islands behind him, Columbus had been able to use the fairly adequate charts of the time which had been compiled by the Portuguese and others since their first voyages down Africa. A chart of that time was made on skin (the Piri Reis map of 1513, to be discussed later, was drawn and painted on a gazelle hide), skin being more durable and less likely to come to grief at sea than parchment. Columbus knew then his point of departure. On these charts were drawn a number of wind-roses, showing the compass direction of winds relative to north, and they were also delineated with rhumb lines marking the quarters of the wind. Such charts carried no meridians of latitude or longitude. It was not until a few years after Columbus's first Atlantic crossing that chartmakers began to draw a line down the centre of their charts and mark degrees north or south of the equator.

Once Columbus had put the island of Ferro behind him he was literally, according to his chart, heading into the unknown – except that he undoubtedly had Cipangu and Cathay sketched in on its westernmost edge. It is possible that Columbus was familiar with the work of a Nuremburger, Martin Behaim, who had been in Portugal in 1484 and who, in the very year that Columbus was crossing the Atlantic, was now busily constructing his famous globe. This shows that he shared the same erroneous views of Columbus – that the world was about 25 per cent smaller than it really is. He puts St. Brendan's island about half way across the Atlantic, and a similar distance on again one comes to Cipangu.

It is very probable that, before leaving Gomera, Columbus had checked his latitude against his chart with the aid of an astrolabe or a

Opposite: *Flying fish weather! From Theodore de Bry, 1594.*

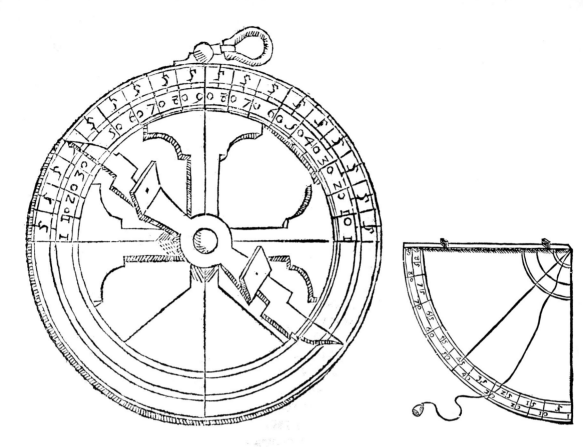

Left: *Astrolabe.* Right: *Quadrant from Palacio's* Instrucion Nauthica, *1587.*

marine quadrant. Both were instruments designed for taking the height, *altura*, of the sun at midday, or the Pole Star at night so as to determine one's latitude. The problem of longitude, or distance east-west travelled around the globe, was not to be solved for centuries to come, when the first accurate clocks enabled the navigator to tell his time accurately. The astrolabe was a comparatively sophisticated instrument, of more use to astronomers than to simple seagoing navigators. It is doubtful if Columbus ever used one on this first voyage – at any rate when at sea. The quadrant, as its name suggests, was a simple wooden, or metal, quarter-circle, with pin-holes for sighting the heavenly body attached along one straight edge. Along the curved edge at the bottom there was a 90-degree scale, while from the top right-angle a plumb line was suspended by a silk thread.

The first known reference to its use at sea occurs in 1456/7 when one of Henry the Navigator's outstanding captains, Diego Gomez, refers to having a quadrant: "When I was sailing to Guinea. I marked on the

The "bosun bird". Drawing by Mark Catesby, c. 1740.

quadrant the altitude of the Pole [Polaris, the North Star]. I found this better than my chart. It is true you can see your sailing course on the chart, but once you get wrong you never find your true position again." The trouble about these early instruments was that, though they were adequate ashore, in the pitch and tumble of a small vessel they were practically unusable. Even in a modern ocean-going yacht, with the perfection of a small sextant to work with, any navigator knows that it requires some practice to adjust to the movement of the boat in order to get an accurate reading. With a quadrant, its plumb line swinging about, it was – as Columbus found out – almost impossible.

Navigation then, on this first crossing and indeed on others to come, was very largely a matter of what seamen called 'dead reckoning'. This has been succinctly described by Mary Blewitt in 'Navigation for Yachtsmen': "Dead reckoning is the name given to the method of plotting the position of a ship by means of distance sailed and course steered: that is by log and compass only. If you cross a familiar room, in the dark,

and arrive without touching or hitting anything, you have achieved this
by Dead Reckoning; by going so many paces in a certain direction, turning slightly to the left to avoid the table and right again to reach the
door . . . The room is only charted in your mind, but you have arrived,
possibly without realising it, by plotting your course and distance . . .
If the sea were like a pool, without winds, tides or currents, and if every
helmsman kept the exact course and if the compass had no deviation and
the log were 100 per cent accurate, D.R. would suffice to take you round
the world with no other form of navigation at all." But of course the sea
is full of winds, tides and currents, all of which deflect a ship from her
chosen course. Helmsmen are unreliable, compasses – especially in the
15th century – not necessarily accurate, and Columbus had no log to
record his speed. Furthermore, he was not "in a familiar room", he was
heading westward in the dark as it were – never to know when he might
bump into Antilia or St. Brendan's Island. As will be seen, when he was
convinced that his ships were nearing land, even though it had not yet
been sighted, he was very careful to make them reduce sail or even heave-
to at night. His experience in the Mediterranean, where men had been
navigating by dead reckoning for centuries (and for centuries before that
without even the benefit of compass), coupled with his voyages in the
North Atlantic, had made a good pilot of him. There was no such thing
as a good celestial navigator in his time.

It is almost certain that Columbus made use of what is called the
traverse board to keep his dead reckoning in some kind of reasonable
order. This was a wooden board which showed the 32 points of the compass, with eight holes designed to take a wooden peg set on the rhumb
line of each point, radiating outwards and representing half an hour of
the four hour watch. It was, in effect, a nautical abacus. The eight pegs
showed the course that had been steered during every half hour. At the
end of the watch the navigator had to convert these readings into the
mean course made good during the past four hours. Primitive though it
sounds, it was not too inefficient a method – especially in the days when
comparatively few men could read or write – of maintaining a record of
"the way of a ship in the midst of the sea". In rather similar fashion the
navigator would "prick the chart". That is to say, from his starting point
he would lay down the course with the ruler and then at regular intervals
he would prick a point on the chart to mark the ship's position according
to his reckoning of course and distance made good. Dead reckoning
navigation in trade wind conditions, as on this outward voyage, was
reasonably adequate for there were practically no course changes. But,
as Columbus was to find out on his return, when head winds were en-

countered, and the ships had to tack, the dead reckoning could only be kept by intelligent use of the traverse board.

It was now, in these early days as they began to draw away from the shores of the Old World, that Columbus and all those with him discovered the delights of trade wind sailing. For the first ten days the ships ran sweetly and easily – making good a distance of more than 1,100 nautical miles. On one day alone they averaged a speed of over seven knots – good going by any standards, and evidence enough that small ships of this period were fine seaboats with sweet hull shapes. The sailors by now will have begun to get used to the eternal rhythm as they lifted and rolled in that steady following sea whose marching lines are lipped with white. Petrels, Mother Carey's chickens, accompanied them on their flight into the unknown – seeming to walk along the water, and then suddenly rising to soar away. These native inhabitants of the oceans, older by far than man, were their constant companions. So too were the yellow-billed tropic birds, with their webbed feet, their rapid wing action, and their long white tails which look so much like a marlinspike that seamen call them 'bosun birds'. These may well have encouraged the men to think that land could not be far away. They will not have known that these types of oceanic birds rarely come ashore except during the breeding season. Black-backed dolphins rose with their snorting sighs alongside the ships, and sometimes played for hours on end in the rushing tumble of the bow wave. Flying fish weather! Sometimes without any effort on their part, they may have had free breakfast out of flying fish that had inadvertently skipped over a dipping gunwale during the night.

Sailors are rarely poets, and yet no real sailor is without the poetic instinct. The officers and men who had the morning watch will have experienced the dawn hours when the sails, cordage, and the wooden decks, are damp with dew and the air smells so fresh that it seems as if one is present at the creation of the world. These moments were not missed by Columbus. "It is like April in Andalusia. Nothing is missing except the nightingales." And on September 16 he wrote: "How great a pleasure is the taste of the mornings!"

The Sea Life

It was now September 16 and they were over eight hundred miles out from the Canary islands. At dawn the morning watch would scrub decks and the officer in charge would inspect the lead of the ropes into the blocks to see if there was any chafing. Usually they would shift the gear a fraction so that a different section of rope took the constant pull of the sails and spars – 'freshening the nips' as sailors call it. They fled on towards the west. And then they began to find themselves sailing into a carpet of floating seaweed, sargaço the Portuguese called it, who had first observed it in the area of the Azores. But this was denser and covered the ocean as far as the eye could see. "Very many bunches of green weed" were recorded. The entry recurs several times, and it is clear that in due course everyone grew quite used to it. But, to begin with, it was alarming – and then hope-inspiring. Weed was always to be found in the vicinity of land. It grew in shallow waters and was torn from the sea-bed by storms, and hurled onto mainland beaches. They sounded with the lead, with two lengths of lead line tied together – well over one hundred fathoms – nothing. Where they were sailing the ocean was about 2,000 fathoms deep.

The Sargasso weed (*Sargassum bacciferum*) is of the brown algae family and is never dense enough to impede the progress of any vessel, however small. Supported on small berry-like bladders, it is to be found between 32° and 70° West and from the Gulf Stream down to roughly 20° North. It is not as Columbus thought, and indeed as was believed for many centuries, torn from the seabed but is a self-perpetuating plant, a permanent native of the ocean. Small crabs and other simple forms of animal life live in it, thus giving rise to the idea that it must have been originally connected with some seashore. Sailing among it the adventurers will also have seen the beautiful but sinister colonies of *Siphonophora*, which sailors have come to call Portuguese men-of-war.

The days were easy, the nights vivid with stars, and the Pole was low on the horizon. There is no evidence that Columbus on this first voyage ever did any celestial navigation. It is doubtful even, whether with the simple equipment at his disposal, it would have been any use to him if he had. He could, as sailors do to this day and age, take an eye view of the Pole Star's altitude against his mast or spars, but to all practical intents and purposes he was, as has been seen, running down his latitude entirely on dead reckoning. At night as the sun went down ahead of them they drove on into its red eye, while all the trade wind clouds burned with the dying light. At dawn it came up astern over far-distant Africa. During the nights Columbus could tell the time by the 'sky clock'. This was a method that had been systematised by the great Catalan mathematician Ramon Lull in the 13th century, whereby the observer imagined the figure of a man in the sky, with Polaris at his navel. The two brightest stars of the little Bear were known as the Guards. Since the Little Bear moves around Polaris every 24 hours of sidereal time, provided that you know the midnight position of the Guards for each month or fortnight of the year (since their position shifts by about an hour for every two

The "little bear", the two brightest stars of which were known as the Guards (the cross-staff shown was not used by Columbus).

weeks) you can use them, and particularly Kochab the brightest in the constellation, rather like the hand of a clock. The 'Sky Man' had his head above Polaris and his feet below. His arms were to right and left. The Guards were described as they stood in relation to his limbs. A simple instrument, the nocturnal, was developed to enable men to read the time by the use of the Guards, but it is doubtful whether one was available to Columbus.

As a monk Felix Faber had described on his Mediterranean voyage nearly ten years earlier: "All night long a lamp burns alongside the compass . . ." This reference immediately brings to mind the all-important questions of fire on board these early vessels – fire for communication signals, and fire for cooking. At night, when in close order, for instance when nearing the Canaries, the flagship will have burnt a brazier over her stern, but in the depths of the Atlantic the ships ran on independently, bearing up and regrouping with the dawn. Columbus, by his alteration of *Pinta*'s rig, had so arranged it that – although *Santa Maria* was slower than the other two ships – all of them, by shortening sail if necessary, could maintain an almost equal rate of advance during the dark hours. Despite the fact that all available spare space will have been crammed with wood for the fires, this had to be as carefully husbanded as water on this sail into nowhere – or to Cipangu as the leader thought. In that part of the ocean, wakes are as phosphorescent as the nights are lovely, and the brilliance of the stars, quite apart from the moon, makes it none too difficult to keep another vessel in sight. (Many who have lived through wars at sea know well enough that keen eyes can follow a wake well enough to keep in station without the benefit of any lights being shown.)

Such lights as were used aboard – and they, apart from the compass light will have been few enough – will have been fuelled with olive oil. (After all, the Romans had run a whole empire on olive-oil lamps.) It is probable that only one hot meal a day was eaten, this being either salted fish or meat with hard-tack biscuits and onion or garlic for vegetable. A simple firebox was all that the cook had to work with, but Latin peoples then as now were unlike Nordics in not requiring a lot of meat and cooked vegetables. The men on this voyage, even when ashore, probably ate cooked meals very rarely. Bread and fruit, vegetables and oil, helped down by a little wine, were their normal diet.

It was on September 17 that Columbus confirmed what he had been suspecting for a number of days – the compass, their only reliable piece of navigational equipment, was itself becoming unreliable. As the ships moved westward the directive force of that great magnet the Earth was causing a variation in the compass needles. Since the needle of a compass is mounted so that it only moves freely in the horizontal plane it is only the horizontal component of the earth's force that directs it. The result is that the direction of the needle diverges towards the east or west of geographical north, depending upon the position of a vessel on the earth's surface – a divergence known to seamen as declination or magnetic variation.

It has sometimes been said that Columbus 'discovered' variation but this is manifestly untrue. The Portuguese had long been familiar with the alteration of the needle and referred to it as "north-easting or north-westing". Columbus uses this term quite familiarly, for he had learned all about variation during his days under Portuguese sail. The men aboard his ships, however, familiar with easterly variation from their coastal and Mediterranean sailing, "were dismayed and frightened". So Columbus did his best to encourage the crews by pointing out that if they consulted "the needles" at dawn they were true against the North Star. What Columbus had observed – and no doubt other navigators of his time had done the same – was that Polaris in his time moved in a radius of nearly $3\frac{1}{2}°$ around the true, or celestial, pole. The result was that the westerly variation of the compass at nightfall was intensified by this amount, whereas at dawn – since they were at this time in the zone of $2°$ westerly variation – the discrepancy was hardly noticeable. Of course, as the ships drew further west, the variation increased considerably. It has also to be remembered that the compass card of this period, based on Mediterranean usage (where strict definition was not too important), was only based on points of $11\frac{1}{4}°$. The common method of checking the compass after sunset was for the navigator to raise his hand in the direction of the North Star and bring it down over the compass card – what was known as "the pilot's blessing" – to check the verity of the needle.

E. G. R. Taylor has the following comment on the discovery of the variation of the magnetic needle: "Some put it down to a poor lodestone or an imperfectly touched or badly hung needle. Others said that it was not because of the needle that the ship appeared to go off course but because of some hidden leeway. And the truth was obscured besides by the action of the compass-makers who tried to correct the tendency of the instrument to stand a little off the meridian [the great circle of the celestial sphere which passes through the celestial poles and the zenith of any place on the earth's surface] by fastening the wires askew under the fly or card and not exactly under the fleur-de-lys [The North Point of the compass]. This is why Columbus found that his Flemish and Italian compasses did not read alike. While the Flemish, French and some Genoese makers used to make a 'correction' of the needle according to the local variation other Italian makers left it alone . . . There were other craftsmen who had come across the variation and dealt with it also in a commonsense way without comment. These were the sun-dial makers of Nuremburg, who had designed and made a portable little instrument set by a tiny magnetic needle. Finding that the needle did not actually stand in the meridian, they cut a mark across its box to show where it should be when the dial was correctly set. The oldest surviving specimen of these 'travellers' companions' as they were called carries the date 1451, but they must have been well known twenty years earlier, for Prince Henry the Navigator's elder brother, King Duarte, when describing the sky-clock, mentioned the little *relógios de alguha* or magnetic time-pieces which came from abroad."

"The needles," Columbus wrote, "always require truth", and he found it to his own convenience in the rotation of the Pole Star around true Celestial north. "He told them to inspect the needles again at dawn, and they found that the compasses were true." In other words, Columbus had divined that the North Star moved around the celestial axis. It does not necessarily mean that he had as yet discovered the reason for the variation of the magnetic needle. One thing this whole episode does prove, though, is the collected calm of the expedition's leader in the face of what at the time must have seemed the dissolution of their only reliable guide. But crowds of seabirds kept reassuring the men that they could not be far from land, and there were "showers without any wind", another sign, they thought, that land could not be far away, and yet again "a whale, which are never found far from the shore". In all their thinking they remembered the seas off the Spanish and Portuguese shores, and the simple Mediterranean, where indeed the whales can never be too far from the land. But they were in the middle of the Atlantic.

Onward! Onward!

On September 19 the day that they sounded and found no bottom with a 200 fathom line, two pelicans came aboard. Columbus recorded that he was sure they were near their destination because "these birds do not go over 20 leagues from land". On the same day, the pilots of the three ships compared their positions, *Santa Maria* making them 400 leagues out from their departure point, *Pinta* 420, and *Niña* 440. Columbus's deliberate false reckoning for *Santa Maria* was probably the most correct . . . All the pilots of the ships, and Columbus himself, would seem to have consistently over-estimated their speed. It is a common enough habit for the captains of sailing boats to think that their much-loved craft are going faster than they really are – but today their enthusiastic optimism is easily enough quenched by log or speedometer.

The following day they ran out of the trade winds. They were now in the area of what are termed 'the variables', roughly between longitudes 40° to 47° West. The weed was all around.

> The fair breeze blew, the white foam flew,
> The furrow follow'd free;
> We were the first that ever burst
> Into that silent sea.

It had been well enough while the 'breeze' did indeed blow, but now in the variables the crew began to murmur amongst themselves. They had – and who can blame them? – the feeling that they would never get back to Spain. Up to date all the winds had boosted them relentlessly away from the shores of the known world, and now even these had deserted them, and they were sailing perforce on a westerly course into this interminable ocean. On September 23 they were practically becalmed and the mood of the crews was ugly. Then suddenly, and mysteriously, a great swell began to lift under their hulls, although there was no wind to have caused it. "This," wrote Columbus, "was very useful to me." It was an omen and a portent. He compared it to a sign such as was given to Moses when the Jews were complaining against his leadership. He too would take his people, however much they might complain, out of Egypt and into the chosen land. This sea that comforted Columbus and astonished the men was almost certainly a dead swell rolling up from a hurricane that had struck hundreds of miles to the south-west of them. At night, at evening prayers – for in those days all shipboard activities were regulated by the Christian observances of the Church – they sang that most beautiful of all hymns: "Saeve Regina Mater Misericordiae..."

On September 25 after five days of this idle sailing, Columbus and Martín Alonso Pinzón had a discussion over a chart Columbus had which showed islands roughly in the position where they now assumed themselves to be. Undoubtedly, Antilia and St. Brendan's island once more raised their hoary, mythical heads. They came to the conclusion that they were certainly in the vicinity of the islands, but that some current had set the ships to the north-east of their presumed dead-reckoning position. Pinzón then went back to *Pinta*, which had drawn up alongside the flagship for their meeting, his head no doubt full of these islands which they must surely raise at any minute. That evening, at sunset, a great cry came from *Pinta*. Martin was shouting from her poop "Land! Land! I claim the reward!" Hands rushed forward, others climbed the masts, and all – including Columbus – agreed that there indeed was land, a mountainous island standing up on the sea's rim against the dying sun. They were now almost exactly half way across the Atlantic. What in fact they were looking at was a towering cumulus cloud on the western horizon, common enough in trade-wind latitudes, but novel to fresh eyes – and especially when those eyes were eagerly determined to find islands. Columbus knelt upon the deck of *Santa Maria* and gave thanks to God. Course was altered in a south-westerly direction.

By the afternoon of the following day they knew that they had been deceived. "Not land, but sky", commented Columbus. Course was resumed towards the west. The disappointment caused by this false landfall, coupled with the fact that they had now been nearly three weeks on the voyage – something that was practically unique for coastal Atlantic or Mediterranean sailors – increased the feeling among the crews that something must be done about this madman who was leading them all to certain disaster. The fact was, of course, that the men were right and Columbus wrong. If they had really been headed for Cipangu and Cathay, with nothing intervening, they would certainly all have perished of thirst and starvation. Columbus was sure that plots were afoot

Columbus aboard ship on his first voyage, with dolphins and mythological figures. From Theodore de Bry, 1549.

to kill him. It is not easy to keep secrets aboard small ships where the slightest gesture, or even the alteration in the tone of a voice, are immediately remarked. (Even in the 20th century yachts have arrived in the West Indies after an Atlantic crossing and the crews walked ashore never to speak to one another again.) Trade-wind sailing is so beautiful – and yet so monotonous. These men were travelling into the unknown, on the rim of the world, led by a wild visionary – and a foreigner to boot.

Columbus was now careful to let it be known that if the ships returned to Spain without him aboard Ferdinand and Isabella would certainly see that his death would not go unavenged. He had them finally cowed, not only by a threat like this, but by the sheer force of his personality. He was Moses, he was the chosen leader, chosen by God. There is no doubt that Columbus was a fanatic in the true sense of the word: a person believing himself to have been divinely inspired. Beneath the Genoese practicality and desire for gain there lurked something else. Perhaps Salvador de

Madariaga, with his theory that Columbus was of Jewish stock, may not have been entirely wrong. Certainly he had in his veins something of that inspired religious feeling that seems to be the prerogative of desert peoples. The blood of the Genoese is very mixed – it is almost as likely that he had Moorish as Jewish among his ancestry. "There is no point in your complaining," he told a delegation who came to tell him that he must turn back, "No point at all. I am going to the Indies and I shall sail on until, with God's help, I find them." There was nothing they could do with him. They were so far from land, and he was the only one who knew – or said he did – where they were going. They could not dispute his reasoning. Surly, part-mutinous, frightened, and each alone with his memories of home, the sailors submitted to the iron will of their master.

On October 1 Columbus gave out to the crews that they were 584 leagues from the Canaries – although his own estimation was 707. Once again he was more nearly correct on his deliberate underestimate. They were now out of the variables, heading slightly south of west, and lying on about latitude 52° West. There is no doubt that during this troubled period the influence of Martín Alonso Pinzón was all-important. "Hang them," he said to Columbus of the potential mutineers. "And if you don't – I and my brother will!" In any estimation of Columbus's achievement, credit to the Pinzón family must never be forgotten. They had not only seen to the provision of two of the ships, but it was their influence – and almost their influence alone – that had managed to raise the crews for the expedition. Now, in the middle of the ocean, with potential mutiny on their hands, it was the Pinzóns who, by backing the future Admiral, made the continuance of the voyage possible. It was the Pinzóns, or probably more particularly Martín Alonso, who now began to urge upon Columbus a more south-westerly course. No doubt they felt that most of the useful discoveries by the Portuguese during the past two generations had been made in that direction. Columbus, however, would not be deflected at that moment from his west, always west, feeling of direction.

On October 7 there was yet another illusion of a landfall, *Niña* firing a gun – the prearranged signal – and hoisting a flag to her masthead to indicate that she had sighted land. But once again it was only a cloud, one of those sunset clouds that look exactly like the ones that hang over the heads of islands. The mood of gloom deepened even further. Where was Antilia? Where was the great island that they should have found half way on their route to the lands of the Orient? Again, observing flocks of birds flying in a south-westerly direction, the Pinzóns advised Columbus to alter course. After all, the flights of birds heading in the

direction of land had been used by mariners since the very dawn of
navigation. Noah's use of the dove was as old as man the seafarer. Even
into the 20th century Polynesian sailors have kept caged birds aboard
their canoes and released them at a suitable moment, to give them an
indication of where islands lie beyond the visual range of a man in a small
boat.

Finally Columbus agreed that the course be altered – one of the most
significant agreements in history. Had he held on for West the ships
would most likely have sailed up into the Gulf Stream. They would have
then inevitably been borne northwards and – if their food and water
had held out – would most probably have ended up on the shore of
Carolina. North America would have been colonised by the kingdom of
Spain. Everything in this extraordinary story was a chapter of accidents.
Or was it, as Columbus truly believed, all a part of the immense design
of God?

"And all the night they heard the birds passing overhead . . ." Four
days later, on Thursday October 11 the sailors had some real reason to
feel that they were not lost in the middle of a limitless ocean, and that
land lay somewhere ahead of them. A reed and a stick were picked up,
and "another stick which seemed to have been carved – and then some
grass such as grows on land, and then a piece of wood". They were nearly
at the end of their desperate journey and, "on seeing these signs, they all
all breathed again and were more cheerful".

But Columbus was not yet out of the wood – or, rather, out of the sea.
If they were indeed approaching the shores of Cipangu or Cathay, now
was the moment when the captains and the navigators had to be even
more careful. Ships sometimes founder at sea, but most ships are lost on
their approaches to the shore. They were scudding along under fresh
trade winds, at times making as much as a steady 7 knots over a 24-hour
run. There was certainly nothing wrong with those ships, nor their
canvas and gear, nor the men who sailed them. Yet even now – and perhaps it is hardly surprising since they were over thirty days out and had
gone further than had ever been anticipated – there were signs of in-
cipient mutiny. As the ships tore along, the trade-wind freshening to
force 7, there were inevitably some who, despite all the signs (the birds,
the wood and the grass), felt that they had been pushed beyond all
reasonable limits. But they were totally committed. They had gone
longer out of sight of land than any men in known history, and there
could be no turning back against these north-easterlies that were hurling
them forward under their squaresails.

At sunset on October 11 Columbus made the signal for the ships to alter course back again to due West. One suspects that his reason for doing this was that there had been sufficient signs of land for him to be sure that they were soon going to sight it. He was determined it should be done on a westerly course. After all, his whole theory – the very idea that he had, as it were, 'sold' to Ferdinand and Isabella – was that all a man had to do to find the Indies was to sail due west. He sensed that the Indies now lay close ahead of *Santa Maria*'s rushing bow-wave. When they reached the golden shores and he truly became Admiral of the Ocean Sea, it should be on the very course that he had always said was the right one.

That night the *Salve Regina* was sung with more fervour than usual. There was a tense expectancy in the air. Columbus made it known that, apart from the 10,000 maravedis which the sovereigns had promised to the first man to sight land, he would also personally give him a silk doublet. *Pinta*, ever the fastest of the three ships, stormed ahead. Men gathered on the fo'c'sles and strained their eyes through the darkness. Columbus was absolutely confident that they were going to make land within a few hours. He was at fever pitch, his nerves strained by the days of incessant sailing, by the troubles among the crews, and by the intense awareness that at last, after so many years of waiting, his dream was going to come true.

It was at about 10 p.m. that Columbus thought he saw a light, "like a wax candle that rose and fell" ahead of the ships. He called one of the seamen, who also agreed that he could see something, but yet another

said that he saw nothing at all. This famous episode which has occasioned so much controversy must be seen in its true context. Columbus could not have seen a shore light of any kind, for the ships at this time – as their true landfall later proves – were nearly 40 miles offshore. He did know however, by all the signs – and perhaps by that sixth sense that some seamen possess – that they were going to make land within a very few hours. Was it his simple Genoese greed, reinforced by his certainty, that made him claim the first sight of the promised land? Quite possibly. Equally possible, as has happened to thousands of seamen when making a landfall, his overheightened senses and imagination led him to see a light where none existed. In any case, he certainly pocketed the Sovereigns' award.

It was at 2 a.m., on the morning of Friday October 12, that there was a turmoil aboard *Pinta* which was surging away in the van of the little fleet. A gun was fired – 'Land in sight'. Another false alarm? The moon was in its third quarter and in the east (astern of the ships), ideal for lighting up anything ahead of those wildly advancing bows. Rodrigo de Triana, a sailor aboard *Pinta*, standing on her swaying fo'c'sle had sighted what appeared to be a white cliff dead ahead. No doubts this time, no cloud illusions. The lookout of *Pinta* had sighted one of the outriders of America.

"Land in sight". The coast of the island of San Salvador. First landing of Columbus.

Another Eden

Throughout the night the three small ships backed and filled under reduced canvas off that unknown shore. They hung in the eye of the wind, with all the Atlantic ocean behind them. Under the moonlight the island waited.

Dawn and the scent and sight of land for the first time in thirty three days. Dawn, and the ships which had been making a south-westerly drift during the night could make plain sail again. They could now see how wise they had been to stand well off during the dark hours. The whole of the coast that faced them was fanged with rocks, where the trade-wind swell flashed and thundered. Softly, timorously almost, they crept along its southern shore searching for a place to anchor. Equally softly, far more timorously, other eyes watched them. As the Spanish sailors pointed, gesticulated, expatiated upon the beaches, the inland green, the lift of morning mists over the small wooded hills, the Caribs to whom the island had belonged watched the arrival of monsters. Fish they knew, and canoes they knew, but nothing like these unbelievable things driven by man-made clouds had ever before haunted their coral coasts.

So, to the slop and sigh of *Santa Maria's* passage through the dawn waters, Columbus came to the promised land. Did he wonder, as they rounded-up under the south-western point of the island – seeing the lee shore also fringed with reefs – at the absence of pagodas and gold-tiled houses? Possibly, but then he knew that he was only at one of the outer islands that fringed Cipangu and Cathay. With the leadsman standing in the bows, the invasion fleet moved stealthily up the coast. They had come in the name of God and of their Most Catholic Sovereigns, Ferdinand and Isabella of Spain, to take possession of all the Indies.

The island which they had finally reached after their long flight across the ocean was one of the Bahamas.

It was most probably the island that is now known as San Salvador, or on British charts "Watlings Island". San Salvador, as Columbus named it after the Saviour of Mankind, was known in the native tongue as Guanahaní. Columbus was later to describe it as having a large lagoon in its interior, and there are to this day not one, but several salt-water lagoons, each separated from one another by small, wooded hills. The first suitable place that the ships found to anchor will have been Long Bay, about half way up the west coast of the island. Here, for the first time in thirty-three days, the anchors splashed overboard to dig their flukes into the coral bed of the New World.

Now was the time for ceremonial. Columbus, who had earned his title Admiral of the Ocean Sea, went ashore in *Santa Maria*'s boat. Along with him in their ships' boats went the other two captains, Martín Alonso Pinzón and Vicente Yánez his brother. The Admiral held in his hand the royal standard of Castile, while the Pinzóns held the banner of the expedition – a green cross bearing the initials of the two sovereigns, over each of which was a crown. The simple islanders, "naked as the day they were born", watched the approaching boats with childlike incomprehension. As the bows grounded the sailors leaped out to steady them and drag them up the beach. Now the strangest thing of all happened. The headman of these mysterious visitors – clearly the chief, to judge by the extraordinary metal clothing that he was wearing and the crimson cloak over his shoulders – fell upon his knees on that simple sand with which they were so familiar. He uttered mysterious sounds. "The Admiral," writes Navarrete, "asked all those with him to give faith and witness how he took possession of this island for their sovereigns, the King and Queen, with all due ceremony."

While they watched, understanding nothing, the god-man and the others who were with him went through a strange proceeding – clearly something to do with the sky from which they were descended. What in fact was happening was that Rodrigo de Escobedo, the secretary, together with the two Pinzóns and other members of the crews who had come ashore, were witnessing the transfer of this island to the Catholic Sovereigns and the Catholic Faith. The sailors, the doubters, the potential mutineers, all now acclaimed Christopher Columbus as Admiral and Viceroy of these new lands. He had proved himself beyond all conscience as a true leader. He was a man of vision whose prophecies were revealed in this sand, this sea, and these golden-skinned people. The Indians, for such they would be called for all the years to come (until only a handful of them were cloistered and artificially maintained like zoo exhibits on the island of Dominica) were not Indians at all. They were a branch of the Arawak group, natives of South America, who had emigrated from the mainland within recent centuries

117

Left: *Natives making wine on the island of San Salvador*. Right: *Natives in canoe. From Benzoni's* Historia, *1572*.

and had enslaved or exterminated an earlier wave of emigrants. Now, as they clustered happily around these bearded strangers with their extraordinary pale skins, they had no fear that it was their turn to become enslaved and exterminated. They were entranced by these men who owned gigantic canoes with birds' wings.

What did the great dreamer himself think of these people whom he had awoken from a dream? "Since they showed so much friendship for us, and because they were clearly a people who would better become members of the Christian faith by love than by force, I gave to some of them coloured caps and to others glass beads for their necks, as well as many other things of little value. [Columbus had come with the usual traders' trash that had served the Portuguese so well in West Africa.] They were delighted with these things and were so friendly to us that it was quite marvellous. Later on they came out swimming to the ships' boats, and brought us parrots, balls of cotton thread, darts and many other things. They exchanged them with us for things that we gave them – little hawks' bells and glass beads. In short, they happily exchanged with us everything that they had . . ."

The Admiral remarked that all went naked, even one young woman whom he saw – but the women in general kept themselves well away from these frightening visitors. So apparently did the elders of the tribe, for Columbus remarked that all the men seemed young. "They were well built and handsome, with coarse short hair." This was worn shaggy over their eyebrows, except for one long lock at the back of the head. He remarked that some of them painted themselves with primary colours all over, and others only their faces or their noses. He noticed also that some of them had wound-scars on their bodies and they indicated by signs that people came from other islands (or from the mainland of Cathay?) and made war upon them.

"They ought," he reflected, "to make good and skilful servants, for they imitate our speech very quickly. They do not seem to have any religion and I am sure they will easily become Christians." Poor creatures, he concluded, for "they neither carry arms, nor do they understand them". And when they were shown the Spaniards' swords one or two of them took hold of that bright, shining – but for them ultimately to prove so deadly – metal, and cut their hands. Their only weapons were wooden spears, sometimes pointed with fishbones. An innocent – or relatively innocent – world!

On the next day, Saturday October 13 1492, the Spaniards again went ashore and explored the island more thoroughly. The one thing which really did attract their attention, and that of their leader, was that some of the natives had rings of gold dangling from their noses. This was what they had come for, the gold of Cathay! "Poor wretches," wrote Sir Arthur Helps, "if they had possessed the slightest gift of prophecy, they would have thrown these baubles into the deepest sea!" Columbus's Arabic-speaking interpreter having naturally proved quite useless among these native Americans, communication could only be conducted by simple gestures. They managed in this way, by touching the gold rings and pointing, to extract the information that the gold came from some land to the south. Their word for this land sounded like "Cubanacan". This was in fact the centre of what is now called Cuba, but Columbus – hot as ever on the trace of his dreams – interpreted it as Kubla Khan. So he was right after all! Despite the primitive condition of these islanders he was on the fringes of the land he had come to discover, and the courts of the great Khan himself. They must sail on.

Next day, after a further expedition along the island in the boats, the Admiral and his men returned and the ships weighed anchor. During their morning along the coast they had met other natives, all of whom had received them in the most friendly fashion, bringing them water and things to eat. As Columbus was later to write in his letter to the Sovereigns: "They are so guileless and so generous with everything they possess that no one would believe it who has not seen it. They never refuse to give away anything which they own if they are asked for it. On the contrary, they invite anyone to share it and show as much love as if they would give away their hearts. Whether the thing be of value or of small price they are content with any trifle that they are handed." He does however add that, "I forbade them to be given things as worthless as broken crockery or bits of broken glass and scraps of leather – although, when they could get hold of them, they thought they had the finest jewels in the world. As for silver coins, for them they would give anything that they had, even as much gold as would be worth two or three of our gold coins or an arroba [about 25 lbs.] or two of spun cotton . . ."

But before leaving San Salvador, as it had now become – little though the islanders knew it – Columbus committed the first great sin in this new Eden. And in doing so, he set the whole pattern for the future of the Americas. "In the first island that I found, I took by force some of the inhabitants. This was in order that they might give me information of everything in those parts." Natural enough in its way but, as Las Casas rightly comments, this was the beginning of the maltreatment of the Indians and the beginning of slavery in this world which seemed so innocent, so wonderful and fresh. Columbus goes on to say: "They soon understood us, either by speech or by signs, and they have been very useful. I still take them with me and they are quite convinced that I come from heaven . . . Wherever I went they were the first to announce this fact. They dashed from house to house and into nearby villages, crying out "Come and see the people from Heaven!" Poor innocents indeed, they had the first plague of Europeans upon their shores.

From San Salvador Columbus sailed south west, a natural enough direction, since the trades still sat firmly in their sails. They fetched up the following day at their second island, which the Admiral named *Santa Maria de la Concepcion*. The British who came along much later (with less religiosity and a northern love of liquor) gave it the name which it bears to this day – Rum Cay. The natives aboard *Santa Maria* had indicated that hundreds of islands lay to the west and south, and Columbus believed that he was hot on the track of Cipangu. A few "Indians" as proof that these islands existed, and a handful of gold was hardly going to be enough to satisfy the investors in this expedition – let alone King Ferdinand and Queen Isabella. Here and elsewhere, in what one must now call "The Indies", Columbus with his seaman's eye was impressed by the speed and efficiency of the native canoes. "They are," he wrote, "like our rowing *fustas* [a fast oared vessel, rather like a miniature galley], some larger and some smaller . . . They are not so beamy, because they are made of a single log of wood. But a *fusta* could never keep up with them, for their speed is amazing. In these boats they navigate throughout all the islands, which are innumerable, and carry their goods. I have seen one of these canoes with as many as seventy or eighty men in her, each with his paddle."

He found out soon enough that the boats aboard his own ships could not catch them, for at this second island one of his native captives jumped into a canoe that came alongside, and was off and away leaving the pursuing Spaniards far behind. This incident alone (quite apart from the fact that one of the men from Guanahaní had already escaped by swimming ashore) should have convinced him that the Indians did not think he was doing them a service by removing them from their native islands. Nevertheless he persisted, always in the hope "that their Highnesses will determine upon their conversion to our Holy Faith, towards which they are very much inclined".

Moving on again, still in search of those gold-tiled houses, they came to the next island downwind, which Columbus named after his Sovereign, *Fernandina*. Its modern name of Long Island fits it better. Long indeed it is, about 60 miles from north-west to south-east, but at the most only 4 miles across. Here again he found the natives completely docile but observed that unlike the more primitive inhabitants of San Salvador, they wore short tunics and were not above driving a bargain for the requirements of these "men from Heaven". Water is short in the Bahamas, there being no rivers at all, only cisterns and water catchments, so this was one of the things that the Spaniards had to bargain for with the Indians. Yet still, although they constantly inquired about it, they did not find the mountains of gold, the heaps of pearls and precious stones with which they had imagined the whole of this Orient to be stocked. Columbus, during this first fantastic experience of these islands – never forget that everything was new – was always convinced that he would find the place, or places, "where the gold is born". As Navarrete puts it: "Because of the heat from which he then suffered in the Indies the Admiral argued that in the regions there must certainly be gold . . . and he believed that he was near its source and that Our Lord would show him where gold is born."

Natives dancing and drinking cocoa. From Benzoni's Historia, *1572.*

In Quest of the Great Khan

From October 12 1492 until his departure for S٫ ١in on January 16 1493 the voyage of Columbus must be seen in terms of a man staggering about in a dark room – a room with which he thinks is familiar, but which in fact is in a house that he never even knew existed. In any reading of his discoveries, such as we have them from his son Ferdinand and from Las Casas, it is quite clear that the original diary must have been largely a piece of self-justification. Over and over again one hears the voice of this impassioned man insisting that he is in the Indies. At any moment now he will be in the courts of the Great Khan, or better still – his eternal hope – in the fabulous island of Cipangu.

On October 17 the ships got under way, with the intention of sailing round the northern end of Fernandina and coasting down its western side before shaping a course for another island which the natives called Saomete. The ships could not in fact have rounded by the west, for there is not enough depth on that coast for the passage of anything larger than a canoe. On their way up, they anchored in a small harbour at the northern end of the island practically opposite Rum Cay. It was here that a watering party which Columbus had sent ashore first saw an Indian village and entered some of the houses. Now, for the very first time, they came across something that was indeed to transform seamen's lives for centuries to come, as well as to give pleasure and relaxation to millions of people all over the world. They reported that the people slept in beds which were "like nets of cotton". These, as Las Casas says, "are called *Hamacas* in Hispaniola". The hammock, which the Spaniards were the first to introduce into their ships, was later adopted by nearly all the navies of the world. (It is only in recent years that the Royal Navy and the United States Navy have discarded its use.) Ideal for giving a man a

Opposite: *The coast of San Salvador as it appears today.*

Frutex Lauri folio pendulo, fructu tricocco Semine nigro Splendente.

Red Wood.

Psitticus Paradisi

The Parrot of Paradise

good night's sleep in a rolling ship, the hammock – little though it may have interested Columbus – was one of the first assets derived from the New World.

The Admiral remarked on the strange barkless dogs that the natives kept as pets, and on the cleanliness of their houses, which were in the shape of tents. Once again, all went naked except what seemed to be the married women who wore a kind of breach clout. Determined to find everything "for the best in the best of all possible worlds", Columbus grew ecstatic about the "fertile, temperate, level and fine land". The vegetation, the parrots – though he noticed the absence of any domestic animals – all had him in raptures. Perhaps it was not entirely part of a desire to please his Sovereigns, but was the genuine expression of a sailor's wonder at this new Eden. The Bahamas in his day will have been far more fertile and wooded than they are now, when centuries of exploitation have reduced so many of them to impoverished husks.

After watering ship he sailed up north, with the intention of coming down the west coast, but – fortunately for him – the wind went round to the north-west and they had to turn back again. All night they ran back on a south-easterly course down the island, heading for Saomete, or Crooked Island as it is now called. (Columbus was to name it Isabella after his other Sovereign.) Throughout the night it rained steadily. Columbus was later to complain disconsolately that nearly all the time he had been in the Indies it had been raining. He had, of course, arrived just in time for the start of the rainy season. Crooked Island likewise charmed him. The scent of the island, coming offshore at night after they had anchored, brought him memories of flowering gardens. The damp earth exhaled the odours of the tropics.

They landed and found the grass "like springtime in Andalusia", bird song, hosts of parrots, and a large lagoon, on the edge of which they came across "a hideous reptile". To see him was for Columbus to attack, one of his adulators later wrote. So Spanish swords were drawn in anger for the first time in the New World – and a harmless iguana was slain. But all this was bringing him no nearer to the real object of his quest. True, these islands were beautiful, and the people seemed friendly, but something was wrong somewhere. Marco Polo could not have been lying. The first flicker of doubt possibly began to stir in his mind.

He listened, though, with great attention when the natives began to talk of some large island called Colba (Cuba) where, if he judged them right, there were ships and much merchandise. "This," he wrote, "must

Opposite: *Parrot of Paradise, by Mark Catesby, c. 1731.*

I think be Cipangu." In any case he was determined in due course to find his way to the mainland and present his Sovereigns' letters to the Great Khan in person. But first of all let them make sail and investigate this Colba.

After being delayed by the intermittent calms and heavy rain that are typical of that season of the year Columbus, following the advice of his native guides (who put him on the route that they would have taken in their canoes) was underway once more. But instead of heading direct for Colba – which he could not do because he had no idea where it was – he followed the indirect, island-hopping route which was the only one his Indian pilots knew. Many sailing vessels, and indeed modern ships, have been lost among these islands, and it is a tribute to Columbus's great skill at pilotage that, with only these Indians and an almost complete lack of communication with them, he managed to make his way across this uncharted stretch of sea. He skirted all the islands of the Great Bahama Bank – which he named the Sandy Islands – and sailed right down the long line of them. He then crossed the area which is now called Columbus Bank and was all set for Cuba, with a fine trade wind breeze astern of him. He was also listening intently to the Indians who apparently were telling him about yet another great island. This sounded like *Bofio* (almost certainly *Bohio*, the word in Arawakan for a 'house'). It proved, in fact to be Haiti.

On Sunday October 28, shortly after sunrise, the ships were off Cuba. This, it was immediately apparent, was indeed something quite different from the little islands that they had investigated hitherto. In fact, it seemed at first sight so large that Columbus could not help wondering whether he had reached the mainland of Cathay. They sailed up the mouth of a river, "very fair and with trees all along its banks". They were in what is now the Oriente province of Cuba, and the river mouth has almost certainly been correctly identified by Morison as Bahía Bariay.

Once again they went ashore, hoping to find all the evidence of a great civilisation, and again they were disappointed. There was a deserted native village, more barkless dogs, and abandoned fish nets and other similar gear. Where was all the gold? True enough the countryside itself was delightful and Columbus was entranced by its natural beauty on a boat trip up river. But he was acutely aware of the absence of everything that he had expected. Presumably, then, he was still on the fringes of the Great Khan's realms? He took note of the superb Cuban mountains and compared them to those of Sicily which he had known from the trading voyages of his youth. But there was nothing else here that could remind him of the meanest Sicilian fishing village, let alone ports like Messina.

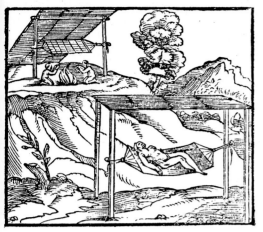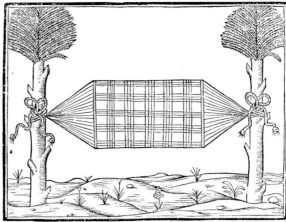

Right: *The hammock which Columbus's men saw for the first time near Rum Cay and which was to transform seamen's lives for centuries to come. From Oviedo's Historia, 1547.* Left: *Indians in hammocks. From Benzoni, 1572.*

In everything he was to be baffled. He heard of gold but saw none, heard of pearls but saw none. The ships up-anchored and carried on coasting westerly.

In his letter to the Sovereigns Columbus was later to declare how he had "gone 107 leagues in a straight line from west to east along the sea-shore of the island Juana [for such he decided to name it in honour of the heir apparent Prince Juan], and as a result of that voyage, I can say that this island is larger than England and Scotland put together. Beyond these 107 leagues there remain two more provinces to which I have not gone. One of them they call Avan, and there the people are born with tails. These provinces, as I understand from the Indians, cannot have a breadth of less than 50 or 60 leagues." Columbus in fact was not so far out in his reckoning as to length, for Cuba is roughly 600 (nautical) miles long, but in depth it is only as much as 100 miles in a very few places. However, it would certainly look good to Ferdinand and Isabella if he was presenting them with an island as big as England and Scotland put together.

But at this point Columbus became more than ever convinced that this was the mainland, and not the island of Cipangu. He noted: "It is certain

The iguana encountered by Columbus. Drawing by John White, c. 1590.

that this is the mainland, and that I am near to Quinsay [the imperial city of Cathay], one hundred leagues more or less . . . this can be noticed from the way the sea is running differently, and yesterday while I was sailing north-westward I found that the air was growing cold." Prevented by the winds from holding to his chosen course any further Columbus put the ships about. They headed back for an anchorage which he had already explored, and which he had named The River of Seas because two rivers, the Coyoyuin and the Gibara, poured out into the large sandy bay where is modern Puerto Gibara. It was a good sheltered anchorage, and here the ships stayed for the next eleven days. Columbus, his imagination still inflamed with this Kubla Khan (Cubanacan), who was said to dwell in the interior, prepared to despatch an embassy with the sovereigns' letter to the mighty monarch so that he might himself be taken at his own true value – Admiral of the Ocean Sea and the elected delegate of Ferdinand and Isabella come to trade with the ruler of Cathay. There can be no doubt that his interpreters from Guanahaní as well as the natives they met in the fishing village all pointed inland. That, indeed, was where their chieftain or cacique resided, less than thirty miles away.

Luis de Torres, Columbus's interpreter, the Jewish convert with a knowledge not only of Hebrew but of Aramaic and Arabic, was naturally chosen to head the delegation. It was thought that, even if the natives they had met so far spoke an unknown tongue, there would be learned men in the court of the Great Khan who would at least be familiar with Arabic. Along with de Torres went a Spaniard, Rodrigo de Jerez, one of the Guanahaní Indians, and a native from the village. Columbus must clearly have set great hopes upon this embassy. While they waited, a suitable site was found for careening the ships, which had by now been three months at sea. Quite apart from the dangers of the wood-devouring teredo worm, they must have been very foul from weed and from barnacles, the latter, particularly in trade-wind seas, getting kicked up in the vessels' passing and growing thickly around stern and rudder.

They scraped the ships off, caulked where necessary, overhauled running and standing rigging, and prepared the tar (which they had no doubt brought with them) by heating it over wooden fires. Columbus, smelling the resinous local wood as the smoke drifted over the beach, pronounced it to be of the mastic tree family – in which he was quite incorrect – and felt sure that, even if he had not yet found the gold, he had certainly found a lucrative source of income for his sovereigns. In everything he was determined (and who can blame him?) to prove that they were at the source of all good and prosperous things. Potatoes, possibly yams, were given them and were eaten for the first time by Europeans.

The delegation returned on November 5. Their report was highly discouraging. There was no Great Khan. True, they had been handsomely entertained everywhere on their route. They had been hailed as visitors from the sky. But the 'Khan', when they had reached him, had proved to be no more than a cacique, and 'the golden city' no more than a collection of native huts. Columbus's envoys had shown the people the samples he had given them of cinnamon, pepper and other spices, and the people had indicated that such things were to be found further to the south. This at any rate was good news for the future. One most peculiar thing, however, that the delegates had noticed on their way was an extraordinary habit of these Indians. While they were travelling they carried small tubes of dried leaves, and every so often they would stop and insert one end of them in a nostril. The tube would then be lit by a small boy with a firebrand, and the Indians would take the smoke up their nostrils and into their mouths, and exhale it. How strange this country was proving – there was nothing about that in Marco Polo! Apparently they called these tubes *tobacos*. Las Casas, writing forty years later, said that he had questioned the Indians about this *tobaco* and they had said that the smoke took away fatigue. He also knew of some Spaniards who had adopted this unattractive habit. When he reproved them, saying it was a vice, they replied that it was one which they were not able to give up. Sir Arthur Helps accurately commented: "It was a discovery which, in the end, proved more productive to the Spanish crown than that of the gold mines of the Indies."

Columbus now heard of a place called Babeque "where gold was collected at night by torchlight on the shore and then hammered into bars". How on earth this information was conveyed baffles the mind – but at any rate they must certainly up-anchor at once and be off from this pleasant anchorage and village of friendly natives. One thought immediately arises when reading the account of the Admiral – there is absolutely no reference to the sailors associating with the native women. They must have done of course. But Columbus was writing for his Sovereigns and, in particular, for the pious eyes of Queen Isabella. Sailors, newly ashore after weeks at sea, are unlikely to be chaste. (In any case, as will be seen later, the Spaniards were to be accused of bringing back from the New World something quite unwanted and unlooked for.) Before leaving in search of Babeque Columbus took a number of young men onboard, as well as "seven head of women". The latter he indicates were to serve as necessary companions to the Indians. He intended to take them all back as a present to his Sovereigns. In much the same way Henry the Navigator's first captains had brought back a few negroes to Portugal – and this had subsequently developed into the prosperous African slave trade. None of these unfortunate inhabitants of Cuba, however, was destined to survive the return voyage.

Columbus now sailed eastward, still apparently convinced that Cuba was part of the mainland of China. At this point, the first rift in the expedition occurred. Martín Alonso Pinzón, apparently disregarding the Admiral's signals, sailed off on his own – determined no doubt to find Babeque first and to get his hands on all those gold bars. Columbus was rightly infuriated. Here they were in unknown waters, only three small ships, thousands of miles from home, and his senior captain had deserted him with one of the ships. Confiding his bitter feelings to his diary, he nevertheless pressed on along the northern coast of Cuba. Needless to say there were no gold bars. (When Pinzón finally rejoined Columbus in January 1493 he seems to have acquired little more than a few gold trinkets such as noserings, bought no doubt in the usual way for hawks' bells and beads.) Babeque was probably what is now called Great Inagua Island. Columbus never went there. It is a strange thought that if at this moment, instead of sailing east, he had gone westward he would indeed have found the mainland of South America. But, convinced that Cuba was the mainland, he was now looking for fabulous Cipangu. He felt sure that this great island Bohio of which the natives spoke must be it. Cathay, what he had seen of it, was beautiful enough – but a bit of a disappointment.

Columbus' men discover the natives smoking the dried leaf of the tobacco.

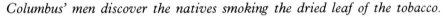

The Golden Island

Cruising along the northern coast of Cuba Columbus admired the beauty of its mountainous scenery. He commented also on the delicious taste of the air, and remarked that not one of the crew had been ill "except for an old man who had long been a sufferer from the stone". He noticed that the natives often referred with some alarm to the *Caniba* (in fact, cannibal tribes of Indians), but again he took this to refer to the Great Khan, and assumed that it meant the Khan's people. Presumably every now and then the Khan's soldiers made a raid and took these primitives off as slaves. Yes, that accounted for it all. The great cities were a long way inland, and the Khan "no doubt has ships, and comes to take these people away as captives and as they do not return the others assume they have been eaten". What a simple people they were, and what a pity about the language difficulty! Yes, he must certainly learn it for future occasions. The Admiral rapt in his dream, which was in fact a dream within a dream, mused in the cabin over his journal.

They now came to Bohio (Haiti) and at first they were still not absolutely sure whether it was another island or part of that same mainland which Cuba seemed to represent. But there was a distinct difference, and Columbus seems to have found this new place even more agreeable than the last. Everywhere was getting better and better. As he wrote in his 'First Letter' to the Sovereigns; "Española [for such he named Haiti] has a circumference greater than all Spain, from Colibre, by the seacoast to Fuenterabia in Vizcaya, since I voyaged along one side 188 great leagues in a straight line from west to east. It is a land to be desired, and once seen, it is never to be left . . ." His reference here to "great leagues" would seem to confirm that Columbus used two different systems of measurement – one for land and one for sea. To judge from his navigational record his "great league" was a little under 3 nautical miles, while his "land league" was about half of this.

The mountainous inland region brought back memories, "the whole country appears like Castile". Again, he wrote that "this island and all the others are as much yours as Castile . . . The people have no weapons and go naked and have no spirit for warfare. They are very cowardly and one thousand of them would not stand up to three [of us]. The result is that they are suitable for discipline and to be made to work, to sow and do everything, to build towns and to learn to be dressed and adopt our ways." Already one hears the voice of the conqueror. Within a brief few weeks the simple joy at the Adam and Eve nature of these natives has been replaced by harsh cupidity. If this is not indeed Cathay or Cipangu, at any rate it can be made to serve the purpose of his masters and his investors.

Columbus, one feels, must surely have begun to suspect by now that he was in the wrong place. But then, according to his reckoning, and according to his conception of the globe as derived from Toscanelli, he really was in the Indies – or at least on the fringes of them. He had gone ashore in Cuba with his quadrant, taken at altitude of Polaris, and got his latitude fantastically wrong. He was almost certainly 'shooting' the wrong star, for he remarks that "The Pole Star looks as high as in Castile". It was this that further propped up his conviction that Cuba was part of the Chinese mainland. The Admiral was totally lost. The fact remains that he was one of the greatest pilots of all time. Time and again he successfully takes *Santa Maria* into unknown harbours, along the edges of immensely dangerous coral reefs, over uncharted seas, and into channels where he does not know whether they are the bights of a mainland or passages between islands. It has been customary to make fun of him as a celestial navigator, but it is doubtful whether, with the instruments at his disposal, any seaman of those days could have done much better. Certainly, there were learned astronomers ashore in European and Arabic countries who could have got their latitudes right, but the point is that they were *ashore*. Columbus, with all his faults, and they were many, had done the unique thing. Like Daedalus he had flown into space – and without any computers to help him. But, like Icarus, the great inventor's son, he was to be destroyed by his ambition.

Opposite: *Hispaniola, c. 1616. The port of San Domingo is shown on the South West coast.*

Overleaf: *Paolo Toscanelli's world map, c. 1457. Toscanelli had been asked by the king of Portugal to illustrate his views about the route to the Indies.*

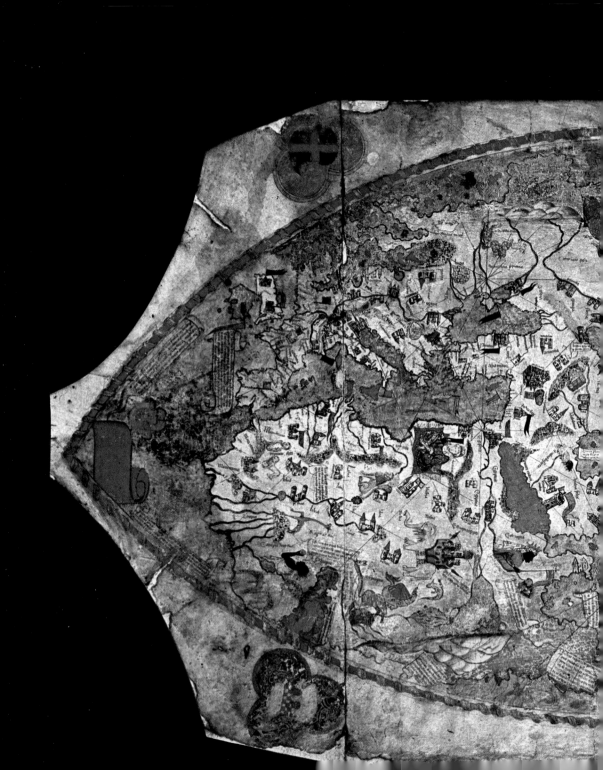

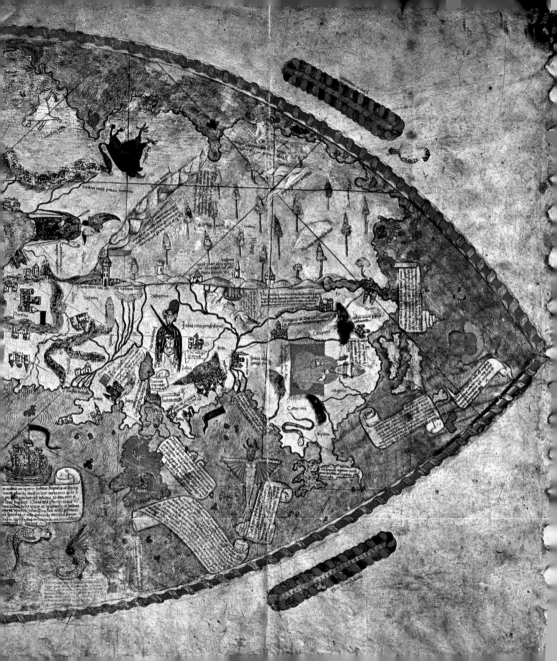

The first harbour he found in Haiti on December 6 was at the western end, and he named it Puerto San Nicolas since it was the feast day of that saint. It was appropriate enough, for St. Nicholas, usually thought of as the patron saint of children, is also the protector of scholars, merchants and sailors – and Columbus was a compendium of all three. This was certainly the finest harbour that they had yet found, with an inner arm that was almost completely landlocked. Here he should surely encounter the imperial fleet of the Khan? But there was nothing: only a few natives who fled inland when they saw the monster-canoes with their bearded masters. Disappointed, although appreciating the harbour's possibilities, Columbus sailed on eastward down the coast.

At his next port of call, which he named Puerto de la Concepcion, for the Conception of the Virgin Mary, he was held up for five days by a strong easterly coupled with heavy rain. On December 12 Columbus had a large wooden cross erected and formally took possession of Hispaniola in the name of the Sovereigns. It was while they were here that some of the sailors captured a native girl and brought her back onboard. She was naked except for a gold nose-plug. Columbus wisely reckoned that if she was given some of his beads and hawks' bells, and some cast-off clothing, she would report favourably to her tribe. Then he might at last begin to do some serious trading for the gold which his natives from Cuba assured him was to be found in this land. The girl was accordingly sent ashore decorated and clothed, and on the next day Columbus despatched a party of seamen inland with a native interpreter. They found the largest village that had so far been encountered in the New World, at least a thousand huts. The inhabitants at first fled in panic, but they gradually came back after the interpreter had assured them that these were not from Caniba, but men from Heaven. The Indians were as friendly as ever and gave the sailors presents of parrots, but again there was a lamentable absence of gold. It turned out that the girl had been wearing a gold nose-plug not because the metal was common, but because she was the chief's daughter. The land though, the sailors reported back to the Admiral, was rich and fertile. Columbus was also heartened by the fact that, while on a boating expedition, a skate leaped aboard, the first fish he had seen, he records, "similar to those we have in Spain".

Since they were now opposite the great long island which Columbus had already named Tortuga (from its resemblance to a turtle's back) it was natural enough that they should sail over and take a look at it – yet

Opposite top: *Natives preparing beverages and* below, *cannibals. Scenes as imagined by Theodore de Bry, 1594.*

another fine acquisition for the Spanish crown. But it was in Hispaniola, as it must now be called, that Columbus did at last manage to justify the expedition financially. Having picked up a solitary Indian in a canoe during a fierce blow in the Tortuga Channel they put him ashore, with the usual assorted presents, near a village on the beach of Hispaniola. He was probably some relative of the local cacique, for the latter "a youth of about twenty-one" soon arrived with a host of attendants. Columbus remarked of these Indians that they were almost as white as Spaniards. Columbus had him aboard and, although the cacique was stark naked, the Admiral was most favourably impressed with the dignity of his behaviour and with the deference with which he was treated by his attendants. "When he came into the aftercastle he made a hand sign for his retinue to stay outside, which they did with all signs of respect. Except for two elderly men, whom I assumed to be his counsellors, they all seated themselves on the deck. The other two came in and sat at his feet. Of the food which I had set before him he took only a very little, and sent the larger part out to his retinue. He did the same with the drink, which he merely raised to his lips before giving it to the others . . ."

One cannot help wondering what the simple palate of this young cacique made of rough Spanish wine that had been tumbled around at sea in a wooden cask for months! He knew, however, what these strangers were after, for he was careful to make Columbus a present of some pieces of worked gold. Columbus for his part, noticing he admired the head of his bed, gave him it, "along with some excellent amber beads which I wore round my neck, and some red shoes, and a bottle of orange water, which he greatly enjoyed". As he wrote in his letter to the Sovereigns,

The Booby. Drawing by John White, c. 1590.

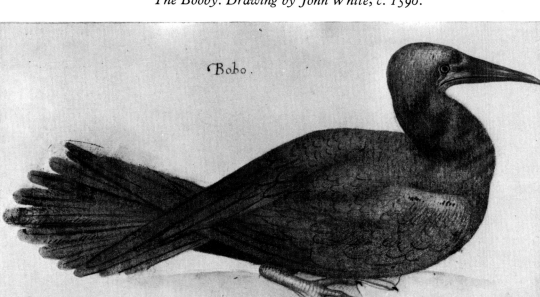

he was quite convinced that the cacique said that "the whole island was mine to command". How this statement was conveyed when "neither of us understood one another" is difficult to comprehend.

Acul Bay which excited Columbus's admiration when the fleet entered it on December 20 – and which he named the Sea of Saint Thomas – does indeed, as the Admiralty Pilot says, "afford excellent, sheltered anchorage, for vessels of deep draught". It is however fringed by reefs and shoals, and it is a tribute again to the seamanship of the Admiral that with no charts and only a hand lead and sharp eye the Spaniards brought up in it without coming to grief. Natural beauty always moved Columbus, who not only had a seaman's eye for a great anchorage, but a poet's for scenery – "Mountains reaching to the sky . . . Compared with these even the peak of Tenerife is nothing." Friendly relations were quickly established with the local natives, Columbus commenting on the pretty bodies of the women, who here went totally naked without even the customary breech clout. But, as ever, it was gold that obsessed him. "Our Lord, in whose hands are all things," he writes, "be my help. Our Lord direct me that I may find the gold."

A messenger now came to visit the Admiral. He had been sent by the cacique of the whole area, who appears to have been called Guacanagarí. He brought with him a splendid gift, a kind of decorated cummerbund made out of cotton but, most important of all, having in its centre the face of a god made out of gold. Columbus, naturally enough, was entranced. Now, he was quite sure, if he understood the natives aright (who kept talking about somewhere called 'Cibao'), that Cipangu lay just around the corner, or that he was possibly already there. The mine

Sketch-map drawn by Columbus, 1492–93.

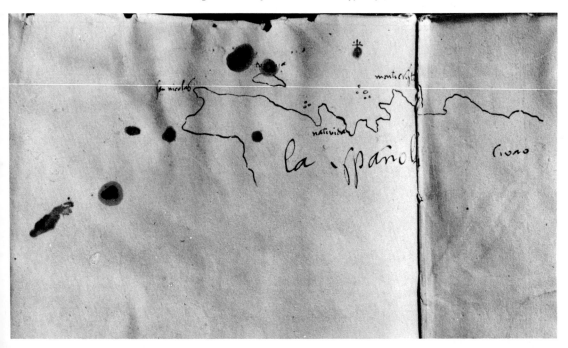

obsessed him. He was all the time imagining something like La Mina on the west African coast, which the Portuguese were happily exploiting. He had to find something like that to convince his investors that the whole thing had been worthwhile.

In the meantime he sent another party inland to make contact with the natives. They came back with three fat ducks, some cotton, and a few bits of gold. Here as everywhere the people were astonishingly friendly. As Madariaga rightly comments: "One is left wondering whether these natives of Haiti were not the only true Christians that ever existed." Columbus noted that "I cannot believe that any man has ever seen people with such good hearts . . . They are the most loving people and without cupidity." They came out in their thousands to see the ships, some in canoes and others swimming – even though Columbus was anchored some way offshore. The islanders were as native to the sea as fish. In their lovely tropic climate they had in fact developed a culture that, even though it was devoid of great monuments or works of art, was perfectly suited to their environment.

Cibao lured Columbus. It was in fact the central area of Hispaniola, but convinced that it was another island, his much desired Cipangu, he up-anchored on December 24 and sailed on down the coast. The wind came from ahead and *Santa Maria* and *Niña* spent the day tacking to windward. They rounded the massive bulk of Cap Haitien, soaring up well over 2,000 feet above the reef-strewn coast, and headed on eastward. At dusk on December 24 the wind fell light, as the trades often do in this area, to spring up again with the dawn. The moon was low and the Admiral, after seeing that the ship was all set for the night and leaving Juan de la Cosa as officer of the watch, went down to his cabin. Here no doubt he made his evening devotions and thought happily on the fact that tomorrow was Christmas Day. It would be the first Christmas ever to be celebrated by Christians in these pagan Indies. How memorable! Perhaps Our Lord on his natal day would show them some sign of his favour. The mine, the island of gold . . . The Admiral, who had had practically no sleep for forty-eight hours, got into his bed.

He was awoken by a gentle bump, to be immediately followed by a mass of confused shouting and the sounds of people running about on the upper deck. He sprang up and found himself involved in disaster. What had happened was that Juan de la Cosa, seeing that the night was quiet and fair, and that there was nothing to do but follow *Niña* as she glided along ahead, had abandoned the deck and gone to sleep. The helmsman, similarly, had turned over the tiller to one of the ship's boys and got his head down. *Santa Maria*, following the shallower draught

Niña, had run gently up on a reef, one of the many along that scarred coast.

Columbus immediately ordered the ship's boat lowered to take an anchor out astern so as to kedge the ship off the reef. It was quite clear that if they were quick about it they could get her bows off before the swell drove her on deep. Now, if we are to believe his subsequent story, the most extraordinary thing occurred – Juan de la Cosa and the men in the boat made off after *Niña* to save their own skins. "Treachery!" Columbus reported. This seems difficult to believe. Juan de la Cosa was part owner of *Santa Maria*. He was also the ship's master, and a seaman to his fingertips. It seems much more likely that he made for *Niña* to acquaint them with what had happened, and get them to put back immediately to lend a hand. This was what in effect happened, and he returned in company with the other boat to lay out a kedge. Whatever the rights or wrongs of this famous episode there can be no doubt whatsoever that Juan de la Cosa was responsible for the wreck of the flagship. In any court martial the verdict must have gone against him. Firstly, he had left his post as officer of the watch, and secondly, even if we accept that his action in making off to *Niña* was not due to cowardice, it prejudiced any chances of salvage. By the time that the two boats returned it was too late to kedge *Santa Maria* off the reef. Columbus, in order to lighten her, had the mainmast cut away, but even this was ineffectual. The long trade-wind swells were gradually driving her ever further onto the gap-toothed coral. No wooden hull can take such punishment for long, and soon the seams began to open.

It was Christmas Day 1492. With what bitterness, with what despair in his heart, Columbus now gave the order "Abandon Ship!" *Niña* stood carefully off up wind on that calm but disastrous night. The ships' boats ferried the men across. The Admiral came last. He had reached the Indies, but he had as yet little to show for it. He must still get back to Spain – and he had only one ship left.

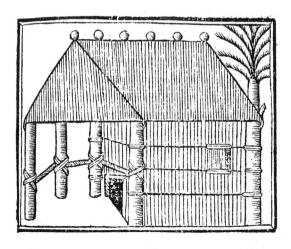

After the Wreck

Christmas Day, which they had hoped to spend in feasting and junketing with the friendly natives and their chief Guacanagarí, was passed in a very different manner. All hands were turned to, and throughout the daylight hours officers and men laboured to get the stores and equipment off *Santa Maria*. Without the help and unremitting concern of Guacanagarí the operation would have taken far longer. The young cacique despatched all available men and canoes to the salvage of *Santa Maria*. Far more than this, he and his relatives personally supervised the storage of all the gear on the beach, making sure that not a single thing was taken – and this by simple men to whom almost every single article must have seemed of immense value! Columbus wrote that "he assures the King and Queen that nowhere in Castile could there have been so much concern and attention, so that nothing – not even one needle – was missing".

The wreck of *Santa Maria* was in every respect the turning point of Columbus's life and fortunes. It changed him from an explorer, navigator and sea-adventurer, into a coloniser. It is a strange fact that his own adaptation of his name into Spanish, Colón, should itself derive from a name left in the language from the Romans: *Colonus*, "one who settles in a new country". Now, with only one ship left, it became clear that he would have to leave a number of the men behind: he would have to plant a colony. As Washington Irving remarked: "This shipwreck shackled and limited all Columbus's future discoveries. It linked his fortunes for the remainder of his life to this island, which was doomed to be to him a source of cares and troubles, to involve him in a thousand perplexities, and to becloud his declining years with humiliation and disappointment."

There can be no doubt that on that Christmas morning God had indeed sent a sign – Columbus himself was convinced of it: "The Lord had ordained this shipwreck so that he might choose this place for a settlement . . . Without this I would not have been able to leave people here, nor to provide them with so much equipment, weapons and supplies." Seeing the hand of the Lord in everything the Admiral was convinced that everything was for the best.

At first, however, he was very naturally distressed, but the cacique comforted him. He had noticed how easy it was to comfort these strangers – the yellow metal always made them happy. So on Christmas Day, with the salvaged gear and timbers from *Santa Maria*, they began the construction of the first European settlement in the Americas (if one excepts the earlier Viking villages thousands of miles to the north). This was to be called *Villa de la Navidád*, in honour of Christmas Day when the wreck of the flagship had compelled Columbus to start a township in this isle of the Indies – Cibao? Cipangu? (certainly not Cathay, he had already touched there and left it behind him). La Navidád was east of Cape Haitien, within the barrier reef of coral that stretches along that shore, and not far from what is now called Caracol Bay. Here Columbus was to leave behind a large part of *Santa Maria*'s crew with instructions that they should "search for the gold mine, and, as I have already said to Your Highnesses, the profits shall go towards the recovery of Jerusalem". He was as determined as Henry the Navigator had been before him that the Holy City should be recovered. Here he was, thousands of miles from Europe, still endeavouring to ensure that Christian arms should one day recover the citadel of their Faith.

There would seem to have been no lack of volunteers to man this fortress-stockade-village that Columbus was planting in the New World. This in itself is hardly surprising. The land was pleasant, the sea warm, the natives friendly, the women golden and indulgent, and they had stores to last them a year, quite apart from what they might get from the land. Columbus left *Santa Maria*'s boat with them so that they could thoroughly explore the coast, find the mine of course, and also other suitable places for settlement when the Admiral came back again. It was quite clear now, and the wreck of the flagship had been God's method of showing it to him, that it was his duty not only to bring the Faith to these Pagans but to colonise them.

While the work was going ahead Columbus received the first news of *Pinta* since Martín Alonso Pinzón's desertion. She was said to be lying at the head of a river some way to the east of him and he immediately despatched some of the natives in a canoe with a message to Pinzón. He was naturally enough anxious that on the return journey the two re-

maining ships should sail in company. He was equally anxious that
Pinzón should not forestall him at the Spanish court and claim the
honour and the glory for himself – for it was he, Columbus, who "had
found what he was looking for".

Of all this he was later to write in his letter to Their Majesties: "In
this Española, in the situation most convenient and in the best position
for the mines of gold and for all communication with the mainland here
as well as that there, belonging to the Great Khan [clearly Cuba], where
there will be trade and gain, I have taken possession of a large town. To
it I have given the name of La Navidád. Here I have constructed a fort,
which by now will be finished, and I have left sufficient men and arms
and provisions for more than a year and a ship's boat together with a
master craftsman to build others [the *Santa Maria*'s carpenter, Alonso
Morales]." He goes on to describe the great friendship he has with the
"King of that land", but adds that "even if he were to change his attitude
towards my men, he and his subjects do not know what arms are. As I
have already said, they go naked and are the most timorous people in the
world. The men that I have left behind would be quite enough to take
the whole land . . ."

The canoe sent to find *Pinta* returned without having made any contact, and Columbus began to fear that Pinzón had sailed back ahead of
him. He hastened on the work, determined to get underway as soon as
possible. On January 2 1493, he had a farewell party with Guacanagarí,
in which the iron hand in the velvet glove was first demonstrated to the
natives of Haiti. He had *Niña* stand off *Santa Maria* and send several
shots from her guns clean through the hull of what remained of the
wreck. That would show them clearly enough what the power of Spain
could do, that would ensure that they understood that these white Gods
had fire in their hands like the fire from the sky. They would be back
again – and let there be no doubt that, if a single one of their men had
been harmed, the whole of this land would be devastated.

It is easy enough some five hundred years later to criticise Columbus
and his methods – and those of the Spaniards and other Europeans who
were to follow him – but it is essential to try and understand the thinking
of his time. The promulgation of an assertive Christianity was bred in
their bones, and especially in Mediterranean men who had suffered so
much from Mohammedanism. The whole of life, as they saw it, was a
battle between the Cross and the Crescent. It was all-important that any
foreign people whom they encountered should be converted in order to
add to the weight of the armies that fought for the true religion.

On the morning of Friday January 4, the conqueror of the Atlantic and the discoverer of the route to the Indies, weighed anchor. He stood out to sea through the treacherous reef, sending the ship's boat to sound ahead of him until he was clear. Then the boat went back and the men rejoined their comrades in their new home. Columbus headed out of the bay and set course for the east. On the following day he anchored off the headland which he called Monte Cristi. On the 6th, having been forced to put back into this anchorage by strong head winds, he was astonished, and no doubt highly delighted, to see *Pinta* running down the coast towards them. Martín Alonso Pinzón had heard of the wreck of the flagship from some natives on the coast and had come back to lend a hand. The scene between the Admiral and his renegade captain was a stormy one. Columbus had right on his side and he was justifiably furious with Pinzón. However, for the moment he must endeavour to contain his resentment, for the two Pinzóns were all-important to the expedition and nearly all the men were either Pinzón recruits or friends. Four men and two girls whom Martín Alonso had captured were ordered to be put ashore. A river which the elder Pinzón had named after himself was declared null and void – and later renamed by the Admiral. From now on, in Columbus's judgement, Martín Alonso could do

Rebuilding a caravel. From Theodore de Bry, 1594.

nothing right. It is not difficult to understand his anger and resentment, but the elder Pinzón was also a fiery-spirited man. It seems clear that he had all along resented taking orders from this foreign adventurer who did not even own his own vessel.

Columbus was slightly cheered up, however, by finding that the nearby river, Yaque del Norte, had grains of gold in it and, despite Las Casas's pronouncement that this was probably "fool's gold", the Admiral was quite right. The river drains the Cibao area of the island – that Cibao where he had already heard there was much gold – and where the Spaniards were to establish their first great gold mine. Meanwhile, as they were detained two days in the anchorage, Columbus had *Niña* caulked, the ships watered, and all made ready for the long passage home. On his boat trip to explore the river "the Admiral saw three sirens which rose fully out of the sea". He is honest enough to comment however that "they are not as beautiful as they are painted, although in some respects they do have human faces." These of course were Caribbean manatees which inhabit bays, lagoons, estuaries and rivers. The face does indeed have a somewhat human appearance and this resemblance is reinforced by the fact that the flippers are very like hands, and the manatee when feeding on aquatic plants push the food into their mouths with these hands. One of the outstanding qualities of Columbus is his fascination in all natural phenomena and his accuracy in reporting them. At the same time he records having heard of another large island to the south, Yamaye (probably Jamaica), where "there is more gold even than in this and where they gather gold in nuggets bigger than beans, whereas here they are no bigger than grains of wheat." He must get back to Spain with all this astonishing news. Then there must be a further and much bigger expedition, in which the Admiral of the Ocean Sea would take possession of even more of these fabulous Indies for his Sovereigns.

On January 12 the two caravels brought up in what is now Samana Bay, and here for the first time they encountered natives who did not welcome them with smiles and flowers and parrots. These were the first they had met in the Indies who were armed with bows and arrows, and a minor skirmish took place in which some of the Indians were wounded. They finally fled the field before the Spanish swords, but they were an early warning that not everything in these new lands was going to be as easy as it had seemed at first.

The Caribbean manatee, "the siren" which the Admiral saw rise out of the sea.

Homeward Bound

Before leaving the 'Bay of Arrows', as he named it, the Admiral entertained a local cacique and sent him back ashore with some of the usual presents – beads and a red cap. As far as possible he was all along determined to establish good relations with the local people. The affray on the previous day had been unfortunate, and he was anxious that it should not interfere with his future plans for the whole of this region.

On Wednesday January 16 1493, the two caravels weighed anchor for the last time in these strange Indies, a place where everything seemed to be seen through a misty mirror – a mirror that Marco Polo had obviously not properly observed. Naked savages, mermaids, superb scenery but no pagodas, only a little gold and very little of what appeared to be spices. Columbus, as a Genoese, must certainly have wondered if the Venetian (all Venetians were liars) had not deceived the world with his false stories of the Khan's dominions. Another thing came to his mind, the Spanish proverb: "Revenge is a dish to be served cold." Yes, these Pinzóns, and particularly Martín Alonso, would have to stand by for the knife in due course. It annoyed him, but also possibly amused him, that *Pinta* was sailing very badly. She had a sprung mast, and "if Pinzón had exerted himself as much to provide himself with a new mast in the Indies, where there are so many excellent trees, as he did in running away in search of gold, then they would not have suffered so much inconvenience".

He was eager before he left for home to see a little more of these islands. He had heard, for instance, of a place called Matininó which was inhabited by an Amazon tribe of women, where they only admitted men for a short season every year, strictly for breeding purposes. How fascinating, and that was exactly what Marco Polo had written about an island called Feminea in the Indies. It would help to prove his contention that he was exactly where he was sure he was, if he went to the

147

island. Possibly he might take a few of the women back to the Sovereigns.

Before leaving Samana Bay he had taken aboard four native youths, presumably with a view to using them as local pilots as he had the previous ones from Guanahani. It is worth noting that, apparently, it was all right for the Admiral to impress Indians, but not for Martín Alonso Pinzón. There is no knowing which was the legendary island of the Amazons, although many have opted for it having been Martinique. How this comparatively complicated story could have been conveyed in sign language is difficult to say. One suspects that Columbus 'read' the natives in whatever way suited him best. In any case, their directions proved faulty, the island was never reached, and the crews of *Pinta* and *Niña* began to grow restive. Both vessels were leaking badly, they were many days sail from home – if they ever made it. They had seen Cathay and Cipangu, and were eager to get back with such gold as they had, their other souvenirs, and their fantastic tales which would certainly make them the idols of all the village girls.

Columbus "observed that the men began to get upset at his not setting a direct course for home", so he followed their wishes. The course for Spain was given: North-East by East. It was not the course for Spain. The right course would have been more like East-North-East. The course that Columbus had ordered would, if they had followed it, have taken them north of Scotland. It does seem, however, that Divine Providence looked after this strange Genoese for, just as he had found the off-lying islands of America by a miscalculation of the circumference of the globe, so he had now by another miscalculation found the ideal sailing route home. By going too far north he came out above the latitude

Martinique. The seashore unchanged since Columbus's day.

of Bermuda and picked up the prevailing Westerlies. Then, at the latitude of Cape Hatteras, he was able to run almost due east until he fetched the Azores. From there on, of course, they knew their way home. The success of the return voyage was, like that of the outward one, a chapter of fortunate accidents.

To begin with, though, they inevitably had to beat to windward. It would have been very hard going for *Santa Maria*, which would have found it impossible to lay so close to the wind as the caravels – luck again that she had gone! *Pinta* and *Niña*, with their finer entry and leaner hulls were, even though both square-rigged, able to lay a far closer course. Very soon they were once again in the Sargasso Sea. This first part of the return passage was delightful: tropic days and nights, the ships rushing onward to the silken sound of their bow waves, while tunny leaped around, and graceful bo'sun birds followed them overhead. They were fairly short on rations, but they managed to catch fish. Anyway, they were going home, back to the familiar world, so spirits were high. On February 2 the Admiral tried to get a latitude on Polaris but, in the swell through which they were running, his instruments were useless. All he could do was make an estimate by eye, and he calculated that the star was about the same height as at Cape St. Vincent. He was, in fact, nearer the latitude of Cape Blanco in Morocco, but even so it was no bad guess – made from the deck of a small vessel rolling heavily in an Atlantic sea. Shortly after this they began to shape a more easterly course, for the weather turned rainy and much colder. Columbus realised he had made quite enough northing.

It was midwinter, and they were in the middle of the North Atlantic, in an area where no ship's keel had ever driven before. They were fine little ships, proof of how good at their craft were the builders of that time. There were days when the caravels were averaging ten knots, something that would be considered good for many a modern ocean-racer with all the tank-tests and technology of the 20th century behind her. On February 10, Columbus reckoned that they were about on the latitude of Flores in the Azores, the other pilots reckoning they were much further north, near Madeira. Columbus was more accurate. They were in fact still south of the Azores and more or less on the latitude of Cape Spartel in northern Morocco. Two days later there were all the signs of an impending Atlantic gale, the wind freshening up, great grey-backs building, and the spume beginning to fly off the long-crested rollers which had all the fetch of thousands of miles of ocean behind them.

In winter the area of the Azores can be one of the most unpleasant in this ocean. Here is an extract from the log of an ocean-racing yacht

"Kay", which was for several days in full gale force conditions slightly north of the islands: "Sea rising again. Big seas now carrying large crests instead of white horses. 2230. Struck by heavy squall, force 7–8. Handed all plain sail, set storm jib and trysail. When the squall struck the helm was put hard up and the main sheet started. She answered slowly due to force of wind. All hands were called." And a few days later: "Caught by a terrific thunder-and-hail-squall blowing a good force 10. Visibility was nil to windward and 20 yards to leeward. The storm jib was pressing the bow under and giving a $9\frac{1}{2}$ knot reading on the Kenyon [speedo-meter] when we ran off before the squall . . . I wonder how long this weather can keep up? Shortly after the above was written we paid her off due East and streamed double lines [the yacht was under bare poles]. Wind gusting 9 and even 10 with rain and lightning. I shall never go to sea again!"

Pinta and *Niña* were in for all of this and a great deal more, and they were not vessels that had been designed for the North Atlantic in winter, nor were they freshly fitted out. They had only been careened once since they had left Palos. All their gear, fittings and sails, were merely the standard equipment that they would have used on their coastal runs around Spain and Portugal. They were a credit to their builders and to the various artisans and craftsmen who had had a hand in them. Their crews were also a credit to their ships.

Columbus reports on February 12 "Heavy seas and full gale. Had the caravel not been sound and well built I should have been afraid of being lost." Both vessels laboured under disadvantages: *Pinta* because

Storm at sea. Detail from painting by Bruegel the Elder, c. 1568.

of her mast, and *Niña* because she was underballasted due to the consumption of her stores during the long voyage: this had been rectified on Columbus's orders by the crew filling up the empty wine and water casks with sea-water, but it did not give her her proper draught stability. The two of them ran before it under bare poles. There was nothing else they could do. In vessels of that type they could not heave-to, but the high stern of the period made them good at running before breaking seas, with only a rag of sail showing to give them steerage way. Without the latter they would undoubtedly have broached-to and gone down with all hands.

On the night of February 13 the two ships lost contact. It was the worst moment of the whole expedition, thunder to the north, a howling westerly gale, and the sea pitched into a cross-confusion which meant that no one onboard can have had a dry shirt to his back. The Admiral may have earlier complained of the bad workmanship of the Palos boatyards, but he must now have thanked God that it was better than he had thought. They all prayed and, as they ran before those monstrous seas, they drew lots as to who should make a pilgrimage of devotion to Santa Maria of Guadelupe – if only they were spared. The Admiral drew the lot – a chick-pea marked with a cross. Another penitential pilgrimage was then proposed, and one of the seamen drew the lot for making a pilgrimage to the shrine of Santa Maria of Loreto. Then a third was agreed upon, a night watch and a mass at Santa Clara de Mogues, not far from their home port of Palos. Once again the Admiral drew the marked chick-pea. Two penances then! After this, since the sea and the storm continued to surround them with their noise and fury, all hands aboard *Niña* vowed to make a pilgrimage to the nearest church

of Our Lady, at whatever place they should first make land – if they ever made it. There is no record as to what happened aboard *Pinta*, but no doubt in that day and age something very similar must have taken place.

The bad weather was very typical of its type in those latitudes at that time of the year and in that part of the ocean. After four days the gale had more or less blown itself out (it might have continued a great deal longer, but for the fact that the vessels were sailing eastward out of the depression area). It was now, with the possibility that at any moment they might be overwhelmed, that the Admiral sat down in his damp cabin and wrote an account of his discoveries. He was determined to the last that Martín Alonso Pinzón – who once again had disappeared – should not claim for himself the credit for this voyage to the Indies which he, Christopher Columbus, had been dreaming about for so many years and had finally, despite so much opposition, achieved. Having completed this on parchment, and wrapped it in waxed cloth, the Admiral had it placed in a cask which he then threw into the sea. There was always the chance that someone would find it. He was quite resolved that his name should ring through the ages as the discoverer of the western ocean route to the Indies.

On February 15 land was sighted. There was wild surmise as to what it might be. Columbus was right about his latitude. It was the little island of Santa Maria, the southernmost of the Azores. They had been lost, and now were found. It took them three days, with headwinds always preventing them from reaching this much-desired land, to find out that they had indeed fetched the Azores. This was the territory of the Kingdom of Portugal. The latter was hardly likely to be friendly to the Admiral of the Ocean Sea, especially if it could be proved that he had been taking, in the name of Ferdinand and Isabella, lands which by all right belonged to Portugal. This Christopher Columbus, or Colón as he might now call himself, was in any case an unpopular character with the Portuguese. He had learned all his seamanship and navigation under their flag, and what was he now doing using that knowledge in the service of Spain? Columbus was well enough aware of the dangers that he was running, in putting into Portuguese waters with this new knowledge of the Indies in his head. But the ship had suffered so severely during the storm that it was really necessary to get ashore, re-water, provision, and give the crew some rest. On February 18 1493, Columbus and the crew of *Niña* were back for the first time, in just over five months, in a familiar world.

The Last Leg Home

Santa Maria has no really good anchorages, being, as the Admiralty Pilot puts it, "on all sides bold". It is a mountainous little island, but fertile. They brought up on the north side and sent the boat ashore. Yes, they were in the Azores and this was indeed Santa Maria. It was the first island to have been colonised by the Portuguese in these parts, and was already settled with small villages, raising in its valleys cereals, grapes and citrus fruits. From where they lay at anchor they could see the clouds scudding over the centre, Pico Alto, nearly 2,000 feet high. What a moment of relief that was to the Admiral and all the crew! They had been *there*, and they had come back.

At first their reception seemed friendly enough, the acting governor of the island, João de Castanheira, having provisions sent out to them – fresh bread (how good after their salt-ridden hard tack) and some chickens. A few hours later they shifted anchor further to the east where, as the villagers advised them, there was more security from wind and weather, and better holding-gound. Columbus had put three men ashore at their first anchorage, near the village of "Our Lady of the Angels", with instructions for them to make arrangements about provisions and water. Near where they were now anchored there was a chapel dedicated to the Virgin. The Admiral, mindful of the vows that they had all taken during the storm, sent half the crew ashore in the ship's boat to perform their penitential pilgrimage and arrange for the local priest to say a Mass. His intention was that, when they returned, he and the other watch would then go ashore and perform their vows.

Unfortunately, the Portuguese governor was suspicious of these salt-stained, sun-burned Spaniards, who said that they had just returned from the Indies to which Portugal had been seeking a sea-route for so many years. Also, he said, he was acquainted with Columbus, and that does not seem to have disposed him in favour of these triumphant sailors. In

153

short, the penitential party was arrested after landing and Columbus, concerned that they did not return, moved berth yet again. Then he saw horsemen on the shore and armed men getting into the ship's boat and coming out towards him. There now followed an altercation between João de Castanheira and the Admiral of the Ocean Sea – the latter producing his credentials from Ferdinand and Isabella to prove his title. The Portuguese was not impressed, he had no use for Spaniards anyway, and he was quite convinced that this non-Spaniard, non-Portuguese, non-Admiral, had been trespassing in the preserves of his own king. And what was all this about being "Admiral of the Ocean", for everybody knew that it was the Portuguese who had discovered, penetrated, and indeed opened up the Ocean and its attendant lands? While João de Castanheira attempted to inveigle Columbus into the ship's boat – *Nina*'s boat which in any case they had illegally acquired – the latter for his part attempted to get the Portuguese aboard his ship. Both had the same thing in mind: immediate arrest and detention. But neither of these two wily characters was to be taken in the other's net. This somewhat absurd confrontation ended with high words: the Portuguese saying he did not give a damn for the Sovereigns of Spain, and Columbus saying that he would come ashore with the rest of the crew and tear the whole island apart. It was a sad homecoming to the old, familiar world, and it was a portent of everything that was to follow.

Columbus was somewhat naturally disgusted with this return to the shores of Europe, and made invidious comparison between the old world and the Indies. There, he said, "at the far end of the Orient lies the celestial paradise. The theologians and the philosophers were right in saying that in the Orient, that most temperate place, there indeed is the true Eden." He was in for even worse troubles, for another storm now blew up and had to take off from Santa Maria and try to make for the next island to the north, São Miguel. Beaten back by the wind and weather he once again headed for Santa Maria – and one must bear in mind that he only had half of his crew. This time everything was better. João de Castanheira had clearly had a conference with the other dignitaries in his small island, as well as interrogating the sailors from *Niña*. It must have become clear to him that these Spaniards had not in fact been interfering in the realms of the king of Portugal. A delegation came forward composed of two priests and a notary, and it seems to have been established that Columbus might be allowed to proceed on his way without any further affront. His detained crewmen – by now, no doubt, thoroughly penitent – were released. The Portuguese governor, having failed to capture the great man himself, clearly felt that there was no possible point in keeping a lot of potentially troublesome sailors in his small island. After all, Santa Maria is only about ten miles long by five miles wide.

Columbus proceeded to up-anchor and sailed round to the south of the island, well away from the area of governmental control. He needed to get stone-ballast aboard for the conclusion of the journey and wood for the fire. On Sunday February 24, Columbus in his sole remaining ship, the caravel *Niña*, left the Azores and set sail for the homeland of his shipmates – Spain. He himself had no homeland. He had a mistress; his wife was dead; and he had two sons. He had discovered the mysterious 'Indies' by the direct sea-route – just as he had said he would do – and now he was bringing them back as a present for their Majesties.

Once again he was to suffer from the weather prevalent more often than not in that stretch of the Atlantic between the Azores and the mainland of Europe in winter. "When we were at the very doors of home," as he reported, "it was more than sad to encounter such a storm." Three days out from the Azores, headed for Cape St. Vincent, the little caravel hit straight into the centre of a major depression, with the wind coming in full strength from the south. *Niña* was forced to run before it, "dry-masted and in extreme danger from the immense tempest of sea and wind which drove at us in two different ways". What had happened was that the caravel had to cope with the old remaining swell from the north, while the storm centre had shifted so that the gale-force winds now blew from the south. The wind had also increased to such intensity

Illustrations from the Basel edition of Columbus's famous "First Letter" to his Sovereign, 1493, which began: "Sire, I know that you will be pleased at the great success with which our Lord has blessed my voyage . . ." Left: Ship of the Santa Maria type. Centre: Imaginative sketch of the islands discovered by Columbus, 1492. Right: Columbus landing on "Insula Hyspana".

that the canvas of the sails – already hard tried by their outward voyage and by the salt and torrid climate of the tropics – split before the wind. Once more the lot was cast as to who should make yet a further pilgrimage if all were spared, and for the third time the lot fell on Columbus. It certainly seemed as if God was determined that the author of this whole enterprise should acknowledge his debts.

On March 3 1493 the secret of 'The Indies' was very nearly lost. The storm increased even more, the wind backing to the North, and *Niña* being driven nearer and nearer onto the lee shore of Europe. Fortunately they still had just enough sail left to manage to claw offshore. They had now sighted the headland under their lee. They had reached Europe all right, but in a very unfortunate place. They were off the entrance to the Tagus, the river-mouth to Lisbon, the kingdom of Portugal – the very kingdom that had just tried to detain the Admiral, and where his recent adventures would be heard with the greatest attention. Columbus recognised the coastline well enough. After all, he had been a sailor in Portuguese ships long before he had made the acquaintanceship of the Sovereigns of Spain. Under the prevailing conditions, however, in a winter gale that devastated the whole of the Atlantic coast of Europe, there was little that he could do but make for harbour.

He came into Cascais, then no more than an obscure fishing village. The people ashore were so astounded at seeing this caravel come flashing out of one of the worst storms that had ever been known that they kneeled and prayed for her safety. They went on up river and finally dropped anchor off Rastelo, near the golden walls of the castle of Belém on the outskirts of Lisbon. They were safely home in Europe, but it was one of the most awkward homecomings in history.

Relations between Portugal and Spain were far from good. Columbus had previously been a seaman under the Portuguese flag, and he had attempted to interest King John II in the Enterprise of the Indies, and had been turned down. Now here he came in a small weather-beaten caravel, with the high sounding title of "Admiral of the Ocean Sea", to announce that he had done on behalf of Ferdinand and Isabella what he had always promised that he could do – find the sea route to the Indies by sailing due west. It has sometimes been suggested that he deliberately

The approach to Lisbon harbour made at the end of the first voyage.

made for Portugal in the hope of getting a better price for his knowledge than from the Spanish Sovereigns. This is nonsense. Given the weather conditions at the time, and his uncertainty as to his true position, he could have done nothing else. In any case his vessel was Spanish and crewed by Spaniards. What is more, he had no idea what had happened to *Pinta*, or whether indeed Martín Alonso Pinzón might not at that very minute be claiming all the honours for himself, safely tucked away in his home port of Palos.

While he had been at sea "off the Canary Islands" Columbus had written his ever memorable 'First Letter' to the Sovereigns. It was most important now that it should be immediately despatched, so that Ferdinand and Isabella should know that he had more than fulfilled his promise and, no doubt, that they should not be concerned about his presence in Portugal.

It began: "Sire, I know that you will be pleased at the great success with which Our Lord has blessed my voyage . . . I sailed from the Canary Islands to the Indies in thirty-three days with the ships you, the King and Queen, our Sovereigns, gave to me. I found there many islands filled with a great number of people. I have taken possession of all of them in the name of Your Highnesses. I did this by proclamation and with the royal standard unfurled. No one opposed me."

After a description of his voyage, he then goes on to say that "It would appear in all these islands that the men are content with one woman, but to the chieftain or king they give as many as twenty. It seems as if the women work harder than the men . . . I have found in these islands no human monstrosities, as had been expected, but on the contrary a good-looking people. They are not like the Negroes in Guinea [Portuguese West Africa] but with flowing hair, for they are not born where the heat of the sun is intense, although it is indeed hot enough . . . I have found no monsters, but the only exception I have to report is in the people of one island, Quaris, the second one finds on reaching the Indies. They

Port of Lisbon from Braun and Hogenburg's Civitatis Orbis Terrarum, *1572.*

Cannibals. From Thevet's Singularitez . . ., *1558.*

are extremely fierce and are cannibals. They have a great number of canoes and in these they range throughout the islands, robbing, and taking whatever comes to hand. They look very much like the others, but wear their hair long like women. They also have bows and arrows made out of cane. At the end of the cane they have a small piece of wood instead of iron, for they do not possess this metal. [These were the Carib Indians, who were quite distinct from the gentle Tainos whom Columbus had met in most places.] In yet another island, which they tell me is even larger than Española, the people are hairless. Here there is any amount of gold. From it and the other islands I bring Indians with me as evidence of where I have been. Finally, just to conclude the success of my voyage, I can assure Their Highnesses that I will give them as much gold as they could possibly want, if they for their part will give me such small help as I may need. More than that, I can also give them spices and cotton, quite as much as they can want – and, as you know, these things have previously had to be shipped from Greece, and the island of Chios, and the Venetians sell these things for whatever price they like to ask. I can also bring aloe wood, as much as is wanted, and as many slaves as you shall order to be shipped." He goes on to say that he believes he has "found rhubarb and cinnamon, and I shall certainly find a thousand other things of value, for the people I have left behind will undoubtedly discover them".

In Samana Bay Columbus encountered the first natives armed with bows and arrows. From Thevet's Singularitez, *1558.*

All along one must take into account the fact that Columbus had brought very little of value back with him. He had lost his flagship, he had left behind subjects of the King and Queen in some unknown island (which he was not quite certain that he could find again), and he had possibly also lost the third ship. He had had no communication with *Pinta* since they had parted in the storm. Not a very good balance sheet. He now had other problems on his mind. A Portuguese man-of-war which was berthed nearby the storm-beaten caravel sent across a boat and demanded to know the reason for the presence of this Spaniard in their waters. The ship was commanded by Bartholomew Diaz, one of the greatest seamen who ever lived, and who had already discovered the true sea-route to the real Indies in 1488, when he had rounded the Cape of Good Hope and found the north-eastward trend of the African coastline. It was hardly surprising that so distinguished a navigator took some exception to the claims of this red-headed Genoese, in the employ of the Spanish crown, to have gone direct to the Indies by just sailing westward. Diaz almost undoubtedly had a better idea of the geography of the globe than did Columbus.

159

Admiral of the Ocean Sea

The real problem was not presented by Bartholomew Diaz – who swiftly accepted the credentials which Columbus was only too ready to show. No, the problem was, what would King John II of Portugal make of his presence in the Tagus, and of the fact that he had achieved for the rival kingdom of Spain the golden and so much desired triumph of the sea-route to the Indies? While, on the surface, Columbus was happy at having been accepted by Diaz and the others aboard the Portuguese warship as what he claimed to be, "a Castilian Admiral", and while he was delighted with the flocks of admiring spectators who came out by boat to see "his Indians" and to hear from his crew of their exploits, he must have been a very worried man. His fears were set at rest on the third day, Friday March 8 when a messenger from the king arrived with an invitation to Columbus to visit the ruler of Portugal at his court.

Admiral Columbus, having smartened himself up as much as was possible in the small cabin of his caravel, went ashore. He took with him some gold souvenirs of the Indies as well as some of his Indians. The latter alone would serve as proof that he had not been to Africa – not been trespassing in King John's territory. No one could conceive that these long-haired, brown-skinned people were any relation to the black, fuzzy-haired Negroes with whom the Portuguese had long been familiar. What the Caribbean natives thought of it all is unimaginable. They had been taken from their simple islands aboard a great winged canoe, had been subjected to the most terrifying weather, accompanied by cold such as they had never known, and they were now on muleback cavalcade through the rainy, windblown streets of Lisbon. The King at this moment – since plague had been reported in the city – had moved the royal residence to a monastery about thirty miles away. It took Columbus and his party two days to get there, two days of rough travelling through mud and mire, and the kind of weather that might well have been expected to kill the Indians.

The Admiral was well received by the King, who acted throughout with dignified restraint, clearly admitting that the Indians alone proved that Columbus had not been into any of his territories. As Columbus commented in his journal: "The King received him with all due honour and was very courteous, bidding him be seated . . . and gave every evidence that he was pleased at the voyage having achieved its desired ends." Pleased the King cannot have been, for it seemed to mean that all the years of Portuguese seafaring, and of their gradual exploration of the Atlantic and the African coast, had been nullified by this foreign adventurer, whose cause he had turned down on the best scientific advice. Barros, the 16th century Portuguese historian, tells of the meeting: "The King received him in friendly fashion, but was unhappy when he saw that the natives with him were not curly-haired negroes, looking like those of Guinea. They appeared in colour and shape to be like those of India – that land which he had striven so long to find. Colón, for his part, told of the new lands in extravagant terms, far exceeding anything that the place really had, and was also rash in his words – even going so far as to scold the King for having turned down his original proposal. His whole manner made some of the gentlemen of the court so indignant, taking into account their dislike of his insolence as well as the sorrow that they saw he inflicted on the King, that they offered to kill him. In this way also they thought that they would prevent him ever getting back to Castille. They pointed out that his arrival would damage the kingdom [of Portugal], adding that it was clear he had been into lands which had been granted the King by the Pope. The King, however, that truly Christian prince, said that though he was distressed about what had happened he would have no harm done to Columbus. In fact, he showed him considerable honour and even had the natives whom he had brought with him, given robes of scarlet cloth."

Columbus had suffered long at the antechambers of princes and kings, and around the doors of the rich. He was an immensely proud man, and now that he had achieved (as he thought) what he had set out to do, he was not going to bother to be polite to those who had rejected him. He was not being very intelligent. Possibly the best thing that John II of Portugal could have done would indeed to have had him killed; to have seized *Niña* where she lay at anchor, impounded her seamen, and with their aid sent out a Portuguese expedition in the spring to refind these Indies and claim them for his own. But he had to consider his relationship with Ferdinand and Isabella, and those monarchs – especially since their recent conquest of Granada – were considerably more powerful than he in his lean, Atlantic-bound kingdom of Portugal. He behaved with considerable restraint, great dignity and, even more, commonsense. The same cannot be said for the Admiral.

The King went so far as to send an escort of knights along with Columbus when he returned to Lisbon and his ship. The weaver's son had come a long way. He had a great deal further to go. The main thing now was for him to return to Spain, be confirmed in his dignities, and arrange for the next expedition which would take possession of even more of these lands. On the morning of March 13 he was aboard his ship again, the anchors were up, and the Admiral and *Niña* were gone for good from the land of Portugal. Perhaps he was lucky – but then he had been lucky so much recently – for it seems very likely that there was a plot afoot to have him killed before he could get back to Spain. He crossed the bar, with his Indians, his gold, his astonishing islands locked in his head, and his knowledge of seas and lands lying far away to the west.

There was a north-easter blowing, excellent for running down the coast, and the sailors during their days in port had had plenty of time to make good the damages to hull, canvas, gear and rigging. Homeward bound, in the real sense of the word at last, they rolled past Sagres, *Sacrum Promontorium*, the Sacred Promontary, as the Romans had called it. Here Henry the Navigator had made his home, so that he could always be conscious of the Atlantic and always in touch with his caravels as they sailed back and forth exploring Africa and the ocean. Sagres may well have been the place that the poet Camoëns had in mind when he wrote "*Onde a terra se acaba e o mar começa*" – "where the land has an end and the sea begins". It was near here that this new Admiral of all that ocean had swum ashore seventeen years before on an oar.

While Columbus was heading home for Palos, still worried in case Martín Alonso Pinzón had beaten him to it, the latter was indeed at sea and only a little astern of him. *Pinta* had fetched up in Bayona a small fishing port near Vigo in Spain. They had, in fact, come out much further north than the Admiral, having made a greater miscalculation in their dead reckoning. Immediately on arrival Pinzón had done exactly what Columbus had anticipated. He had sent a messenger to Ferdinand and Isabella, who at that time were in residence at Barcelona, saying that they had found the Indies and were back. This was not entirely, as some have claimed, a malicious act on his part – after all, how was he to know that Columbus in *Niña* had survived the storm? But it was almost certainly an attempt to secure for himself all the honours and dignities that would go with this unique discovery. He was to be unlucky, for the Sovereigns were prepared to wait until they heard from their own appointed commander. They would no doubt have sent for Pinzón within a short space of time if Columbus and *Niña* had not appeared.

Now at last, here he came, sailing into Palos which he had left 224 days before – thirty-two weeks which had changed the history of mankind. Nothing would ever be quite the same again. Although it is easy to say that the Portuguese would undoubtedly have reached the Americas within a very few years, it was nevertheless a Genoese in the employment of Spain who first made the voyage. He had already sent the 'First Letter' to Ferdinand and Isabella, in which he had concluded: "Since Our Redeemer has given this victory to our most illustrous King and Queen and to their renowned kingdom, so all Christendom should be delighted

La Rábida, 15th century cloister of the Monastery.

and make great feasts and give solemn thanks to the Holy Trinity. Everyone should make solemn prayers for the great glory which Christendom shall have in bringing so many peoples to our Holy Faith, as well as for worldly benefits. Not only Spain but all Christians will gain honour and profit by it." But now for the moment all was put aside in the sheet excitement of the return, the citizens of Palos seeing the caravel come in, their husbands, sons and fathers returned from the unknown. (But how about those who had been left behind in Hispaniola? Even by the Admiral's standards that would take some explaining.)

Hard on Columbus's heels came *Pinta* – an extraordinary coincidence that, despite the parting at sea, they should both make port on the same day. Martín Alonso Pinzón was considerably older than Columbus and the strain of the voyage had completely exhausted him. It is sad to record that this other great seaman, who had after all been largely responsible for the success of the voyage, should have enjoyed little of the success of the homecoming. He died on March 20. Meanwhile there were the natural feastings and junketings of returned sailors meeting their friends and families – and with such strange tales to tell, unbelievable places and extraordinary seas, and golden-skinned people. And here were some of these natives talking outlandish words to prove it. Columbus meanwhile had despatched a second copy of his letter, just in case anything had happened to the first between Lisbon and Spain. Ferdinand and Isabella were at this moment at Barcelona and Columbus must await the reply to his despatch. It seems likely that he stayed at La Rábida, where in a sense it had all started – La Rábida where he had received so much encouragement in the days when no one was prepared to believe in his dream.

In due course the royal reply came back over the wet and wintry roads of Spain. It was dated "From Barcelona on the 30th day of March 1493". It opened in such a way that there could no more be any doubt what Columbus had achieved for himself and for his descendants. The King and Queen began their letter by addressing Columbus as "Don Cristóbal, our Admiral of the Ocean Sea and Viceroy and Governor of the Islands which have been discovered in the Indies". They desired him to come to court at his earliest convenience. They gave him every assurance that "what you have begun will be continued and even further advanced". At long, long last, after years of waiting in anterooms in his snabby cloak, he had achieved knighthood. He had been accepted as Admiral and Governor of an area that far exceeded the territory of his Sovereigns even. Unfortunately Columbus, who was a good loser (or patient in waiting), was a bad winner. He could never forgive or forget those who had slighted him, and the dignity of his titles and position was destined to go to his head.

Ferdinand and Isabella were rightly eager to get another expedition under way. They had very good information that King John of Portugal was not completely convinced that their Admiral had not been poaching on his preserves. The King in fact had already made up his mind to send a fleet to these Indies. He was only to be finally deterred from this enterprise by a superb piece of diplomacy – one of the world's most remarkable coups – which was achieved by Ferdinand and Isabella and their advisers. They sent news of the discovery to the Pope, and on May 3, 1493 Alexander VI issued his famous bull. He granted them the Indies in the same way as he had already granted the King of Portugal such territories as he might discover *"in partibus Africae"*. The world was now divided – Africa for the Portuguese and the Indies for the Kingdom of Spain. Columbus had set in train a division that would provoke innumerable wars and stud the seven seas with the sails of fighting ships. The time would come when the Dutch, the French and the English would deny that any Pope, at any time, had had the right to apportion giant areas of the globe to other countries.

Meanwhile the most remarkable procession was making its way to the court at Barcelona. The Admiral was passing through Spain in the manner of a Roman general celebrating a triumph. Here he came with these unknown people, these Indians from the far side of the world, and with him went parrots and strange types of vegetation and gold and unknown spices (or so it was rumoured). Nothing quite like it had ever been seen before – nor indeed would ever be seen again. For the first time in the history of Europe and the world a connection had been made between two land-masses that had hitherto been unknown to one another. But then Columbus would probably have maintained that they had been known for a long time – ever since Marco Polo had returned to Venice after his years in the Far East and Cathay.

Pope Alexander VI.

The Very Magnificent Lord

He arrived in Seville on March 31 appropriately enough at the right moment to take part in the ceremonies of Holy Week. Here he came, "the Christ-Bearer", with his pagans who were shortly to be baptised. He was bringing souls to God, and had every intention of bringing thousands and thousands more. His arrival was a sensation. As Las Casas put it: "The news had begun to spread all over Castile that new lands had been discovered, which were called the Indies. There were many people there and quite different from us, and everything was quite new. The man who had discovered them was coming by such-and-such a road, and he was bringing with him men from these people. Not only those from the towns through which he passed, but others from townships quite remote from his route, came to see him. Everywhere the towns and villages were emptied and the roads were crowded so that people could see him and welcome him."

His reception by Ferdinand and Isabella was so favourable and hospitable that not even Columbus could ever have dreamed it. The Sovereigns gave him their hands to kiss, expressed their greatest pleasure at the immensity of his discoveries and of all that it could mean to the throne of Spain. It was early April, a lovely season in the Mediterranean, and Columbus had every reason to feel happy. On his triumphal progress through the land he had naturally called in to see his mistress, Beatriz, and had told her that her cousin was now in command of a Spanish settlement in a totally new land. He had seen both his sons, and here he was being entertained by their Majesties and treated to a degree of courtesy such as only a Spanish 'Don' (and now he was one) ever received. After all these years everything was justified.

The Sovereigns bade him rise from his knees, and sit beside them and

Opposite: *Seville. Detail from painting attributed to Alonso Sanchez Coello, 16th century.*

167

their son Don Juan. The Indians, the gold, the various plants, and other curios like his cummerbund with the gold head upon it – all were examined. "And more and more the wonder grew . . ." Something quite strange had happened, and the world had shrunk. The scholars, savants, and astronomers were all proved wrong, and the Indies were only thirty days or so sailing distance from Europe. How curious that no one had ever gone there before, and that for all these centuries Europeans had been dependent upon the vagaries of Moslems at places like Alexandria to allow them to buy the spices, gold and jewels of the East! The Genoese had been right – all you had to do was sail due west.

As Justin Winsor wrote in 'Christopher Columbus' (1892): ". . . it seems quite evident that this season at Barcelona made the only un-alloyed days of happiness, freed of anxiety, which Columbus ever experienced. He was observed of all, and everybody was complacent to him. His will was apparently law to King and subject. Las Casas tells us that he passed among the admiring throngs with his face wreathed with smiles of content. An equal complacency of delight and expectation settled upon all with whom he talked of the wonders of the land which he had found. They dreamed as he did of entering into golden cities with their hundred bridges . . . It was a fatal lure to the proud Spanish nature, and no one was doomed to expiate the folly of the delusion more poignantly than Columbus himself." Peter Martyr d'Anghiera, another Italian, and a contemporary of the Admiral, wrote in one of his letters: "I am here at the source of much intellectual activity. Welcome news of new found lands . . ." and elsewhere, "Christophorus Colonus of Genoa has returned from the western side of the globe. With some difficulty he had obtained from the Sovereigns three ships to make this expedition for they did not believe that the lands ever existed. Now he is back with the evidence of many valuable things, and especially of gold, in which these lands are rich."

On May 20 his coat of arms was bestowed upon him – no unimportant event in those days when the difference between noble and commoner was as profound as between priest and peasant. Meanwhile the Indians were baptised, one of them being given the name of Diego Colón after the great discoverer. As a memory of the lands from which he had come, the third quartering of the arms of the Admiral consisted of "gold islands in the waves of the sea". It was also later officially confirmed that all who sailed upon the Atlantic to the south and the west of a line drawn between

Opposite: *John II of Portugal (anon.). The inscription referring to John IV is incorrect.*

ANNES · QVARTVS PC
TVGALIÆ RE

the Azores and Cape Verde islands were to be subject to his authority. Few men ever had such supreme responsibility placed upon their shoulders. Compared with the theoretical control of the unknown islands that was being given to Columbus the empire that Alexander the Great had carved out for himself was comparatively modest. But then neither the Sovereigns, nor the Admiral, had any idea just how big a territory he had newly acquired for Spain.

Meanwhile preparations were rapidly being made for the second expedition to the Indies. Columbus had proved his point that they existed, and the great thing now was to get a Spanish fleet across there and in possession before the Portuguese forestalled them. Columbus carried in his head the chart of this mysterious world – and there can be absolutely no doubt that he had in fact plotted the outlines of all the places that he had actually visited. It is tragic that this original 'Columbus chart' has not survived. It would have been one of the world's most important historic documents. But then, it is even possible that it went over the side on that memorable day when he had assumed that they might never make home and had put his documents into a wooden cask and hurled it into the Atlantic.

Curiously enough, perhaps the nearest we can come to Columbus's conception of the western hemisphere is contained in a Turkish map which has been dated as having been drawn between 1513–1517, at which time the cartographer presented it to Sultan Selim I, conqueror of Egypt. The author of this map was Piri Reis, a nephew of Kemal Reis, one of the Turkish admirals in the Mediterranean in the last quarter of the 15th century. It was originally a "mappa mundi" (the whole world as it was then known), but at some time unfortunately it has been torn in half. However, what remains shows very clearly the west coast of Africa, the Azores, Canaries, and Cape Verde islands, the basic position of the West Indian islands, and a large part of the coast of Brazil. Dr. Yusuf Akçura, President of the Society for Turkish Historical Research, in a treatise on the map has translated the passages which are written in Turkish on the land-masses. One of the most interesting reads: "The names which mark the places on the said islands and coasts were given by Colombo that these places may be known by them. The coast and islands on the map are taken from Colombo's own map." Dr. Akçura goes on to explain how he thinks that the map was indeed copied from an early Spanish one (either by Columbus or one of his fellows) "Piri Reis's

Opposite: *Pope Alexander VI. Detail of fresco by Pinturicchio (c. 1454–1513).*

claim to have used Columbus's map, which until now has not been found, may be thus validated: during a naval battle in the western basin of the Mediterranean in 1501, the Turkish sailors captured Spanish ships and in one of them found objects that came from America. As is known, Columbus returned from his third trip in 1500. It is therefore very likely that his map was among the objects found by Kemal Reis on board the Spanish ships." It seems more likely that, by this date, what was captured was a standard Spanish map of the period which would of course have included the results of Columbus's discoveries. However Piri Reis's own comments are interesting enough. After saying that he drew his own map in Gallipoli in the month of Muharrem of the year 919 (that is between March 9 and April 7 1513) he goes on to describe some of the places and to give his own version of how they came to be discovered. Of the mainland of South America he writes: "These coasts are named the shores of Antilia. They were discovered in the year 896 of the Arabian calendar. It is reported that a Genoese infidel, his name was Colombo, discovered these places. For instance, a book fell into the hands of the said Colombo, and he found said in this book that at the end of the Western Sea, on its western side, there were coasts and islands and all kinds of metals and also precious stones. This man, having studied this book thoroughly, explained these matters one by one to the grandees of Genoa and said: 'Come, give me two ships, let me go and find these places.' They said: 'O foolish man, can an end or a limit be found to the Western Sea? Its vapour is full of darkness.' The above mentioned Colombo saw that no help was forthcoming from the Genoese, he sped forth, went to the Bey [King] of Spain, and told his story in detail. He too answered like the Genoese. In brief, Colombo talked to the king for a long time, and finally the Bey of Spain gave him two ships, saw that they were well equipped and said: 'O Colombo, if it happens as you say, let us make you *kapudan* [admiral] to that country.' Having said this he sent the said Colombo to the Western Sea. The late Gazi Kemal had a Spanish slave. This slave said to Kemal Reis that he had been three times to that land with Colombo. He said: 'First we reached the Strait of Gibraltar, then from there we sailed straight south and west between the two [illegible, possibly the two groups of islands, Cape Verdes and Canaries]. Having advanced straight four thousand miles, we saw an island facing us, but gradually the waves of the sea became foamless, that is the sea was becalmed, and the North Star little by little became veiled and invisible, and he also said that the stars in that region are not arranged as here. They are seen in a different arrangement. They anchored at the island which they had seen earlier across the way. The population of that island came, shot arrows at them and did not allow them to land and get information. The males and the females shot hand arrows. The tips of these arrows were made of fishbones, and the whole population went naked and also very [illegible]. Seeing that they could not land on that island they sailed to the other part of the island where they saw a boat. On seeing them the boat fled and the people in the boat dashed out on land. They [The Spaniards] took the boat. They saw that inside of it there was human flesh. It happened that these people were of that nation which went from island to island hunting men and eating them. The

The Turkish map of the Western hemisphere made by Piri Reis

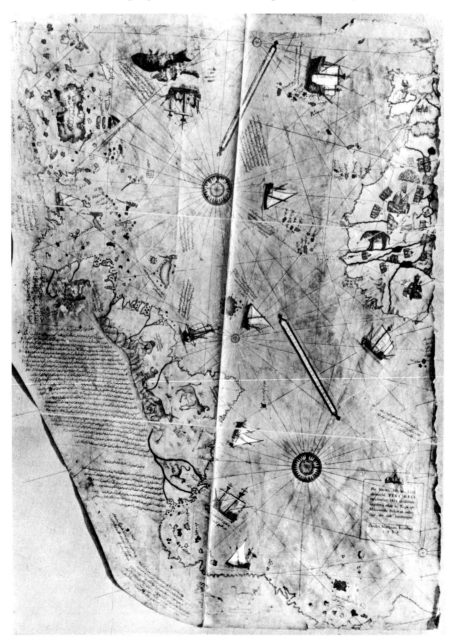

said Colombo saw yet another island, they neared it, they saw that on that island there were great snakes. They avoided landing on this island, and remained at anchor for seventeen days. The people of this island saw that no harm came to them from the people of the ship so they caught fish and brought them in their small canoes. These [Spaniards] were pleased and gave them glass beads. It appears that he [Columbus] had read it in a book that in that region glass beads were prized. Seeing the beads they brought still more fish. These [Spaniards] always gave them glass beads. One day they saw gold around the arm of a woman, they took the gold and gave her beads. They told her: bring more gold we will give you more beads. They went and brought them much gold. It appears that in their mountains there were gold mines. One day also, they saw pearls in the hands of a person. They saw that when they gave beads many more pearls were brought to them. Pearls were found on the shore of this island, and in a spot one or two fathoms deep. And also loading their ships with logwood trees and taking two natives along, they took them that year to the Bey of Spain. But the said Colombo not knowing the language of these people, they traded by signs, and after this trip the Bey of Spain sent priests and barley. The Spaniards taught the natives how to sow and reap and converted them to their own religion. The natives had no religion of any sort. They walked naked and lay there like animals. The names which mark the places on the said islands and coasts were given by Colombo, that these places may be known by them. And And also Colombo was a great astronomer. The coasts and islands on this map are taken from Colombo's map."

What is particularly fascinating about Piri Reis's account (quite apart from the value of his map) is that so much of it is based on the information given by the unfortunate sailor who had been on the first three of Columbus's voyages. Who he was we shall never know, but one gets from his report a very good idea of how the New World looked to an unsophisticated seaman. One also sees how the impact of these discoveries was beginning to affect every country, so that a distinguished Turkish cartographer (later to become Admiral of the Red and Arabian Seas) devotes a large part of his material to "the Infidel Colombo". Interesting also is his statement that Columbus had originally tried to interest his native Genoa in the project. Although there is no evidence for it, this seems more than likely, for he remained a Genoese at heart to his dying day.

The preparation of the second fleet, which was to be a considerably larger venture altogether, took, as might be expected, a great deal longer than had been anticipated. In charge of the main task of organization was

Coat of arms of Christopher Columbus, bestowed upon him May 20, 1493.

Juan Rodriguez de Fonseca, Archdeacon of Seville, a worldly prelate and a man of considerable ability. This time things were not as simple as equipping little caravels and one small merchantman. In view of the threat from Portugal, and the news of the discovery having been bruited all over the continent, Ferdinand and Isabella were determined to send a real fleet. The plan was for seventeen ships, all equipped for a six month voyage, and up to fifteen hundred men to man them. The Admiral was going to go to the Indies as head of an armada that befitted his title, his rank, and the Kingdoms of Ferdinand and Isabella. In terms of the logistics of the period this was no easy venture, and it is to the credit of

175

Fonseca, Columbus, and everyone who worked on it, that it was ever achieved at all. It has to be borne in mind that the whole expedition was something quite new in history. No one had any experience of such a type of enterprise. They were going thousands of miles across unknown seas to colonize unknown lands. True, in the history of Europe there had been plenty of colonial activity in the past, but this had always been undertaken within a known area, and where there had long been sufficient communication between the countries concerned for interpreters to be available. But they were going to countries where there was a complete language barrier and where, apparently, nothing even as simple as an iron nail could be obtained.

Inevitably the merchants and middlemen ashore made all they could out of the whole transaction. Indifferent wine was supplied, and in casks so poor that a good many of them burst open on the voyage. The horsemen – for they were taking horses for the first time to the New World – having been given the money for good bloodstock, appeared on them at a ceremonial parade in Seville. They then quickly resold them and bought themselves cheap old nags, thus giving themselves a bit of profit before they had even left. All down the line it was much the same. But certainly this time there was no lack of volunteers. As Sir Arthur Helps puts it: "The fever for discovery was universal . . . Untold riches were to be acquired, and probably there was not one of the 1,500 persons who took part in the squadron that did not anticipate a prodigious fortune as the reward of the voyage. Nor was one of the great objects of these discoveries uncared for. Twelve missionaries, eager to enlighten the spiritual darkness of the western lands, were placed under the charge of Bernard Buil, a Benedictine monk, who was specially appointed by the Pope, in order to ensure an authorised teaching of the faith, to superintend the religious education of the Indians." Chief Guacanagari, who by now had had time to learn something more about the nature of these white "god-men", little realised what was being prepared for his edification across the distant ocean.

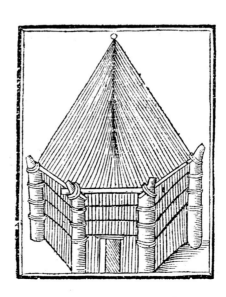

Another Landfall

The prime object of the second voyage – at least as far as Queen Isabella was concerned – was to bring the Faith to these people who lived in darkness. There can be no doubting her sincerity, nor indeed that of the Admiral himself. (He had not forgotten during the months while the fleet was assembling to make his pilgrimage to Santa Maria of Guadaloupe in Estremadura.) Unfortunately, as Morison comments: "[Although] the first European colony in America was conceived of as a means of converting infidels and acquiring gold; in practice the higher object became completely submerged by the lower."

But, for the moment, all that was far away. High religious hope inspired the leader and the Queen, as well as the priests who had been chosen for the task. What totally absorbed the monarchs, the Admiral, and everyone else concerned with the project, was getting the vessels assembled at Cadiz and everything shipshape, stores aboard, and all the gear ready. The months dragged by. Relations between Columbus and Juan de Fonseca deteriorated. There were arguments about trifles and about privileges – how many body-servants, for instance, the Admiral might be allowed. On de Fonseca fell the burden of organisation, for Columbus was long at court and then on his pilgrimage. No doubt de Fonseca felt that while the one was enjoying all the honours, he was bearing all the brunt – interminable rows with shipbuilders and contractors, and the mass of paperwork which, even as early as the 15th century, was one of the delights of officialdom in Spain.

Seventeen ships gradually assembled in Cadiz. Three of them were transports, *naos* or cargo ships, one of these being designated as Columbus's flagship. These larger vessels (about 200 tons) would provide accommodation for the horses and domestic animals that they would need in the settlement. The bulk of the fleet consisted of caravels similar to *Niña* and *Pinta*. *Pinta* in fact was not coming on the expedition –

neither were any of the Pinzón family. The rift between them and the Admiral seems to have been complete. A few of the ships were a special type of light caravel, shallow-drafted and designed for exploring creeks and inlets. These may possibly have been specially built on Columbus's orders. He was determined to explore and thoroughly chart every aspect of these new lands.

There was no lack of gentlemen volunteers any more than of seamen. Many of them were to be further heard of in the history of the Indies; among them Diego, Columbus's younger brother. One who was certainly destined to make a name for himself was Juan Ponce de Leon, the future discoverer of Florida. There was also Juan de la Cosa, a chart-maker, whose map is the first we have of the New World, and Alonso de Ojeda, who had been active in the Moorish wars and was a favourite of the Duke of Medina Celi, Columbus's early patron. Both the father and the uncle of Las Casas, from whose conversations with the Admiral the future historian would gain much of his material, were embarked, as well as Diego Chanca, a physician from Seville, who wrote a narrative of the voyage. The quality of the crews was better, for Columbus could now pick and choose from the hundreds of volunteers who flocked to the great port. It was fitting that the fleet should start from Cadiz, for it was from here (Gades as it was then known) that the Phoenicians had first begun to open up the Atlantic sea-routes. All in all, the grand fleet was a far call from the old *Santa Maria* and the two caravels with which the first expedition had been launched from Palos on what most experts had felt was a thoroughly foolish mission.

Columbus had hoped to get under way by the middle of August, but the weeks dragged by and it was not until September 25 that the fleet weighed anchor. We get some idea of the colour and vitality of the scene

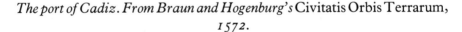

The port of Cadiz. From Braun and Hogenburg's Civitatis Orbis Terrarum, *1572.*

Juan Ponce de Leon, the future discoverer of Florida.

from a letter written by a contemporary: "The usual religious rites were performed by the sailors. The last embraces were given. The ships were decorated with brilliant cloths, banners flying from the rigging, and on the stern of every vessel there waved in the breeze the royal standard. Pipers and harpers held in thrall the Nereids and even the Sirens. The shores echoed with the sound of trumpets and the braying of clarions. Cannons thundered across the water. Some Venetian galleys, happening to enter harbour at that moment, joined in the jubilation. The cheers of united nations went up, as well as prayers for the men who were setting forth."

Now they were standing out to sea, the first of the many great Spanish fleets that were to sail between Cadiz and the New World over the centuries to come. Columbus had been warned by the sovereigns that they were not happy about the disposition of King John, and that the Admiral must steer well clear of any Portuguese possessions. His reception in the Azores, and later in Lisbon, had already taught him that he and his Spanish venture were not popular. He shaped course for the Canaries, the ships driving along happily under a refreshing norther. Seven days out, and the islands lay ahead of them. On October 2 they were anchored off Grand Canary. They stayed for a day while repairs were made to one of the ships, and then sailed on down to Gomera. Dona Beatriz was wait-

CADIZ, olim Gàdes, eiusdem no: minis Insulæ oppidum nobile, por: tu maris Herculeo freto, remploquè memoratum.

ing to greet the Admiral – really an Admiral this time, and in command of a fleet greater than any she had ever seen. Possibly she envisaged him as a future husband, but almost equally soon dismissed the idea. It was quite clear that with these new islands and great land-masses swirling in his head – over all of which he was to be Viceroy – he was hardly likely to settle down with her in Gomera. He was eager to be gone. The fleet only stayed a few days, just long enough to water, take aboard fresh supplies, fodder, and further animals for shipment to the colony. More seeds, melons, oranges, lemons and other fruit were embarked so that they could emulate in this new uncultivated world the garden-like quality that was presented by Gomera.

It was calm and the sails hung idle. Where were these winds they had heard about? All hands must have raised a cheer when the Trades began to pipe up on Sunday October 13, and they were able to put Ferro behind them. Now the Admiral gave his course-order to the fleet – West by South. The reason that he took a more southerly route this year was that he was determined to find the islands which the natives had indicated lay below Hispaniola, especially the one they had talked of where the gold came "in nuggets bigger than beans". His other reason, recorded by Diego Chanca, was that "these islands were nearer to Spain". They were indeed, and it was a good judgement – if no more than a lucky one – for the more southerly heading took him deeper into the trade-wind zone.

It was a perfect passage, the fluffy clouds by day, the ships flashing on, everyone of them with a bone between her teeth – though the flagship was a slower sailer than the others. They encountered gulf weed once again, a marvel to them all as it parted with a lazy sigh before the bows. The bo'sun birds were hovering overhead. Even to sailors used to summer days and nights in the Mediterranean, this was something new. The regularity of the winds drove them always onward, blowing at a strength that was ideal for their canvas and their hulls. They were among the first ever to know:

"... the blazing tropic night, when the wake's a welt of light
That holds the hot sky tame,
And the steady fore-foot snores through the planet-powdered floors
Where the scared whale flukes in flame!"

They had only one piece of bad weather, and that was on the night of October 26, St. Simon's Eve, when they ran into an electric storm. Guigliemo Coma, a Spaniard, who wrote about the discoveries in letters that were clearly based on interviews with some of those who took part, records that everyone was comforted when they saw that electrical phenomenon, St. Elmo's Fire, shining on the flagship mast. "It is certain," he says, "that two lights shone through the darkness of the night on the topmast of the Admiral's ship. Quite soon after, the tempest began to abate, the sea to calm and the surface of the waves became as smooth as polished marble." Once again the ships ran on into a sunny day. But even with all this good weather there were inevitably mutterings, and complaints about the food, the water (or lack of it), the leakiness of some of the ships, and the fear of this sea that seemed boundless. "They longed for land . . ."

Columbus had already begun to discern all those signs which indicated that land was not far below the horizon. On Saturday November 2, he was so confident that he ordered all ships to shorten sail. He had observed flocks of birds flying westwards, and noted how the usual night clouds ahead were building up quite differently from the way they did on the high ocean. Sunday was always a good day, in every sense of the word, for this extraordinary man. In the small hours of Sunday morning, November 3, 1493, the watchman at the Admiral's masthead saw what he had been told by his inspired pilot he would indeed see – Land!

There it lay, dead ahead, and all hands aboard the fleet must have been up on the dew-stained decks, feeling the cool of the morning and seeing the promised land. Feathered with cloud, the high peak of an island made its sharp statement against the misty-grey of the horizon. The Admiral summoned all hands to prayer, and they knelt and sang the *Salve Regina*. The Queen of Heaven had led them across the endless waters, and devoutly "they gave thanks to our Lord".

Introducing Christianity to the Indians, as imagined by Philopono in Nova Typis Transacta Navigatio, *1621.*

The island was to be named by Columbus Dominica, Sunday – a name it bears to this day. As the sun rose other islands began to lift out of the sea. The one they had first sighted soared up nearly 6,000 feet to the peak of what is now called Morne Diablotin. A range of forest-clad mountains traversed the island from north to south. (Dominica is of romantic beauty, and remains to this day one of the few islands in this sea that can have changed comparatively little since Columbus first saw it.) As the American sailor Carleton Mitchell has said: "Dominica seems timeless – mountains swathed in green, a mass of vegetation so luxuriant that nature is almost an enemy . . . I felt I was exploring a strange sea, a sea of lush vegetation. Waterfalls tumbled into wet green glades; giant bamboo and towering trees festooned with orchids arched above; and, tying all together, lianas strangled their hosts."

The fleet had fetched the Leeward Islands, the moon-crescent ring that guards the eastern end of the Caribbean Sea. They could have made no better landfall. The British Admiralty "Ocean Passages for the World" gives as its best route for sailing ships, "bound to the Leeward Islands, Jamaica, Belize, or to ports in the Gulf of Mexico", one almost identical to that which Columbus had taken. It was a miraculous feat of navigation – in any sense of the word – to have come out at the very point that provides one of the best entrances to this sea.

The small island just to the north of them Columbus named Maria Galante after his flagship, and the larger one to the west of it Santa Maria de Guadalupe. Unable to find anchorage on the iron-bound eastern coast of Dominica, they passed on to the north and found shelter on the lee side of Maria Galante. He went ashore and, in his usual fashion, formally took possession. It appears to have been uninhabited, or else the natives had fled inland. For the first time the Spaniards were to discover that there were unknown dangers in this Eden. Some of the sailors tasted a fruit resembling an apple, and were severely burned. This was the poisonous manchineel, with a milky sap which the Caribs used to tip their arrowheads. Guadalupe proved to be a better place altogether, scenically wonderful, with its great streams falling in all directions from the high peak of La Soufrière. So bright was one of these that the sailors argued among themselves whether it was the light reflected from snow or the surface of some much-used road (they were thinking of the hard, white dusty roads of Spain). Trade-wind clouds broomed the mountain's head and everything looked green and fertile after the long acres of the sea. Soon they would go ashore.

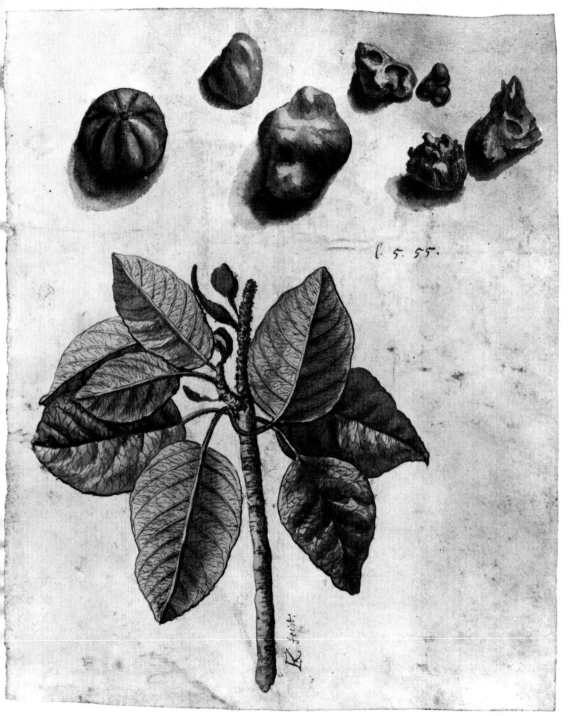

The poisonous manchineel resembling an apple with a milky sap which the Caribs used for their arrowheads. The sailors of Columbus who tasted them were severely affected. Drawing made c. 1705.

Many a Green Isle . . .

They dropped anchor in a cove on the west. They were already beginning to learn how different in these islands were the western shores from the eastern; the latter thunderous with the Atlantic and the former quiet and golden-sanded. Shore parties were landed, the men eager not only to get their feet on dry land, but to explore this wonderful world. They quickly found out that if the natural beauties were astonishing human life was far less prepossessing. Guadalupe was one of the islands inhabited by the Caribs, the *Caniba* whom Columbus had heard so much about on his first voyage. They found plenty of evidence of the unattractive habits of these natives (who were to give the word 'cannibal' to Europe). In one of the first villages they entered they found human bones, slices of human flesh (recently prepared by the Caribs who had fled at the sight of these intruders), skulls which had been trimmed to form domestic utensils, and shinbones out of which these man-eaters used to make their arrowheads. The Caribs were quite unlike the other gentle Taino and Arawak Indians who, indeed, provided them with their living larder. Warlike, distinguished in their appearance by the fact that they bound their legs above the ankle and below the knee so as to make their calves bulge out, the Caribs would raid the other islands and carry off the young women and boys. The latter were castrated and fattened for the pot like capons. The girls were used like battery hens to produce the *pièce de resistance* on the Carib menu – roast baby. (Their children by their own women were, of course, treated quite differently.) The Caribs seem to have regarded the other peoples inhabiting the islands as no more than human fodder. The fact was that they had no domestic animals for consumption, and cannibalism had possibly been forced upon them by this lack in their diet. Among the other Indians the strange barkless dogs, which Columbus had remarked upon in his first expedition, provided the meat dish. This was hardly golden and ultra-civilized Cathay!

The shore parties found much else to interest them: hammocks, excellent cloth made out of cotton, pottery and calabashes, mallard ducks which had been domesticated, tame parrots, sweet potatoes, and pineapples. They also found what seemed to be signs of Europe – such as a piece of timber which they were sure came from the stern of a ship, and even an iron pot. It is possible that a Portuguese caravel had already come this way. Throughout the whole of the Columbus saga it is difficult not to feel that he had been anticipated – perhaps by the Portuguese, who would have kept the secret as closely as they did that of the Grand Banks off Newfoundland – but also many centuries before by the Phoenicians. It always seems unlikely that the men who could circumnavigate Africa in the 6th century B.C. would not at some time or another, either by accident or by intent, have crossed this ocean and found themselves in America. Some of the customs, particularly the religious ones, and the temple buildings of the pre-Columbian civilisations in South and Central America, suggest a Middle-Eastern or Semitic origin.

Meanwhile some of the Caribs's captives, only too happy to escape from the peculiar culture of their masters, gave themselves up to these bearded strangers. A number of "beautiful and plump girls" were later embarked on the ships, where they must surely have provoked more than a little jealousy and rivalry between these many womenless men. One of the shore parties got lost in the course of exploring the island, which was hardly surprising in view of the density of vegetation in the rain-forests of Guadalupe. This was the reason for Columbus staying on for several days, since he had to send search parties out to look for them. The Admiral was naturally worried, particularly in view of the fact that it had now been established that the Caribs really were human-flesh eaters. It was with great relief that almost on the day that he was about to abandon the search the men turned up on the beach. It would have not been

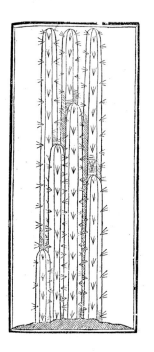
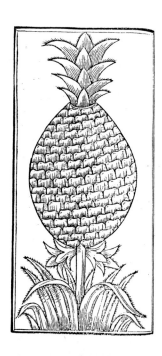

Left. *Cactus.*

Right: *Pineapple. Found by Columbus. From Oviedo, 1547.*

pleasant to report to Their Majesties that a number of their subjects had been eaten by the inhabitants of Cathay. It was time to move on. The island, though beautiful, had yielded not a trace of gold.

On November 10 the fleet made sail from Guadalupe and went by way of the next island to the north, which he named after Santa Maria of Monserrat near Barcelona. It is called Monserrat to this day. He passed on, naming islands as he went, moving in a steadily north-westerly direction around those beautiful Leeward islands (over which the Dutch, English and French were to battle centuries later). Columbus was in a hurry. He was naturally anxious to get back to his settlement at La Navidád, to make a real town out of it, and to find this mysterious Cibao, where all the gold came from. If it had not been for the wreck of *Santa Maria* on the first voyage it is more than likely that on this second occasion Columbus would indeed have found the mainland of South America. He had broken through the necklace of islands at exactly the right point. But the very fact that he had planted a colony in Hispaniola compelled him to keep on tne circuit of islands until he had got back to it. There can be no doubt that he was worried about what might have happened to his fellows – especially since he now had proof that the warlike Caniba really existed. (The only reason, it seems, they had had no trouble at Guadalupe was that all the men were away on a raiding party.)

The Admiral was annoyed by the delay and allowed no more shore leave at the next islands. It was important that he should keep his ships' companies intact. But, at the island which he named Santa Cruz (St. Croix today), the first skirmish took place between Caribs and Spaniards, the herald of many others throughout the years to come. They were now to find out that, primitive though they might be, these Caribs were as good fighting material as any to be found in Europe. Not intimidated even by the arrival in their waters of these incomprehensible winged ships, one of their own 'hollow log' canoes, which had been cut off by a ship's boat, briskly engaged the Spaniards, wounding two of them with their arrows, one of them mortally. According to Chanca's account there were four men and two women in this canoe and all of them took part in the engagement, the women no less than the men.

The newcomers were undoubtedly a little frightened by this whole incident. Even when the natives were captured and brought aboard they showed their Spartan nature. One of them, who had been shot through the stomach, was pronounced by the doctor as certain to die, and was accordingly thrown overboard. The man held his intestines in place with

Opposite: *The Virgin Islands, named by Columbus after St Ursula.*

one hand and struck out for the shore. He was now used for bow-and-arrow and arquebus practice until, riddled with bolts and arrows, he finally sank into the blue Caribbean. Aroused by all these alarms and excursions – in the sea which they had hitherto dominated, the Caribs of Santa Cruz came down to the shore in great numbers. They were ferocious-looking, "with dark coarse hair, their eyes encircled with red paint" – and all of them, as the Spaniards now realised, largely sustained on human meat.

One of the first Caribs to be captured was a young woman who was presented to Michele de Cuneo of Savona (where Columbus had worked at the weaver's trade and whom he obviously favoured). Cuneo, who wrote a lively account of the voyage described how he took her down to his cabin "she being naked, as they all are, and I wanted to have my pleasure of her". He found that he had something like a tigress on his hands, the woman attacking him and lacerating his face with her nails. The infuriated Italian "took a rope's end to her and gave her a good thrashing". Naturally she screamed enough to alarm the whole ship, but then "finally we came to an agreement – to such an extent that I don't mind telling you she seemed to have been raised in a school for whores". The rape of the Indies had begun.

Passing on to the north-east the fleet came to the teeming archipelago of islands which Columbus named The Virgins, after St. Ursula and her martyrs. Ursula, so the story goes, was the daughter of a king residing "in partibus Britanniae" whose hand was demanded in marriage by the son of a powerful pagan ruler. She was told in a dream to demand a respite from the marriage for three years. She then collected 11,000 other young women as companions, all of whom were determined not to surrender their virginity, and sailed off on a pilgrimage to Rome. On their return by way of Cologne they were all slaughtered by the Huns who happened to be attacking the city at the time. They died, if the story is correct, still with their virginity intact. Columbus was a master at name-giving, and the Virgin Islands retain to this day – at any rate when seen from sea – a look of pristine innocence.

They altered course westward towards what is now known as Puerto Rico, but which Columbus named San Juan, for St. John the Baptist. It was here that Ponce de Leon was later to found the city of San Juan de Puerto Rico, which would finally give its name to the whole island. The glamour of that southern coast enchanted them. They stopped two days

Opposite: *Spanish gold coin with the heads of Ferdinand and Isabella. Columbus showed gold coins to the Indians hoping to be led to riches*

189

at Boqueron Bay in the south-west to water and take on fresh provisions, noting that the land was well kept, and a village which they investigated (the natives had all fled) was neat and well laid out.

With a fresh north-easterly trade wind funnelling through the Mona Passage the fleet ranged easily across to the great island where the colony had been planted – to Hispaniola, where this time they would certainly find the source of the gold. Anchoring in Samana Bay they put ashore one of the Indians whom they had captured and taken back to Spain the previous year, hoping no doubt that he would spread the Faith and give a good report of the wonders of Europe. Here also they buried the seaman who had been fatally wounded in the fight with the Caribs. The priests officiated over the first Christian burial in the New World. The fleet did a little trading with the Indians and then passed on, heading for Monti Cristi, where Columbus had found gold in the river. Everything seemed peaceful enough. There was no hint of disaster, only an empty bay with the usual beautiful scenery. And then, while they were all at anchor off Monte Cristi – which Columbus envisaged as being a better site for a settlement than La Navidád – they found the bodies. First of all they found two, so decomposed as to be unrecognisable, and then on the next day two more. One of them showed traces of a beard. The Indians were beardless.

On November 27 1493 the fleet dropped anchor after sunset outside the reef that fringed La Navidád. They lit flares and fired a cannon. (They had left a cannon with the settlement.) The darkness confronted them. No answering shot, no lights, only the heavy silence of the tropic night, and the slop of the sea against their hulls. From that moment on everything was to change. The bodies at Monte Cristi were the first ominous drum-tap.

Snakes in Eden

La Navidád was desolated. The first European settlement in America had been wiped out. A canoe came out from the nearby land and brought the news to the Admiral. It was all difficult to decipher, even with the help of one of the Indians who had been back to Spain. It seemed that in search of gold the Spanish colonists had fallen foul of another island chieftain, Caonabo. He was not so gently disposed as the young Guacanagari, whose friendship Columbus had so carefully cultivated the previous year. Caonabo had been affronted by the behaviour of these strange bearded men and had fallen on the fort and destroyed it. (It seems possible that Guacanagari was also somehow or other involved in the affair.) At first it seemed unbelievable. How could these gentle and practically unarmed Indians have killed forty armed Spaniards? Columbus was unwilling to believe, for instance, that Beatriz's cousin, Diego de Harana, was dead, and that so many of that fine crew who had made the first crossing in *Santa Maria* had perished in this land which had looked so good and tranquil. One thing was certain – the white gods were gods no longer.

What had happened was simple enough and, in the light of later colonial experiences, was only to be expected. But here, as in his first crossing of the ocean, Columbus was the original – he could have no preknowledge. The Spaniards left behind in an unknown land had fallen prey to those two human failings, lust and greed. They had disputed the authority vested in Diego de Harana and finally a band of them under Pedro Gutiérrez, the former royal butler, had gone off into the island in search of gold. They had got into the territory of this inland chieftain

Opposite: *Spanish ships being attacked by cannibals. The first skirmish took place on the island of Santa Cruz. From Philopono, 1621.*

Caonabo, who seems to have been a Carib or part-Carib, and who was of very different mettle from Guacanagari. The Spaniards with Gutiérrez were wiped out, and an attack was then directed at the fort where there was only Harana and ten other men, together with a number of native women. They were overwhelmed. Hence the bodies on the beach and the silence from La Navidád.

In any analysis of this first colonial disaster in the New World, some account must be taken of the responsibility of the leader. Columbus had appointed as head of the settlement the cousin of his mistress, a man about whom we know nothing except his failure to keep discipline among his men. Columbus was always to show that he had a peasant-like distrust of delegating authority to any except those who were related to him in one way or another. This in itself is comprehensible enough: he came from a world in which the family clan was very much the basic unit, the only one that could be trusted. At the same time a leader of any real calibre is able to look beyond such narrow confines. The real cause of the disaster seems not to have been any fighting over the women – the native women were indulgent enough – but the quest for gold. Columbus cannot be exculpated here. From the very moment of his arrival in the Caribbean gold had been the leitmotiv of his wanderings. Bringing souls to God seems to have come a long way second. Indeed, even if that had not been his intention, the forcible capture of the Indians whom he had taken back to Spain had been the beginning of the Spanish slave trade. Furthermore, the very reason for the dissolution of the colony – the men wandering off into the interior in search of gold – had been promoted by Columbus. It was he who had all along been fascinated by the story of this inland place called Cibao. The settlers, when he had left them behind, had been instructed to seek for the place where the gold was mined.

From now on, even though Guacanagari seemed to remain friendly enough, the relationship between Spaniards and natives was to change. Columbus had told all the sailors and gentlemen-adventurers that these people were gentle and trustworthy. He had painted a picture of pastoral innocence and of completely docile creatures who could be taught to work for the Spanish interest. They had now seen the Caribs – hardly innocent or gentle those! – and had lost one companion at their hands. Then they had arrived in Hispaniola to find that all the settlers had been killed. This Eden was proving in some respects only too remarkably like the world they had left behind. Columbus now begins to be discredited. He had promised everyone from the very beginning the golden-tiled pagodas of Cathay. That had been proved false – or else they were only on the fringes of the world which Marco Polo had described. He had been wrong about the nature of the natives. And where was that "village" about which he had talked to Their Majesties – merely a stockade that had been stormed, and where they found the rotting bodies of some of their fellows – ? It is true to say that, on the quiet night when *Santa Maria* had run onto the reef, there began the wreck of Columbus.

Despite the protestations of friendship from Guacanagari, who pretended to have been wounded in the leg during a fight to save the garrison, Columbus and his advisers felt suspicious. In any case the memory of La Navidád was unattractive, and Dr. Chanca said furthermore that the area was unhealthy. The Admiral decided to go back east down the coastline, for it was inland from there, as he understood it, that the gold mine lay. It was now that they found the disadvantages of squaresail, that rig which was so excellent for running down the Trades. Going eastward along the coast they were not only bucking the prevailing wind, but they had a strong westward-going current against them. "It was more trouble," as the doctor wrote, "to make thirty leagues upwind than the whole crossing from Castile." It took them nearly a month to make good some forty miles of easting – a month in which the tempers and the health of the crews were hardly improved, and the livestock sickened and died.

Finally, on January 2, 1494, the fleet dropped anchor off a small peninsula which gave shelter from the prevailing wind. It seemed a suitable site for the settlement which Columbus had in mind. This was designed to resemble the trading posts with which he was familiar from his days under the Portuguese flag on the west African coast. What he could not have foreseen was that the area was infested by the malarial mosquito.

Isabella, as the foundation was called after the Queen who had been so responsible for the whole venture, was a disaster from the start. One thing Columbus could not have envisaged was that, though sheltered from the prevailing trade winds, it was wide open to the north winds of winter – with which he was hardly familiar. The other drawback was that the nearest water-supply was a river a good mile away. The only reason one can imagine that he planted the colony in this particular place was that the long days of battling against the Trades, the dissatisfaction of crews, and the sickness among the livestock, determined him to make a settlement at the first place that seemed even remotely suitable. Again, it is easy to be wise after the event, as some of the critics of Columbus have been. It is important to remember that everything which happened here was for the *first* time. As Dr. Chanca said: ". . . We had to land on the best site and position that we could find (the weather being so contrary). Here we found a good harbour and plenty of scope for fishing. We were in great need of this owing to our shortage of meat."

193

One thing that cheered everybody up was the extreme fertility of the soil. The warm and moist tropical climate – the almost eternal summer of the Indies – was more than clement to the seeds they had brought from Europe. Como remarks that: "Five days after they were sown, garden seeds came up . . . the land was quickly covered in green, plenty of onions and pumpkins, beetroots and radishes." Dr. Chanca added his comment that "In eight days there the vegetables have grown more than they would in twenty in Castile". Agriculture then, gold possibly, but all the time the nagging uncertainty as to where they were, where the cities lay, and where the Great Khan might be found. All were moving in a day-dream, and daydreams can sometimes turn into nightmares.

The first real town organised by Europeans was now established in the Caribbean. A church, a military store-house, and a dwelling suitable for the Viceroy – for Columbus was now Viceroy as well as Admiral – were set out. Naturally enough the patterns of Spain were copied, the whole place being designed around a central piazza (which had itself derived from the forum – or market-place – of the Romans). Day after day the men toiled to make streets, build houses, and erect upon the unfamiliar terrain of this island something that was reminiscent of the world they had left behind them. Day after day, also, the invaders found themselves weakened by disease, some undoubtedly from malaria, and others from unfamiliar food and lack of that animal protein to which, as Europeans, they were accustomed. It was not long before Dr. Chanca was so engaged in his profession that he thought fit to ask Columbus to transmit to the Sovereigns a demand for an increase in pay. He was worn-out looking after these sick, whose illnesses did not seem to correspond with those with which he had been familiar in his native Spain.

The Admiral's great concern was to find gold. It was bad enough that the first settlement at La Navidád had been wiped out, but if he did not return this time with some really substantial profit from the venture, what would King Ferdinand and Queen Isabella make of this 'Don' and 'Admiral' who had promised them Cathay and returned with only a few illiterate natives and some golden nose-plugs? He seemed to gather from the islanders through his interpreter that the area where all the gold came from was not far away. Good, then they had made their settlement in the right place – and, moreover, they were some distance from where all the trouble had happened the previous winter. Here, possibly, they were still gods – always a great advantage in this strange world.

While the bulk of the crews were engaged on the construction of the

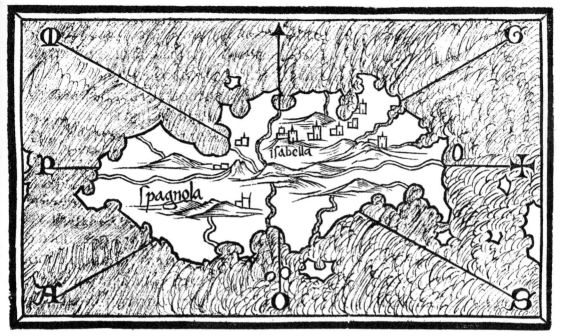

Isabella, the second colony founded on Hispaniola, on the second voyage.
From Bordoni's Isolario, *1534.*

new town, an expedition was mounted to penetrate the interior and to
find out the truth of the rumours that there really was a gold mine
somewhere in the central area known as Cibao. The whole of Columbus's
predicament can be seen as being set around this absurd and inedible
commodity. Gold, pearls, emeralds – so many of the products of the
New World – had no real relevance to human life. "They dig it out of
the earth and they bury it again" – Fort Knox is the saddest joke in the
world. Any being from another planet who penetrated our own would
find totally maniac the habit of digging up this yellow metal, making it
into bars, and putting it deep underground, guarded by armed men.
Columbus was not to blame for the absurd values of the human race.

The expedition set off under the command of a Spaniard called Alonso
de Hojeda, a fiery-tempered man, who was "always the first to get into a
fight, whether it was a war or a private quarrel". Columbus himself fell
ill and, while the party of Spaniards set off for the interior of Hispaniola,
the Admiral for part of the time was laid abed. Meanwhile the work on
the township went ahead, and gradually the ships were cleared of all
their stores. The first mass was celebrated in a temporary chapel on
January 6.

Hojeda and his companions, who had been prepared for trouble
because they thought they were going into the territory of the warlike

Caonabo, found on the contrary that everywhere they went the natives welcomed them with the utmost friendliness. They found also plenty of evidence of gold in the rivers, and they managed to obtain a number of good specimens – enough to convince themselves that if mining was started in real earnest the land would yield what the Sovereigns wanted. After reaching the central valley of the island Hojeda and his men ran into bad weather. He decided to return to Isabella, but not before he had sufficient evidence from the streams, and from barter with natives, that the inland mountains were truly rich in gold.

Their return cheered up everyone. They brought with them the first really good news since the fleet had reached the Caribbean. Columbus decided that now was the time for the bulk of the ships to return to Spain. A great many of the men were sick, the doctor had run out of drugs and provisions were short. Now that Hojeda had brought some worthwhile samples, it was time to communicate all the news to Ferdinand and Isabella. On February 2, under the command of Antonio de Torres, twelve of the seventeen ships left the anchorage and headed eastward for Spain. They took with them not only the gold, not only specimens of the spices and wood of the island, but a cargo of Indians. On this second voyage Columbus without any doubt initiated the Spanish slave trade with the Indies.

It is still widely debated by medical historians and scholars as to whether or not the returning Spaniards did not bring back something much more sinister than their human cargo with them – syphilis. It is certain that very shortly after the second voyage there was an epidemic of syphilis in Europe, the worst affected area being Italy (and many of the sailors were Italians). Subsequent to that the disease in its most virulent form swept the whole continent. Books have been written on the subject, some arguing that it was always endemic in Europe, but that it just flared up owing to the wars and military movements taking place at the time of Columbus's voyages. Both Las Casas and Oviedo confidently state that the disease was given to the Spaniards by the Indians, while a 16th century Spanish physician asserted that the disease was first noted in Barcelona in 1493. One writer has it that the Indian males, to increase the size of their genital organs, were in the habit of stinging them with mosquitoes, that these were malarial, and that in fact syphilis originated as a kind of malaria of the reproductive system. Grenfell Price in "The Western Invasions of the Pacific and Its Continents" has the following comment: ". . . there is [also] a theory that syphilis evolved from the tropical disease yaws . . . The organism *treponema pertenne* closely resembles the organism *treponema pallidum*, which is responsible for syphilis. The two diseases have many points of clinical resemblance and they give cross reactions of immunity but, unlike syphilis, yaws is not handed on by sexual contact."

Yet another viewpoint is that the disease was a completely new one, originating from the union of the different spirochetal parasites of Europeans and Caribbean Indians. P. M. Ashburn in "A Medical History of the Conquest of America" thinks that, although venereal diseases were carried to the Americas by the Europeans, the transfer of syphilis was probably in the opposite direction. One thing is certain: within only a few years of Columbus's discovery of America, Europe was invaded by syphilis. There is no reference to it in classical literature. There is no reference to it prior to the Colombian voyages.

St Ursula and the eleven thousand virgins after whom Columbus named the Virgin islands.

Admiral or Viceroy?

Columbus sent back with Antonio de Torres his own report of the conditions and the state of things in these lands which he had annexed in the name of the Spanish Sovereigns. The Indians, the gold, the trivial herbs and spices, were hardly sufficient to justify the expedition. The ships were not going home laden with all the riches of the Orient, merely the scrapings from the edge of some unknown world. Few can have believed that they were really in Cipangu or Cathay.

In his despatch Columbus begins by informing Their Majesties of the expedition led by Hojeda. This was all-important. It proved that inland in Cipangu, Cibao, or wherever it was, there were gold-bearing rivers running down from the mountains where the metal must certainly exist. The original copy of Columbus's document has been lost, but a copy still exists – with the comments of Ferdinand and Isabella in the margin. Against the second paragraph, which outlines the discoveries that have been made up to date, the king and queen have written: "Their Highnesses give much thanks to God, and consider that all the Admiral has done so far is of considerable service." They were, of course, envious of the Portuguese trade in gold and slaves on the African coast, and it looked now as if Columbus had pulled off the coup of all time. He had found – as he had said he would – the true route to the Indies. Spain, which had recently expelled both the Moors and the Jews, was about to become the richest and most powerful country in the world; and largely, they reckoned, because of its monarchs' devotion to the Christian Faith. They had chosen in this strange Genoese, who bore the name of 'Christ-Bearer', the right man to promote the true religion among peoples thousands of miles away – and the right man to bring wealth and glory to Spain.

The report goes on to explain why the Admiral has not been able to send home more gold. There had been a great deal of sickness in the new town, the diet was insufficient, and he begs for some ships to return with more of the kind of food and wine to which Spaniards are accustomed. Columbus was right enough in this: you cannot transport people from Europe and expect them to be able to live solely on local fish, yams, and maize. The same problem was to beset European settlers in different areas of America for centuries to come.

Columbus, once again, had arrived at the beginning. There was no possibility of anyone being able to advise him as to the way to live in the Tropics. The Caribs had, in their own fashion, solved it for themselves, but meat – as Europeans understood it – was unavailable. Everything, in fact, was unavailable: leather for shoes, beasts of burden, medicine, arms and armaments, and trained miners to go out into the hills of Cibao and bring back the gold. Ferdinand and Isabella were faced with a problem that they had never expected; the Indies had to be supplied with practically all necessities over thousands of miles of the Atlantic ocean. Instead of finding a country from which they could just draw riches, they appeared to have on their hands some territories which needed to be supplied with almost everything from somewhat penurious Spain. They still felt however that their Admiral and Viceroy had added immense dominions to their realm, and disillusionment had not yet set in.

Columbus went on to say that a fort must be built near the place where the gold came from (he was clearly thinking in terms of La Mina in West Africa) and their Highnesses approved, commenting, "This is right, and must be done". On the question of the supply of provisions they also made the marginal note: "Juan de Fonseca to see to this." His complaint about the faulty wine casks was also remarked upon: "Juan de Fonseca to find out who were responsible and see that they make good from their own pockets any loss." But the real crux of the document occurs at the point where Columbus speaks of the Indians whom he has sent back. He says that they are all from the Cannibal islands (one very much doubts this), and that their souls may be saved if they are converted to the Faith. They should also be taught Spanish so that they can return and become interpreters. Against this Ferdinand and Isabella commented: "This is good and so it should be done," but they added the rider that "it might be better if it could be done there (in the Indies)."

Columbus went a great deal further than this, however, for he proposed that ships should be sent every year to carry Indians back to Spain and that this would help to pay for the livestock and other necessities required for the colony. He was familiar enough with the Portuguese slave trade in Africa. He was now proposing to Ferdinand and Isabella that they should institute an exactly similar trade from the Indies. He takes care to stress that these people are cannibals, and that therefore they will not only be enjoying the benefits of Christianity but that they will be weaned from their evil habits. What he omits to say is that the people whom he thought of enslaving were certainly not the warlike Caribs but the peaceful Indians of Hispaniola.

The fact was that Columbus was in a cleft stick. The gold did not seem to be available in the quantity that he had envisaged, his "cinnamon" was not cinnamon, and the various "spices" he sent back were certainly not the spices that Europeans had been used to expect from their trade via Venice with the East. Something was very wrong. Furthermore, as the contemporary chronicler Bernáldez remarked, his planting of a colony was not a deliberate act of policy but had been entirely due to the loss of *Santa Maria*, "since there was no way of bringing the men back". He had now got the Spaniards involved with what seemed, on the surface, to be an extremely costly operation, and the exchequer was not very healthy after the cost of the Moorish war; it would be some time before Andalusia would begin to show a profit to the crown. The reports of those who went back with the bulk of the fleet cannot have been particularly healthy for the Admiral's reputation – islands inhabited by cannibals (nothing about that in Marco Polo), no great cities, nothing much to eat except fish, the original settlement at La Navidád wiped out, bodies on the beach, and precious little else.

The Admiral was no good ashore. There is no doubt that he was a great sailor, and an excellent pilot if an inefficient celestial navigator, but when it came to being a Viceroy and an administrator Columbus was out of his element. He had been a merchant seaman, a chartmaker, a small-time business man, the husband of a noblewoman, a dreamer after riches hanging around the courts of the great, and a man who more by luck than by judgement had happened upon a number of islands in an unknown sea. He was now faced with the problems of administering a small town-fortress in a place that was the wrong place. First of all, though, he must get to the gold. Nothing else could possibly justify the expense which Ferdinand and Isabella had incurred.

On March 12 1494, the Admiral and Viceroy personally led an expedition inland, to follow up the initial probe made by Hojeda into the area known as Cibao. The natives who traded with the settlement had already learned one thing about these white and bearded strangers – their true religion. They would hold up a piece of gold and say "Behold the Christians' God!" Columbus was now leading a pilgrimage in search of the holy shrine. They left in great style, with the blowing of trumpets and the firing of muskets. Let Caonabo or anyone else who was

Ovando, governor of Hispaniola during Columbus's fourth voyage imported negro slaves to work the gold mines. From Theodore de Bry, 1595.

hostile know that the great leader and his invincible men were on their way! There was, in fact, no reason for such a display. Everywhere they went the natives proved more than friendly, willingly giving the Spaniards their food or their few possessions. One habit they had, which Columbus respected and taught his men to respect: if they desired privacy they would lay a few pieces of cane in front of the entrance to their huts, a symbolic door. They were simple, trusting creatures. With mounted caballeros to the fore – and it must be remembered that the horse was something that had never been seen before in the New World – the expedition cut its way through the island, making the first road in Hispaniola. They climbed to the summit of Santo Cerro and then came by way of a pass, which Columbus named El Puerto de los Hidalgos, the Gate of the Gentlemen, after his gentlemen trail-blazers, and came in sight of a luxuriant valley. They had crossed the Cordillera Setentrional, and what now lay in front of them was the plain between the mountains on which they stood and the desired regions of Cibao on the southern side. The valley, as Las Casas put it, "was so fresh, so green, so colourful, so open and full of beauty that they felt they had arrived in some part of Paradise". Columbus with his usual instinct for place-names called it Vega Real, The Royal Plain.

It was a happy expedition. Everywhere the land was so beautiful, the natives whom they met were so friendly, and the whole of this world – unlike tired old Europe – seemed like a child's first experience of Spring. It was new, clean, unsullied and simple. They crossed a great river, and everyone bathed and played about like boys in its pure and sparkling water. Their objective lay ahead. They now made their way up the Cordillera Central, and here in the heart of Cibao (it meant no more than "stony land" in the Indian language) Columbus planted a fort. He called it San Tomás after St. Thomas the Doubter, because one of the cavaliers in his company doubted that there really was any gold at all in this land. There was. The natives, who had learned from Hojeda's previous expedition what these mysterious people wanted, came flocking with their offerings of nuggets of gold. Columbus seemed to be vindicated. Some fifty men were left behind to build and garrison the fort under the command of a certain Pedro Margarite. This, the first inland Spanish establishment in Hispaniola, was designed to provide a base from which the miners would later work, as well as to guard the whole area where the precious metal was to be found.

On March 29, Columbus and his men, after a bad return passage under heavy rain, arrived back at Isabella. It was a sad homecoming. All was very far from thriving in the colony. A number had died, the provisions from Spain had almost run out, and the discontented men were only too eager to get back to their homeland. If this was the fabled Orient, let the Orientals have it! "Without flour, the mood is sour" runs a Spanish proverb, and flour was running short. On the other hand, and indeed almost the only encouraging thing, the crops that had been sown were doing very well. While this at least was reassuring, bad news came hot on the Admiral's heels from San Tomás. Caonabo, who had destroyed the original settlement at La Navidád, was raising the country and preparing to attack the fort. It was the same story all over again, the licentiousness and rapacity of the Spaniards was provoking the inevitable response. The golden natives (who seem to have been in their initial state more Christian than any Christians) were not prepared to be permanently used as a cross between a whorehouse and a slave farm.

To Sea Again . . .

With the fort and the township of Isabella Columbus felt that he had now established a real Spanish presence in the island. Despite the disaster of La Navidád he felt fairly confident that with the several hundreds of men under his command he could now control Hispaniola quite easily. But troubles continued to mount, mainly brought about by sickness. One wonders whether this was not entirely malarial in origin but also syphilitic. So many of the work-people were laid up ill that Columbus was forced to draft the gentlemen, and even the priests, to daily tasks which they felt beneath their blood or calling. No one is prouder than an upperclass Spaniard, and these caballeros had not come to the Indies to do manual labour, but to acquire riches. To be told to work at ditching or grinding flour by an upstart, low-born foreigner was hardly acceptable.

Columbus very quickly realised that he had to take some decisive action, something that would prevent what was clearly on the horizon – open mutiny and insurrection. He had already, according to Oviedo, been forced to have several men hanged and he was consequently in conflict with Fra Buil who had accused him of cruelty. Now Fra Buil was the Queen's own appointee as the representative for spiritual affairs, and Columbus must have realised that he was likely to report back unfavourably on his behaviour as Viceroy. Two things must be done. As soon as possible he himself must get to sea again. In the meantime, the best way of solving the disaffection in Isabella would be to get the gentlemen ringleaders and the most troublesome soldiers out of it.

Another inland expedition was accordingly organised, again commanded by Alonso de Hojeda. Their instructions were to proceed to the fort and relieve the garrison there. After that, the bulk of them were to go out under Margarite, the current commander of the fort, and explore the island in depth. They were to live off the land, but they were not to molest the natives. On the other hand, if any Indians were caught stealing, an example was to be made of them. They should cut off their nose or ears so that "the people will understand that, while the good are well treated, the bad are punished". Harsh justice, but they all came from a world in which it was administered in just such a way. Furthermore, Caonabo must be caught alive. This murderous troublemaker must be given a formal trial. "See that he comes to you," were the instructions, "and, since he goes about naked which would make it difficult to seize him, you are to give him a cap and a shirt, putting the latter on at once, and a cape and a girdle. Then you will easily be able to hold him and he will not be able to slip away." It was all very ingenious, even down to the last detail.

On April 9 the expeditionary force of some four hundred men marched out from Isabella. Columbus must have heaved a sigh of relief. That seemed to have solved the major problem. The next thing was to get the three light-draught caravels fully equipped, provisioned, and ready for sea. It was quite clear now that Hispaniola was an island, and no part of the main. He must make back westward and try to establish whether Cuba (Juana as he had called it) was an extensive peninsula of Cathay. He still had those despatches from the Sovereigns for the Khan, and he still needed to get down to some steady trading for the riches of the Orient.

In the meantime, there was further trouble – the first real difficulty with the Indians that had occurred on this second voyage. Alonso de Hojeda on his march north had come across three of the San Tomás garrison who had been robbed of some of their clothes. He had promptly seized one of the offending natives and cut off his ears. He then laid hold

Cuba, from Bordone's Isolario, *1534.*

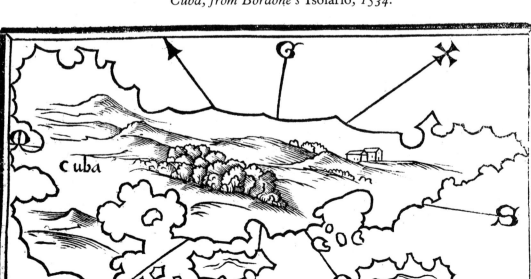

of the cacique of this tribe (not the wanted Caonabo) and sent him and some of his relatives back in chains to the township. Columbus seems at first to have been in favour of executing them publicly, but at the pleading of another local chieftain he let them free, thinking probably that a show of clemency would be better propaganda for the Spaniards. It was all a storm in a teacup – except for the man who lost his ears. The three Spaniards had only lost a few old clothes to natives who, generally speaking, gave freely of everything that they had. It was nonetheless a bad augury for the future.

Columbus proceeded to set up a council to rule the island in his absence. At the head of it, in comformity with his nature, he put his brother Diego. To assist him were Fra Buil (whatever Columbus thought about him, he could not omit him), Pedro Fernandez Coronel, Alonso Sanchez Carajal, and Juan de Luxán. Good, now he felt that he could safely get about his real business and leave this administering of a township, a fort and an island in other hands. Discovery and navigation were where his talents lay. On April 24 Columbus put to sea in the trusty *Niña*, accompanied by the two smaller caravels, *San Juan* and *Cordera*. *Niña* would serve as his flagship, while the other two would be useful for exploring creeks and inlets in the mainland of Cathay. He dropped anchor at the site of La Navidád, noting that his former friend Guacanagari avoided them. It seems very possible that he and his tribe, even if not responsible for the massacre of the garrison, had killed some of the errant Spaniards. From what one knows of the subsequent behaviour of the conquistadors in the New World no one can blame the Indians. Although by nature gentle, tolerant and non-acquisitive, they were not without courage and dignity.

The Admiral sailed on westward. After four days they were off the north-west corner of Hispaniola, with Cuba just in sight ahead. They Crossed the Windward Passage and dropped anchor off the eastern cape of the other island which Columbus on the first voyage had named Cape Alpha and Omega, the Beginning and the End. He had been fairly confident then that this cape was to the mainland of China as Cape St. Vincent was to the mainland of Europe. He was convinced it was, he was determined to remain so, and nothing was going to shake his conviction. Once Columbus got an idea in his head it could not be removed. He had not yet found Cipangu, but he had found Cathay. It was this obsessive quality in his nature – in both the good and the bad sense – that made him the man he was.

A conference was held aboard and it was decided to run down the southern coast of this "peninsula". At the end of April the three small

Philopono's (c. 1621) imaginative view of life in the "Indies". Natives eating iguana, pineapples and smoking tobacco. In the background are shown sea monsters, idols and musicians playing bagpipes.

ships came to anchor in an immense and beautiful bay which he named Puerto Grande. Its modern name is Guantanamo Bay. It was, until the change of regime in Cuba, the main American naval base in this part of the world. Here surely the Mandarins would have immense trading fleets? Nothing. Only a few small native huts, where they found iguanas being roasted. One of the interpreters they had with them managed to lure some of the natives back and a friendly talk ensued. They ate some of the fish that was being cooked, though not the fearsome-looking iguana (Iguana, in fact, which lives only on tender leaves and fruit, is very good eating and is still regarded as a delicacy in some parts of South America). Columbus made the Indians a repayment with the usual trade-trinkets.

The word quickly spread along the southern shores of Cuba that strange men in vast canoes were moving along the coastline. The people came to meet them in their dug-outs, everywhere bringing them fresh fruit and water. It was a triumphal procession over a springtime sea, with the winds gentle in their sails, and the hope always in their hearts that somewhere, just round the next corner perhaps, they would come to the places they were seeking. Golden days – and so much better than all the trials and tribulations in Hispaniola! The inhabitants of Cuba had still had no real relationship with these strangers. There had been no La Navidád as yet on the coast of their island.

When Columbus reached the south-westernmost point of Cuba, he named it Cabo de Cruz, Cape of the Cross, since he arrived there on May 3, the day when St. Helena is said to have discovered at Jerusalem in 326 the true cross on which Christ was crucified. Columbus had now heard more from his native interpreter, who had been in conversation with all those they had met along the coast, of the great island to the south where bean-sized gold nuggets were to be found. This was the place he had heard of, the previous year – Yamaye, or Babeque – so difficult to follow the native pronunciation – in fact, Jameque, or Jamaica as it is now known. Obviously it was time to leave this peninsula of the mainland and sail south. As always in this strange saga, the lure of the elusive metal took him in the wrong direction. It was as if that God, in whom he so firmly believed, was determined to show him by a series of object lessons that the quest for Mammon will always end in disaster.

Strong winds drove them down towards the island, winds so strong indeed that part of the time the small vessels had to run under bare poles. The trade-winds funnelling through the Windward Passage (so aptly named) between Hispaniola and Cuba taught them the lesson that all is not always calm in this apparently indolent sea. After two days he and his companions had another of those miraculous experiences with which this magic world seemed to be filled. They saw ahead of them the forested mountains of Jamaica lifting out of the south, swirling with clouds, green and unbelievably beautiful. They ran down to anchor in a bay which impressed the Admiral so much that he named it Santa Gloria. The whole island he thought "the loveliest and most graceful of all that he had yet discovered". He was equally impressed by the native canoes – Jamaica was extremely populous – and these Indians had evolved a more sophisticated sea-going vessel than any they had previously encountered. Some of the canoes were as much as 96 feet long and 8 foot in the beam, prodigious, and all carved from a single tree-trunk. They were made out of the giant mahogany trees of the rain-forest, and the men who manned them showed at first a spirit of resistance such as the Spaniards had not encountered since they had met with the Caribs. But, when presents were given them and every evidence of friendship shown – at Columbus's orders – they proved that they were prepared to be as helpful and courteous as the people of Hispaniola had originally been. Leaving Santa Gloria, which was to prove the scene of his humiliation some years later, Columbus coasted along to the west where he anchored in yet another Puerto Bueno (a name it bears to this day).

Spaniards attacking an Indian village. From Theodore de Bry, 1594.

Here the reception was not so friendly and, as he needed to land to water and carry out some running repairs to the caravels, Columbus was forced to put on a show of power. Arquebusiers were landed, a number of spear-throwing natives were killed or wounded, and a hound was unleashed upon them. This practice of using large dogs against the local inhabitants was to become standard in the Spanish occupation of America. It was later to be copied by the Dutch, English, French and other settlers in the Caribbean islands. They were trained as protectors of their plantations, but by then the 'natives' would have almost entirely become Negroes. The Indians would have been wiped out.

Jamaica was certainly beautiful, but there was one salient thing wrong with it – no gold. Again, this was not the right place. Having sailed west as far as Montego Bay, Columbus decided to return to Juana (Cuba). The weather had turned against him for any further westward exploration. By May 14 1494, they were back at Cabo de Cruz. The Admiral decided that he would stand up to the north and prove conclusively to his own and everyone's satisfaction that this was indeed a peninsula of the Orient mainland.

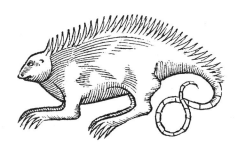

"This is the Mainland . . ."

The land trended north-easterly. The ships followed the Cuban coast-line into the Gulf of Guacanaybo. It then ran westerly again, suggesting that this was certainly no island, but that, if they kept coasting along, they would finally reach the real, civilised mainland they were seeking. Then, on May 15 they sighted on the port bow a cluster of islets, almost uncountable and brilliant with trees and greenery. (They are so no longer, but when Columbus first saw them not even the Indians had laid a hand on them.) Columbus was entranced and named them The Queen's Garden. There was another reason for his excitement. Both Marco Polo and Sir John Mandeville in their accounts had said that hundreds of islands lay off the coast of Cathay. He felt he was drawing very near to the heart of his desire.

It is a tribute to the pilotage skills of Columbus and his captains that they managed to thread their way through these innumerable cays. But they were expert with lead and line, and the two leading caravels were very shallow-draughted. All along, one must never forget that these sailors were in a totally uncharted sea. Few small-boat sailors would care to tackle this area even now without a local pilot aboard. Regularly every afternoon thunderstorms would boil up over the land, and they would be drenched by heavy tropical rain. They were weaving their way through narrow channels dependent entirely upon their sun- and salt-burned sails, or upon sending the ships' boats ahead of them to give them a pluck when they had had to hand their canvas. Inevitably there were a number of groundings, necessitating lowering the boats, laying out kedge anchors, and hard work for the crew. But the hardest work lay always on the Admiral. He had brought them here and it was his duty to see that in due course he brought them safely back. The burden of command is always arduous and breaks many men. The Admiral afloat, unlike the Viceroy ashore, was competent to bear it – although in the end it would exhaust him totally. It is probable that it was during this period of his life that he began to develop that arthritis which was to sadden his later days. (It is curious that Mandeville only wrote his famous books of travels because the same illness forced him to retire home from the East.)

Everywhere were marvels. They saw their first flamingoes and were astonished at their vermilion colour. Then they met some natives who had an extraordinary method of fishing. They had a fish as tame as a domestic dog, to whose tail was attached a line. When they wanted to catch other fish or a turtle they would send their fish away from the canoe and, when like a falcon of the sea he had swooped on his prey, they would reel in him and it. They would then reward their tame fish with small bits of flesh and he would stay swimming alongside their canoe. This must have been encouraging to Columbus, for Mandeville had described how the Chinese employed tame beasts to go into the water to catch fish for them – but Mandeville was writing about the Chinese custom of using cormorants to catch fish. What the Admiral was seeing was something even more unusual. The natives in this part of the world, having observed the habits of the remora or sucking-fish, which will attach themselves by their suctorial disc on the spine to sharks, turtles, and large fish – using them as free transport – had decided to capitalise upon this curious freak of nature. They caught young remora and hand-raised them; then, when they were old enough, the Indians took them out alongside their canoes and used them just as men in other parts of the world used hunting dogs or hawks. At one village on the coast, from which the natives had all fled, the Spaniards even tried the best meat dish of the non-cannibal Indians, roasted barkless dog. Everything was curious here.

They went on westward, communicating here and there with the natives, but they now had to rely on sign language for their own interpreter could not understand these Cuban Indians. Then the coastline began to trend to the south-west – Marco Polo had said it would – and Columbus was sure he was on the fringes of the 'Golden Chersonese' (the Malacca peninsula). He was now only about 150 miles from the western end of Cuba. Had he sailed on he would have found the truth,

Remora or sucking-fish, used by the Cuban Indians to hunt other fish. Watercolour drawing by John White, c. 1590.

that Cuba was indeed just another island, even if a very large one. He would have found the Yucatan Channel and the mainland of America. There, awaiting him, would have been all the gold and wealth of Mexico, which it was to be left for other Spaniards to discover and exploit. Many things militated against him, not least the fact that off the Zapata Peninsula they ran into the shallows "where the water was as white as milk" (from stirred up white marl), and then when they tried to come to anchor the anchors dragged in the poor holding ground. Worse was to come, for next they found themselves in an area where the sea turned black (black volcanic sand this time) and the men were inevitably reminded of those old stories about the Ocean of Darkness. It says much for the Admiral's determination and the courage of his seamen that they still pressed on, going ever westward along the southern coast of Cuba. Columbus came to the conclusion that he was half way round the world (he was in fact about one quarter) so why not sail on, and return by the Cape of Good Hope and astonish the Portuguese? He would have astonished himself by finding South America. But the fact was that, with so many groundings, the conditon of the caravels was such that there was nothing for it but to return to Isabella and give them a complete refit. The amount of water they were taking in had also ruined some of the stores, another salient reason for putting back.

It was a very sad end to this second voyage of discovery. He had had reports of white-robed men seen by one of his shore parties in a forest – that sounded encouraging, not naked savages, more like the people of Cathay. (These were probably fictitious, for the Cuban Indians went naked as did the others.) But he had no alternative other than to return, and without gold or pearls or any real evidence of this being what he claimed it to be. The crews naturally enough were growing restive after all this hard work and were eager to get back to the limited comforts of Isabella even. He had to have something to convince Their Majesties that next time they would really establish contact with the great and rich civilisation that he had promised. It was obvious: he would do what Diaz had done when his crew had forced him to turn back at the moment when he had unlocked the sea-route round the Cape of Good Hope. He would get everyone to take an oath. They would swear that they really had found the place they were looking for. Then, all that would be needed was one more expedition to achieve complete success. Accordingly, Fernando Pérez de Luna, the notary public of Isabella who was aboard with the Admiral, was instructed to take the testimonials of everyone in the three ships, particularly the pilots and captains as to their opinion: Was this a peninsula of the mainland or not?

On June 12 when they were at anchor off the Cuban coast, almost opposite the small group of islands called San Philip Cays, the notary went round the fleet. Everyone was asked to say whether "they had any doubts that this was the mainland at the beginning of the Indies". The ordinary seamen were naturally enough eager to swear to anything that would get them out of this interminable work in leaky ships under a hot sun. Everyone had had quite enough – and no profit to show for it. This world was beautiful but it was not making them the returns that they had all expected when they left Spain. Back, then, to Isabella, and back as soon as possible to Spain with its wine, onions, meat, garlic, green vegetables, and – of course – its girls. Everybody signed the declaration that they were quite sure this immense stretch of land was part of the main.

Something like eighty men in the three-ship squadron now agreed to the statement that they had indeed found the continent. It was even laid down that any officer who should later deny this would be fined a large sum of gold, and that seamen should have their tongue cut out if they did the same, while the ships' boys should receive a hundred lashes for a similar offence. A curious way of establishing the truth! One can only conclude that by now Columbus was beginning to wonder whether his whole theory of the world might not be wrong, and whether he had possibly hit upon some extraordinary place that was blocking his passage to Cathay. The only other reason that he would have bothered to get these depositions taken down was that he really believed he was on the edge of the world he had promised, and that this was the only way he could ensure that Ferdinand and Isabella would back another expedition which would finally prove his argument. The Admiral had a great capacity for self-delusion, and once he had determined on believing in something it was impossible to change his mind.

The ships now turned back, called at the Isle of the Pines, and then made their way eastward along the Cuban shore. Once again they became badly involved among the shoals and cays that fringe the shore of southern Cuba, as well as being constantly forced to beat to windward. At one point *Niña* ran aground and Columbus very nearly had another 'Santa Maria' situation on his hands. Fortunately they managed to kedge his flagship off but she was badly damaged – even more reason why he had to make his way back to Isabella. Still, although despondent at their lack of real success, they continued to find marvels in this strange sea – at one time turtles so dense in the water that it seemed as if the

Opposite: *The flamingo which astonished Columbus and his men during their third voyage. Watercolour by John White, c. 1590.*

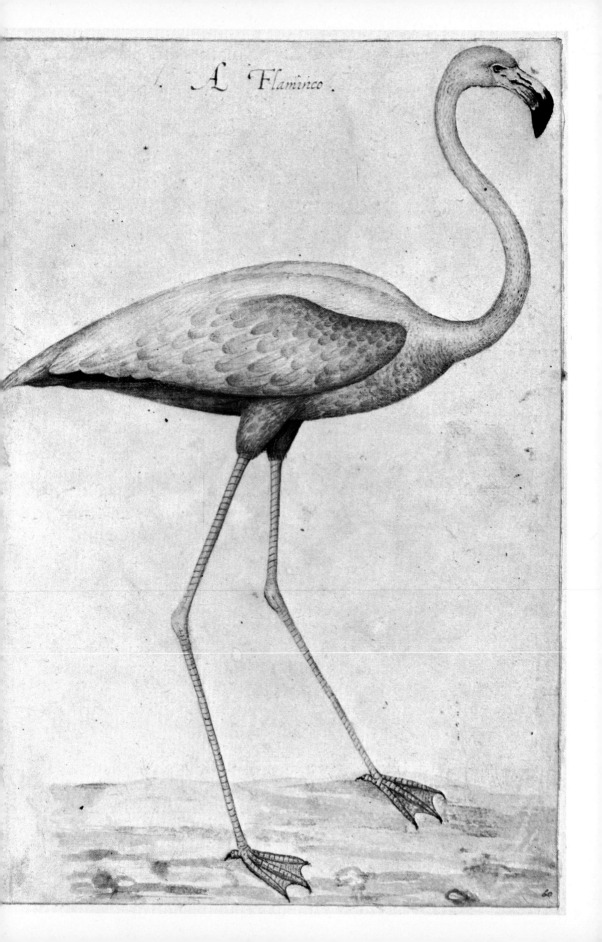

Fl. Flamineo.

ships might become grounded on them, showers of butterflies like living confetti, crested cormorants, the fine-fleshed conch which they rightly enjoyed eating, and great oysters which inspired their hopes but which proved to be palatable – but pearl-less.

Putting Cuba behind them at last they sailed south once more, to take another look at Jamaica. Columbus was determined to complete the circumnavigation of the island, hoping perhaps that in the southern half they might find the area where the nuggets of gold came from. All along one senses his growing desperation as he fails to find any of the things he had promised the Sovereigns, or any of the things that he had been dreaming about for so very many years. The Indians certainly proved a great deal more friendly than those they had previously encountered in the north, and everywhere they brought fresh fruit and vegetables for the hungry Spaniards. Bernáldez describes how at one point the cacique of a local tribe came out in his own massive canoe to see the ships, "together with his wife and two daughters, one of whom was very beautiful, and about eighteen years old. They were of course completely naked as they all are . . . He had a herald in his canoe, and he stood in the prow wearing a cloak of red feathers and carrying a white banner in his hand. Some of the men had their faces painted in the same colours, each wearing a large feather headdress . . . The cacique wore some copper ornaments round his neck, pretty-looking, rather like gold, made from a metal which they call *guanin*. [It was an alloy of copper, gold and silver which they got from the mainland of America]." The chief, who had heard about Columbus, proposed that he and all his family should come back with him to Spain. This was something of an embarrassment, for there was little enough food in the three small ships, and Columbus was very probably worried about the safety of the cacique's beautiful daughters shipped in a small vessel and surrounded by sex-starved sailors. He managed to convey that he would certainly take him back next time, and sent him and his party ashore with the usual gifts.

After riding out what was probably the side-blow of a hurricane under the lee of Saona island, Columbus made an attempt to determine his longitude during a total eclipse of the moon on September 14. He used the tables of the German astronomer Regiomontanus, which had been printed in 1474. They were not so inaccurate as some have made them out to be, but difficult enough even for a good mathematician – and Columbus was never that. The result was that his calculations gave him five and a half hours time difference from Seville, which was about an

Opposite: *Portrait of Columbus as an old man. Attributed to Ghirlandaio*

hour and a quarter too much – thus confirming his impression that he was a good eighteen degrees further west than he really was. This would, in fact, have put him somewhere on the Pacific coat of Guatemala – and even that was hardly half way round the world.

When the weather moderated, the three ships stood out again to the east. They ran right along the southern coast of Hispaniola, heading for Puerto Rico where the Admiral had decided to raid the Caribs who lived there. His avowed intention seems to have been to frighten them and destroy their canoes so that they could no longer make their murderous descents upon the natives of Hispaniola (who, whether they knew it or not, now came under the protection of Ferdinand and Isabella). In the channel between the two islands, now known as Mona Passage, they came across the island which the natives called Amona and which the Spaniards accordingly renamed La Mona (The Monkey).

At this point Columbus collapsed. As Navarrete puts it: "He fell into a slumber caused by pestilence. This deprived him of all his strength and of his mind. He seemed like dead and everyone thought that he would not survive another day."

The Admiral had been taxed to the utmost in the task of pilotage and of conducting his small fleet over unknown seas for all of five months. That in itself would be exigent enough for any commander. It seems likely also that the arthritis that was to plague him for the rest of his life had already taken a hold. At the same time, with the benefit of hindsight, it is almost certain that he was suffering from a severe nervous breakdown. He was in his forties, something that meant in those days more like sixties now, and he had lived a hard life physically and mentally ever since he had been a youth. The climate of the Tropics is not the most healthy, and he had been on short commons along with his crews for weeks on end.

The illness which was to lay him low for the next five months was possibly more in the heart and the head, metaphorically speaking, than in the ordinary functions of the body. He had failed. The golden bowl was broken, the dream shattered. He had found 'The Indies', and yet in some mysterious way they were not the Indies. The first voyage of Columbus, exulting over the wonderful new ocean is Triumph. He arrives and finds that it is all where he said it would be. The second voyage – especially from the moment when he makes the crews swear that they have found the mainland – is Tragedy. Farce also was always present in this man's life, but from now on the tragic element could only deepen.

The Sickness of Hispaniola

On September 29 1494, *Niña* and the other two caravels brought up in the roadstead of Isabella. It was not a happy homecoming. They had not found what they were looking for, and the Admiral seemed to be on the edge of death. The colony, although he was not to know it as yet, seemed to be disintegrating. The central area was seething in revolt against the Spaniards. Worse was to come. There was only one thing to cheer the sick man: his brother Bartholomew had arrived in a ship from Spain. Bartholomew was not only nearer to Columbus in age than the young and somewhat weak Diego, but he was a man of great strength of character. It was some years since the two brothers had met, but they had always got on well together. Bartholomew provided that element of practicality which counterbalanced the visionary in Columbus.

The coming of Bartholomew was a godsend. Here was someone he could really trust. He was a good administrator (as Columbus knew well from their days together in the map-making business), he would stand no nonsense from anyone, and he was completely loyal. The overriding factor was – he was a member of the family. The Admiral-Viceroy proceeded to appoint his brother Adelantado of Hispaniola. The title was equivalent to Governor. It meant that, second to Columbus, he was the head of the colony, and presided over the council meetings if Columbus himself was not present. Since Columbus was seriously ill for several months, his brother became in effect the head of the administration during this period.

It was hardly likely to be a popular move as far as the Spanish caballeros were concerned. Here was another one of these damned Genoese Colóns being put in a state of authority over true-born Spanish noblemen! Despite the genuine capabilities of Bartholomew, as well as his numerous other qualities, the appointment was a bad tactical error. Columbus would have done better to put his brother on the council –

where his abilities would soon have shown themselves – and left it at that. Columbus was a poor politician. Indeed, the qualities that go to make a good sailor are hardly those that make for success in political life. By this appointment Columbus had not only affronted local Spanish pride, he had done far worse – when the news got back, the monarchs were extremely annoyed. As Las Casas tells us, they thought that their Viceroy had overstepped himself. They, and they alone, had the power of conferring titles.

The situation in the colony was very bad indeed. Columbus must be held largely to blame for this by his despatch of Margarite, with his four hundred men, and instructions for them to "live off the land". The land did not produce much, the Indians lived frugally and, as Las Casas remarks, a Spaniard ate more in a day than an Indian in a month. The simple hospitality which the natives had originally practised, offering whatever they had to the passing stranger, was soon abused. Then again, the appetite of these soldiers for the native women was not likely to make them popular, particularly since they could not – and did not – discriminate between the daughters or wives of chieftains, and those of the commoners. To them they were all just naked women, and the political implications of raping a chieftain's daughter or wife were not immediately obvious.

Long before Columbus had returned, the damage had been done. The happy area of Vega Real had been largely despoiled. Margarite, a hot-blooded Catalan, had subsequently objected to taking orders from Columbus's younger brother, Diego, and had embarked for Spain with a number of men. With them also went Fra Buil, another Catalan, a man who had never had any use for Columbus. He was determined to tell the Sovereigns, when he got back, what his opinion was of this so-called colony and its Viceroy. While the Admiral had been battling his way back from "the mainland", Margarite and other dissident colonists were already on their way to Spain.

Although on a larger scale, the situation was much the same as it had been at La Navidád. Individual bands of soldiers were scattered about the country, looting, raping, and compelling natives to act as their slaves. Meanwhile Hojeda in the fort at San Tomás had come under siege. Caonabó, after failing to take the fort with its garrison of some fifty men, had resorted to the sensible stratagem of trying to starve them out, and cutting off their foraging parties. Hojeda was a very small man but he had the heart of a lion. It was he who ultimately was to capture the warlike cacique – though by a stratagem a little more elaborate than Columbus's shirt and cap. Knowing that the Indians were all fascinated

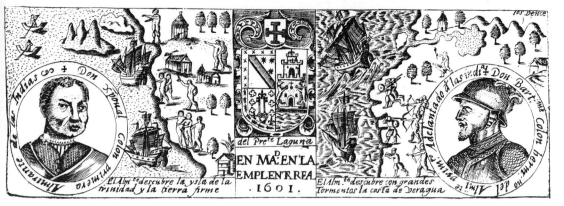

Columbus (left) *and his brother Bartholomew* (right). *Detail from title page of Antonio de Herrera's* Historia, *1601.*

by the sound of the bronze bell in the little church that had been built at Isabella, Hojeda had the message conveyed to Caonabó by an interpreter that if he would only make a treaty with the Spaniards he would give him the bell. Caonabó fell into the trap. He came to a meeting with Hojeda. The latter was well aware that the Indians were as intrigued by ordinary metal as the Spaniards were by gold, so he prepared a handsome pair of polished handcuffs and foot fetters. When the cacique arrived Hojeda proposed to him that he should ride in his company on one of those heaven-descended, extraordinary animals – a horse – to visit the Admiral in Isabella. Furthermore, he should ride like the king he was, wearing magnificent metal on his hands and feet. Entranced by the horse and by the beautiful gifts of metal, the unfortunate cacique had lost his liberty before the guard he had brought with him realised what was happening. His followers were quickly dispersed by Hojeda's men, and the wily Spaniard brought Caonabó back to Columbus. In later days, as Las Casas tells us, chained in the hall of the Admiral's house Caonabó would not stir when Columbus passed by but, if little Hojeda came in, the cacique would rise and bow low. He explained that, even if Hojeda was only a subordinate of the Admiral, it was he who by his courage and cleverness had managed to overcome him.

The land that had at first seemed a heaven had rapidly become a hell. Over and over again in the history of the confrontation between the aggressive European with his advanced technology and the more primitive tribes of the tribe that is Man, the same series of events would occur. The whole history of colonialism (an inevitable event in any case) was foreshadowed by the experience of Columbus in the Caribbean. Men from the Iron and Steel Age descended upon men from the Stone Age. The unfortunate fact that the human animal advanced in varying degrees throughout various parts of the world is not something that can be laid

Indians pouring molten gold down Spaniards throats as retaliation against the manhunting conquerors. From Benzoni, 1572.

at the door of the Genoese adventurer. He had come with the best, as well as mercenary, intentions of establishing communication with the Orient. He had found himself in a situation for which there was no precedent. As Colin Simpson has written of the Australian experience in New Guinea in the 20th century: "On the way in we had been greeted as supernaturals, and with awe. Now there was either the realisation at first that we were people come back from Paradise looking for our homes. Later on we were regarded as rejects who had been thrown out of Paradise."

In the autumn of 1494 a further four provision ships arrived from Spain under the command of Antonio de Torres. He brought with him a letter from the King and Queen, from which it is clear that they had not yet lost faith in their Admiral and Viceroy. They commended his enterprise "which for the most part has come true just as if you had seen it before you spoke about it". They told him about the amicable agreement that had been made with Portugal (The Treaty of Toedesillas) in which the demarcation line of the two spheres of influence had been set at a point 350 leagues west of Cabo Verde. They would like, however, to discuss the whole matter with Columbus. On the other hand, if he felt he

Indians committing suicide rather than be enslaved by the Spaniards.
From Benzoni, 1572.

could not come in person, he was to instruct his brother or someone else
of authority, regarding his opinions, and send him back in the first
caravel.

Columbus could well have taken this as a good excuse for returning,
leaving Bartholomew at the head of the council in Hispaniola. It was to
his grave disadvantage that he did not do so. Instead, he sent back young
Diego. But he also sent back a great deal more than his younger brother.
Fifteen hundred Indians, who had been captured on a recent punitive
expedition into the interior, were enslaved and put aboard the returning
caravels. Thus Columbus definitely established the slave trade from the
Indies. In place of the spices, the gold and the gems, which he had
promised the Sovereigns, he was despatching a cargo of the gentle Taino
Indians – not the man-eating Caribs of whom he had spoken to them.
Two hundred of the Indians died before they reached Spain and the
others, "naked as the day they were born", were sold in the market of
Seville. Even in this, this sad human substitute for the wealth of the
Indies, Columbus was providing, as it were, 'second rate material'. The
Indians could not adapt to the climate of Spain – a cold country in

winter. Bernáldez records: "They are not very profitable, for almost all of them have died." Neither Ferdinand, not especially Isabella were to be very taken with their Viceroy's reaction to their suggestion that he Christianise the Indians in their own islands, when they received a cargo of dejected and sick slaves. Las Casas rightly indicted Columbus for his treatment of the native inhabitants of this New World. Justin Winsor commented much later: "The merit which Columbus arrogated to himself was that he was superior to the cosmographical knowledge of his time. It was the merit of Las Casas that he threw upon the reeking passions of the enslaver the light of a religion that was above sophistry and purer that cupidity. The existence of Las Casas is the arraignment of Columbus."

On March 27 having heard that various caciques had now leagued themselves together against the Spanish invaders of their land, Columbus himself led out his small army – about two hundred infantry and twenty horsemen and a similar number of bloodhounds. Guacanagarí, who had now come to the conclusion that the Spaniards were invincible, and that the best thing was to be their ally, came along behind them with some of his followers. He was to be as shocked as the opposing Indians – and even further reinforced in his opinion – by the massacre that followed. The Spaniards came down through the Pass of the Hidalgos into that green and glowing Vega Real – where only a year before they had thought themselves in Paradise. The arquebuses, the drums even, the braying of the trumpets, all terrified the large band that had gathered against them under the leading cacique Guatiguaná. And what use were their primitive weapons against armoured men? The culminating stroke was a charge by the horsemen, accompanied by the dogs. Horsemen always terrified these poor primitives who imagined that, centaur-like, the man and the horse were one beast. They were cut to pieces. Those who did not escape into the surrounding woods were quickly rounded up by the exultant Spaniards. Soon there was another large batch of slaves ready to be taken back to Isabella for transhipment to Spain.

It was shortly after this action – if one can call it such – that Caonabó was taken by Hojeda's stratagem. Good, the Admiral must have felt, he was gradually getting this island under control. Eden was being tamed. The process went gradually ahead, more forts being built in the interior. There were further skirmishes with the natives, the acquisition of more slaves, and the victorious Spaniards now marched boldly about the interior, demanding the payment of yet more gold. Columbus, as he slowly mastered the whole island, imposed a tribute system upon all the native inhabitants of Hispaniola. Every Indian over fourteen years old, who lived in the area where the gold was panned and mined, was to bring every three months a hawksbell full of gold if he was a commoner, and a calabash-full if he was a cacique. Natives who lived in the non-goldbearing regions would pay their tribute in cotton, twenty-five pounds-weight every three months. The inhabitants of this beautiful island, who had idled in the sun, caught fish, eaten fruit that needed no cultivation, made love without shame, and had feared only the occasional attack of the Caribs, were now to enjoy the benefits of European civilisation. The punishment for non-payment of the tribute was death.

The people were unused to labour, and it was difficult for them to secure gold. Inevitably many of them took refuge in flight into the mountains, hoping that there they could once again live in their former happy indolence and freedom. The conquerors evolved a new sport – manhunting. Mounted caballeros accompanied by dogs would set off on expeditions into the interior, rounding up the natives and killing any who made a show of resistance. One authority has estimated that, at the time the Spaniards first landed in Hispaniola, the population was over a quarter of a million. Within three years, a third of them were dead. Oviedo in 1548 estimated that only about five hundred Taino Indians remained in the island. The voyage through flying-fish weather, the wonderful winds, the green – and golden – islands, all were turned to dust.

One of the methods the Indians used for making bread. From Benzoni, 1572.

Return

The Indians had a word for an immense wind that occasionally struck the islands: they called it *huracan*. And in June 1495 a hurricane struck Hispaniola and the township of Isabella. Peter Martyr, an Italian priest who knew Columbus well and who coined the expression 'New World' in his chronicle *De Orbe Novo* has the following description (the translation is by the Elizabethan, Richard Eden): "This same year in the month of June they say there arose such a boisterous tempest of wind from the south-east, as hath not lately been heard of. The violence hereof was such that it plucked up by the roots whatsoever great trees were within the force thereof . . . It beat down to the bottom of the sea three ships which lay at anchor, and broke the cables asunder: and that (which is the greater marvel) without any storm or roughness of the sea, only turning them three or four times about. The inhabitants also affirm that the same year the sea extended itself further into the land . . ."

Columbus had lost all but one ship (*Niña*) of the small fleet which he needed to garrison Isabella and maintain communications with Spain. Fortunately he had shipwrights in the colony and they were immediately set to work to build a caravel on the lines of *Niña*, a vessel which Columbus recognised as about the finest he had ever sailed in. The new caravel was nicknamed *India* by the sailors since she was the first to be built and launched in the Indies but Columbus, true to his nature, officially named her *Santa Cruz*. In October a relief force of four caravels from Spain dropped anchor off Isabella. Besides useful stores and provisions, and more colonists, they brought considerable trouble for the Viceroy. Fra Buil, Margarite, and others had made their complaints to the Sovereigns. Returning soldiers and colonists had not painted a picture of a superb country to which all should wish to emigrate. On the contrary, they had talked of disease and privation, hostile natives, and above all of the autocratic behaviour of the Viceroy who hung men out of

224

Ships despatched by Ovando, governor of Hispaniola, meet disaster in a storm. From Theodore de Bry, 1594.

hand and behaved in Hispaniola as if he was a ruling monarch. Also, at the time that they had all left the island, Columbus had been gone for months and there was no knowing whether he would ever return. He and his three caravels might well be wrecked, or else he was engaged in planting yet another colony in some unknown place. Ferdinand and Isabella had listened with growing disquiet. Things in their new territory did not sound quite as the Admiral had painted them in his despatches, nor as he had told them on his last visit to Spain. It definitely called for some form of inquiry. Juan de Aguado, who had been on the second voyage and had returned with Torres, was sent out as a commissioner to investigate the state of affairs in the colony. He carried with him a singular document, singular because it was addressed over Columbus's head to all the colonists. It read as follows:

225

"The King and the Queen.

"Cavaliers, Esquires and other persons, who by our command are in the Indies: we send you thither Juan Aguado, our Gentleman of the Chamber, who will speak to you on our part: we command that you give him faith and credence.

I the King: I the Queen."

The letter was dated "Madrid, the ninth of April, one thousand four hundred and ninety-five".

At the time when de Aguado arrived in Isabella Columbus was away on another expedition inland. The Commissioner was met by Bartholomew, acting in his capacity as Adelantado. Aguado proceeded to show him that his orders were direct from the monarchs and that Bartholomew could step aside. From now on, as Columbus realised when he returned, his powers were to be seriously curtailed. The Very Magnificent Lord Don Cristóbal Colón saw the writing on the wall. Meanwhile de Aguado and his scribes were assiduously investigating the state of things in Hispaniola. From all they heard, and from their own observations, almost everything that Fra Buil and Margarite had said at court was true. The main cry of the colonists was "God take me back to Castile!" All were hungry for good food and for a beaker of wine. As Las Casas tells it: "All they got was a mere plateful of wheat from the King's granary. This they had to grind in a handmill, many just eating it boiled. Other than that they might get a slice of rancid bacon or a piece of rotten cheese together with beans or chickpeas. As for wine, it was as if none was left in the world." Something – practically everything, it seemed – was wrong in Hispaniola. This was hardly the bright jewel in the Sovereigns' crown that had originally been proclaimed. From now on "neither the Admiral nor his decisions were as respected and obeyed as they had been earlier".

Aguado had some other unpleasant news for Columbus. It had been proclaimed that any native-born Spaniard who cared to fit out a vessel might make his way to the Indies, to trade or settle there if he wished. Columbus's monopoly was broken. It was not until some years later that he managed to convince the Sovereigns that this irresponsible voyaging was to their detriment, and to that of the royal exchequer. Aguado also brought with him a personal royal letter for Columbus, in which they ordered him to reduce the number of colonists to five hundred. This had probably already happened through the departure of so many with Torres, as well as deaths by sickness, accident and warfare. Nevertheless, it was a clear enough statement that the King and the Queen had come to the conclusion that, if these 'Indies' had to be almost entirely supplied from Spain, there was a very definite limit to what they could afford. Aguado had also brought with him a skilled metallurgist, Pablo Belvis, who had been given special privileges in working the mines (when they were discovered). Again, Columbus was being reduced. He realised, during the months the commission was investigating the colony, that he must get back to Spain, confound his detractors, and once again win Ferdinand's and Isabella's trust. To add to his embarrassment, even the native caciques were now coming in and laying their charges and complaints against him before Aguado. He could not possibly stay on in Hispaniola and let the commission get back before him.

Meanwhile a more suitable site for the island's capital had been discovered. Isabella, as the hurricane had shown, had a poor harbour – really no more than an open roadstead. Also, as had happened at La Navidád, the surrounding countryside had been despoiled. The story goes that a young Spaniard, Miguel Diaz, who had wounded another Spaniard in a fight, had fled into the interior of the island. He had ultimately come to the river called Ozama in the south, where he had become the lover of a local chieftainess. She had told him that the richest gold mines were all in her territory, and had suggested that the Spaniards come and build their town and settle down there. Whether all this was romance or not, the fact was that Columbus, before he sailed, gave orders for the new capital of Hispaniola to be sited at what is now Santo Domingo, the capital of the modern Dominican Republic. During his absence in Spain all the colonists moved to this new territory and built their township there. Isabella the unhappy was abandoned. Like La Navidád it had never proved anything more than a disaster area. Nothing but a few carved stones still indicate that this was once the first European capital in the New World. Ever after it was reputed to be haunted. The ghosts of long dead caballeros were seen in its ruins and the area was avoided by all later colonists.

Sketch map by Alessandro Zorzi showing the coasts of Central and South America, based on a map by Bartholomew Columbus.

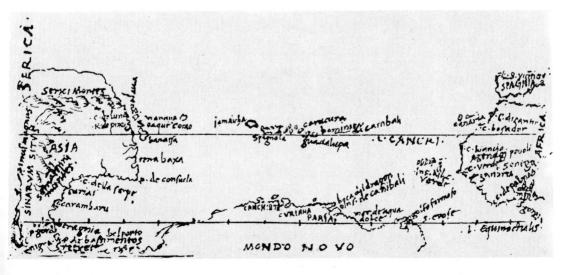

On March 10, 1496 the Admiral finally managed to get his two caravels out to sea. They were small ships and they were badly over-crowded. Fifty men would have been quite enough to man them, but they carried over two hundred Spaniards, some sick, and all discon-tented, as well as about thirty Indians. Among the captive natives of Hispaniola was the stout-hearted Caonabó, destined never to see his own land again, nor even the wonders of Spain. The Admiral had in-tended to impress him – before returning him – so that he could tell all the people that they could never defeat these strangers. But Caonabó died at sea.

Columbus left behind him in charge of the colony his brother Bar-tholomew, having given him instructions to found the new capital on the south coast. It was a bad return voyage, and it seems to prove that Columbus's first return in the high latitudes was no more than a lucky accident. He sailed in *Niña*, while the man who had all the reports about the colony, Aguado, sailed in *India*. They immediately had trouble bucking the trade-winds, and it took them many days before they were even clear of Hispaniola. They learned now, if they had not learned already, that the lateen rig – while awkward to handle under the pre-vailing winds of the ocean – was a good one when working in the Caribbean. Later documents and pictures show that, while square-rig was used on the Atlantic passages, the lateen remained a favourite in the islands.

It took the two ships four weeks to beat their way from Isabella to the vicinity of Guadalupe (a direct distance of about 600 miles). At this rate they would be out of water and provisions in their overcrowded ships long before they made the crossing to Spain. The Admiral decided that he must put in and re-water, as well as get some fresh provisions. All the Carib men, as it turned out, were away on the far side of the island, and the strangers were met by a crowd of screaming women. They probably thought that these shipmen were a new and even more dangerous tribe of cannibals than themselves. Landing in the face of a shower of arrows, the Spaniards pressed on inland and managed to capture a number of natives, including a woman of Guadalupe who was probably the wife of a cacique. Columbus, finding that there were practically no men about, concluded that this was undoubtedly the Island of the Amazons. A further proof of his whereabouts. The women of Guadalupe now taught these strange bearded men how to make cassava bread from the roots of the potentially very dangerous, bitter cassava. Its sap contains hydro-cyanic acid, and it can only be used for food after drying out, careful cleaning, and grating. The cassava was to prove a boon to them on the long voyage home – for Columbus had decided to repeat the success of his first outward voyage, due west, by going back due east. It was nearly a fatal mistake.

De Torres on his return to Spain followed much the same route as Columbus on the first voyage, when he had stood north and come back via the Azores, driving along with the westerlies above the latitude of 35° North. By heading out on the 22nd parallel Columbus was facing the prevailing easterlies of summer. Conditions aboard the ships were very bad, and by late May they were down to a basic ration of six ounces of cassava bread and a cupful of water. In Guadalupe they had captured and taken aboard some of the Carib women, and it appears it was even suggested that they should be eaten just as they ate the other Indians – either that, or throw all the Indians overboard as being no more than useless mouths. Columbus would not tolerate the idea of cannibalism, nor would he have his Indians drowned. They were to be brought back to Spain to be turned into Christians. (They ended up in the slave market.) Whatever his error in taking the southern route, the Admiral's dead reckoning was as good as ever. While the other pilots seem to have lost all track of their position he confidently asserted on June 7 that they were nearing Cape St. Vincent, and ordered sail shortened. He was almost dead-right. The next day they made their landfall off the coast of Portugal. Three days later, putting on as brave a show as possible with banners and pennants, the two weather-beaten caravels sailed into the harbour of Cadiz. It was a far call from the triumphant fleet that had set out in 1493. Columbus had been away for two years and nine months.

The Admiral brought back with him a crowd of half-starved yellow-looking colonists, a few Indians, and little else. There were two caravels and a ship commanded by Peralonso Niño in the harbour when they arrived, preparing to sail for the colony with provisions and supplies. Niño, who had been with Columbus in *Niña* on the return voyage in 1493, must have been as dismayed as the rest of the newly embarked sailors and colonists when they contemplated the appearance of these former inhabitants of Hispaniola. One cannot help wondering whether one or two of the potential emigrants did not change their minds at this late hour and make off down the docks for home. Columbus and his Indies were discredited. Whatever he had found, it was not what he had promised. As a sign that he considered his misfortunes a chastisement inflicted upon him for the sin of pride he adopted the coarse brown habit of a Franciscan Brother. The Very Magnificent Lord had reached the conclusion that he must pay attention to those all-important virtues – Poverty, Chastity, and Obedience.

"Once more into the breach . . ."

On July 12 1496 Ferdinand and Isabella despatched a letter to their Admiral requesting that he come to court. It was couched in friendly terms and expressed regret at the hardship which they knew he had suffered. As his reception would also show, the Sovereigns still had respect and affection for Columbus. He might have erred in some of the things that he had done in the Indies, but they did not forget that it was he and he alone who had fished these great islands out of the deep. Although himself remaining in his penitential garb, Columbus made sure that his progress through Spain should remind everyone of the brilliance of the world that he had discovered. Men went ahead holding cages of parrots, whose screams alerted each village or town, as they approached, that Columbus was on his way. Indians bedecked with feathers and with gold ornaments combined to excite the simple on-lookers by the strangeness of their appearance and by the evidence of gold, elaborately-worked in the native fashion. Bernáldez, who witnessed it, describes the whole ornate style in which the wily Genoese put on a parade designed to prove once again that he had done what he had said he would do. It was also no doubt designed to win colonists. He describes a crown which had belonged to the cacique Caonabó "very big and tall, with wings on its side like a shield" as well as "crowns, masks, girdles and collars". All in all, it was a show that no one who saw it would ever forget. It would also impress the Sovereigns.

From Cadiz the cavalcade had to traverse almost the whole length of Spain to reach Burgos in the north, and nothing could have suited Columbus better. He was received by Ferdinand and Isabella with every mark of affection. They were delighted with the gold dust and nuggets that he brought them, as well as with all the native curiosities, the cotton garments and wood carvings, the gold crowns and ornaments. Columbus for his part must have been pleased to see his two sons, Diego and Ferdinand, both of whom were pages at court to the Infante Don Juan. He had seen little of either of them in his wandering life. Columbus had great charm, as several who knew him testified. He was also clever in his anticipation of a hostile reaction by donning his penitential robe well in advance. Although the Sovereigns now had Juan de Aguado's report on the colony, and although they had heard from other sources much against their Admiral and Viceroy, when they saw him again and heard all the stories from his own lips their trust was renewed. They remembered how they had disbelieved his proposal in the first instance, and how they had been proved wrong. They yielded to his persuasiveness as well as to the evidences of this world that he had laid before them. They agreed to his proposal for a third expedition.

Columbus asked for eight ships, but it was to be a very long time before he got them. His reason for asking for this number was, as he said, that five would be required to carry stores and settlers, while three would be caravels with which he would press on down the peninsula (Cuba) and reach Cathay and the Khan. Nothing would change his mind about that. Father Bernáldez, as he himself records, had earlier made the tentative suggestion to the Admiral that he might be wrong. He had argued that "a great deal of time would be required to reach Cathay, for the Great Khan had been in the past Lord of the Tartars". Now everybody knew that Tartary was east from Spain, or as Bernáldez put it, "where the sun rises in the longest days of the year. It was in that direction that merchants used to travel to those lands. But in the direction in which the Admiral looks for Cathay, it is my opinion that even if he goes another twelve hundred leagues round the globe, he will not get there." Father Bernáldez, of course, was just as right as the learned men who had originally discounted the Columbian theory.

The reason why Columbus was now delayed nearly two years in Spain was due to a number of factors. One of them may well have been that Ferdinand and Isabella had already sent off a new commander for the colony. "Because we fear that God may in some way have disposed of the Admiral of the Indies while on his way, since we have not heard from him for so long, we have therefore decided to send thither Commander Diego Carrillo and another person of rank in charge, so that in the Admiral's absence, he may see to all the business over there and, even in his presence, he may put a remedy to all that might need it, according to the information we had from those who came from there." Although they welcomed Columbus home and treated him in an openly friendly manner, the Sovereigns could not entirely ignore what they had heard from Fra Buil and others. The initial enthusiasm about the Indies which had led to sending the fleet of 1493 had waned. The discovery had not proved half as profitable as the Portuguese discoveries in West Africa, out of which gold, spices and slaves flowed abundantly.

Up to date, if one could make an accurate profit-and-loss account, it would seem likely that these Indies were costing Spain considerably more than they were bringing in. Then again, there were other and far more urgent political reasons that militated against the expenditure of any more money or the despatch of any more ships. There was trouble with France, and Ferdinand had to look north towards Perpignan, which was then Spanish and threatened by the French. "As for the Queen," as Madariaga has summarised the situation, "she was busy with the naval arrangements in connection with the marriage of two of her

The Cantino world map, 1502.

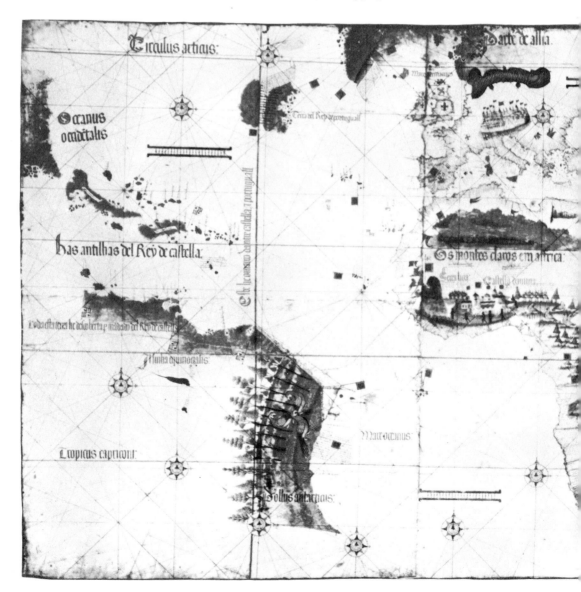

children: the Infanta Juana, betrothed to Philip the Handsome of Burgundy, son of Emperor Maximilian; and Prince Juan, the heir to all the Spains – but Portugal – who was to wed Margaret, Philip's sister. A fleet of one hundred and thirty vessels, with an army of twenty-five thousand men, was to escort the Infanta to Flanders and to bring Princess Margaret to Spain. No lesser escort was needed in view of the war with France. The Admiral of Castile, who commanded it, could indeed look down upon the Admiral of the Indies who had landed in Cadiz, in Franciscan garb, at the head of two caravels . . ."

It was hardly surprising in view of these martial and marital enterprises – all of which were heavy burdens on the depleted Spanish exchequer – that Columbus had to wait. It is astounding really that so harsh and relatively unproductive a country as Spain (though it had been rich in metals in classical times) could ever have afforded the outlay to

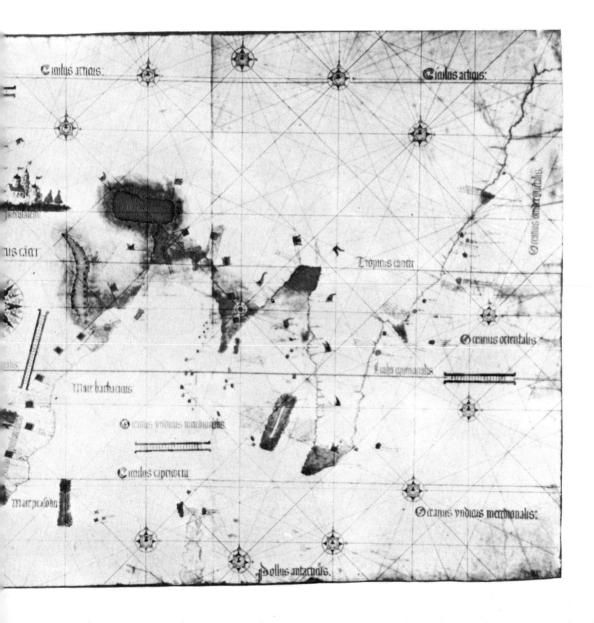

become the empire that it did. The reason, of course, was that after the discoveries of Columbus the vast wealth of the New World ultimately came into its hands. His adulators have demanded everything for him – including canonisation. His detractors have not even been prepared to concede that as the first (known) man to make the voyage to South America, he did thus ensure that the wealth of the Indies became Spanish. The deterioration of the South American continent over subsequent centuries may be put down to two factors: inefficient Spanish colonial administration and the ministrations of a Church so rigid that, despite true Christians like Las Casas, it never made any attempt to understand the nature of man in a different area of the world. Many Spanish prelates were to show by their behaviour in the Indies that they were as proud and power-conscious as any of the worst Popes of Rome.

It was not until 1498 that Columbus got under way for the third time. It was the month of May, a lovely season in Spain, but the Admiral had been chafing at the bit for a long time to get back to those "flowers of the sea". Although he could be charming, and although he could be cunning, he was really no good ashore. The year before he sailed two edicts were published by the Sovereigns, supposedly on the advice of Columbus. They were hardly likely to improve the state of things in the Indies. The first of them authorised the judges to sentence criminals to transportation to the Indies, and the second granted an indulgence to all who had committed any crime (with certain exceptions such as heresy, sodomy, and treason) to be allowed to go at their own expense to Hispaniola. Whether it was on his advice or not, Columbus was later to remark: "I swear that many men have gone to the Indies who did not deserve water either from God or from man."

Before Columbus's departure, his titles and privileges were confirmed but he was relieved of bearing one-eighth of the cost of the past years' provision fleets. In return for this he was to surrender all rights to the profits over that period, while for the future he should have one-eighth of the gross and one-tenth of the net profits. There were various other instructions about bringing the Faith to the Indians and points of detail about the administration of the colony. Finally, the Sovereigns confirmed Bartholomew, his brother, as Adelantado of Hispaniola. All in all, the Admiral had done well from the months that he had spent at court. Three hundred and thirty persons, gentlemen, soldiers and artisans, were to accompany Columbus on this next expedition at the Crown's expense. Any others he took with him were either to be at his own charge, or were to pay their own way. All hardwoods, such as brazil-wood, and precious metals were reserved for the Crown. Columbus was also authorised to take with him – if he could find any willing to go – thirty women, roughly one for every ten men. Finally, before he left, Columbus made a will and testament in favour of his legitimate son Diego but protecting the rights of Ferdinand, Beatriz's son, and then those of his brothers and their sons. Whoever should finally inherit would automatically become Admiral, and receive one-eighth of the income of the Indies. Columbus never forgot his native city. He laid down that a percentage of the revenue was to be paid into the Bank of St. George in Genoa.

There can be little doubt that he was eager to be gone. Returned sailors, disillusioned caballeros, colonists weakened by privation and disease, all had spread the word that Hispaniola was a nightmare. It was time. The shore was a prison to this man. There was always the conflict, the deviousness, the endless chicanery (he had hit a crooked ship-chandler) and the whole seediness of the land. Although avaricious, he was at heart a romantic dreamer. It is probable that the only real happiness he knew in all his life was during the days and nights he spent at sea. In some ways he foreshadowed Arthur Rimbaud:

"Et dès lors, je me suis baigné dans le Poème
De la Mer, infusé d'astres, et lactescent,
Dévorant les azurs verts; où, flottaison blême
Et ravie, un noyé parfoir descend . . ."

They left from the mouth of the Guadalquivir river on May 30 1498, putting gracious Seville behind them, outward bound for this world that the Admiral had presented to the Spanish crown.

The Third Voyage of Christopher Columbus is best detailed by his own account – a long document which he sent to Ferdinand and Isabella in the October of that year. "I left, in the name of the Most Holy Trinity, on Wednesday May 30, from the town of San Lucar [at the mouth of Guadalquivir] . . . I navigated to the island of Madeira by a route I had not used before to avoid any trouble with a fleet from France which was awaiting me off Cape St. Vincent. From there I sailed to the Canary Islands, whence I departed with one ship and two caravels, having sent the other ships on the direct route to Española in the Indies. So I sailed southwards, with the intention of reaching the equinoctial line and from there following it westward so that the island of Española would be to the north of me. I reached the Cape Verde Islands (a false name since I saw nothing green in them and all the people were ill, so that I did not dare stay there) and I sailed on to the south-west for 120 leagues . . . At this point the wind failed me and I came into a region of such great heat that I really believed all the ships and people would be burned. We were in such a state of exhaustion that no one dared go below decks to attend to the water casks and the provisions. This heat lasted for eight days. It was fine on the first day, but on the following seven days it was cloudy and rainy, and yet we found no relief. I really believe that if it had remained sunny as on the first day we should never have been able to survive."

There are two important things to be noted about the document so far. Firstly, Columbus denigrates the Cape Verde islands, because they belong to the King of Portugal, and secondly he exaggerates the heat of the equatorial zone. Cecil Jane comments in the Hakluyt Society edition of 'The Voyages of Columbus': "This was within the traditional 'burning zone' (although constantly passed and repassed by the Portuguese), and Columbus paints an exaggerated picture of the sufferings of himself and his crew in order to enhance the supposed advantages of the hemisphere that lay beyond the Pope's line."

Columbus was lying. The temperature in the Cape Verdes is not so very different from that in the Canaries. But he had to lie in order to convince his Sovereigns that they were getting control of a better part of the world than the Portuguese. He goes on to say that he recalls how, "when sailing to the Indies, whenever I passed westward of the Azores by 100 leagues, there I found the temperature change". This was perfectly true, for he was at least 20°, or something like 120 sea miles, further to the north. Columbus may have convinced Ferdinand and Isabella, he may even have convinced himself, but he does not convince anyone who has ever navigated in his wake.

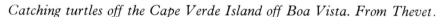

Catching turtles off the Cape Verde Island off Boa Vista. From Thevet.

Unrecognised Mainland

Nearly a year before Columbus made his departure from the Cape Verde islands his great contemporary Vasco da Gama had already made his way to India – the true India.

Columbus's letter to Ferdinand and Isabella tells how, "after seventeen days, during which Our Lord gave me a favourable wind, on Tuesday, July 31, land appeared to us, which I had expected to sight on the previous day . . . As the strength of the sun increased, and because we were short of water, I decided to go to the Carib islands and took that route. The Divine Majesty has always shown mercy to me. A sailor went to the maintop to look out, and to the westward he saw three mountains close together. We all said the *Salve Regina* and other prayers, and we gave many thanks to Our Lord."

If by 'the Carib islands' Columbus meant Dominica and Guadalupe he was nowhere near them. He was off the coast of what is now Venezuela, and what he had just sighted was the island which still bears the name that he gave to it, Trinidad, the Trinity, after its three distinctive peaks. His first consideration was to water ship. On August 1 he anchored just past what is now Erin Point, which he named Punta de la Playa. In the bay here he had observed several streams pouring down over the sandy beach. He was now on the south coast of the Orinoco delta. He was looking at the mainland of America. From its shape and from the way it faded away at the edges he decided that it was just another island and named it Isla Sancta, Holy Island.

The first encounter with the natives served to encourage the Admiral's belief that he was drawing near to the civilization that he sought. ". . . There came from the east a large canoe with twenty-four men in it, all in the prime of life and well equipped with bows and arrows and wooden shields. They were well-built, not Negroes, and whiter than the others we have seen in the Indies, graceful and handsome. Their long hair was

237

straight, cut in the manner of Castile. They had scarves made of cotton wrapped around their heads. These were colourful and elaborately worked, very like the gauze veils of the Moors. Around their body they wore another of these in place of drawers." Columbus's attempt to attract them onboard proved unsuccessful. ". . . I caused to be brought up to the aftercastle a tambourine and got some of the young men to play and dance, thinking that they would draw near to see the festivity." The Indians, on the other hand, clearly thought that this was some tribal war dance, for they immediately let fly with a shower of arrows. "I then ordered some crossbows to be discharged."

Columbus went on round the south-western end of Trinidad and anchored in that narrow neck of water which leads to the Gulf of Paria, between the island and the mainland. He accurately named it Boca de la Sierpe, the Serpent's Mouth, for the current which pours through here – particularly when the Orinoco is in flood – can be very alarming. "And in the night, when it was already very late. I was on deck and I heard a terrible roaring which came from the south towards the ship." Naturally enough, as captain of his vessel and being in overall charge of all the ships, Columbus stayed up top and witnessed what was either a tidal wave caused by some volcanic activity or a sudden immense discharge of water from one of the mouths of the Orinoco, caused by flooding in the interior. "A wave advanced roaring with the same fury of roaring as that of the other currents, which, as I have said, sounded to me like the waves of the sea breaking on rocks. I remember to this very day how afraid I was that the wave might overwhelm the ship when it reached her." Next morning he sent the ships' boats on ahead to sound the way and, finding that there was a good 6 or 7 fathoms in the passage, Columbus thankfully moved his ships out of the Serpent's Mouth. The green-clad hills of Trinidad, bright with humming-birds, were on his starboard hand and all of South America to port.

Between the western tip of Trinidad and the Paria peninsula of Venezuela he passed through the narrow channel which he named the Dragon's Mouth. Prior to this he had made contact with the natives of the mainland and had observed that they wore ornaments of gold as well

Opposite: *Sunset over Trinidad.*

Overleaf: *The Fountain of the Four Rivers in the earthly paradise, or the Garden of Eden which Columbus believed he had found. 14th century French manuscript.*

as pearls. They had told him that their land was called Paria and he had naturally enough assumed that this was once again just another large island like Jamaica or Hispaniola. Cuba was the peninsula of the mainland, that was the one and only definite geographical fact. He took his latitude again and, as usual, got it wrong. Quite apart from the fact that the quadrant of his day was a primitive instrument, Columbus was sick. It was not only his arthritis that was plaguing him but – worst thing of all for a seaman – his eyesight. His eyes, according to his own account, were giving him great pain and even "running with blood". After those many days at sea, always peering ahead over an ocean that bounced with wavy light, he was suffering from severe eyestrain.

What did indeed surprise him, and all those with him, was that at one point on the coast they found that the sea was no longer salt, but almost completely fresh. They were of course receiving the outpour of the Orinoco, a river system which embraces nearly all of Venezuela south and east of the Andes. Even this was not sufficient to convince the Admiral that he was on the edge of a huge continent. At the same time he felt quite sure that he was touching upon some mystery, perhaps the fringes of that heavenly Eden about which he had read. St. Augustine and others had placed the Garden of Eden somewhere far in the East. He had the feeling that the world was not a sphere, not round as everyone had always held it to be, but "like a woman's breast, and at the part of the nipple it is highest and closest to heaven. It is under the equinoctial line, at the end of the Orient. I call the end of the Orient the place where all lands and islands end."

Columbus had given Ferdinand and Isabella far more than Africa or the Indies, or ordinary islands in the Ocean. He had given them the Terrestrial Paradise itself. "I think that this water may come from there. All these are definite signs of Paradise, for the situation conforms with the opinion of great theologians. All the facts point that way, for I never heard or read that so much fresh water could mix with salt and penetrate so far into it. The gentleness of the climate strengthens my belief. And if the water does not flow from Paradise, then it is a still greater marvel. I do not think there is in the known world a river so great and so deep." His mind obscured by medieval theology, Columbus still remains an acute observer and is not entirely blinded by his prejudices and preconceptions. At one moment he hovers on the edge of the real truth: "I believe that this land which Your Highnesses have now had discovered is very large and that there are many more in the East, which

Opposite: *Trinidad beach today.*

243

have never been known . . . I am convinced that this is mainland, hitherto unknown, and am prompted to think this on account of this great river and sea which is fresh." But then again he inevitably has to fall back on his intellectual background: "I am reinforced in my belief from the saying of Esdras in Book IV, Chapter 6, a book approved by St. Ambrose and St. Augustine, which says that six parts of the earth are dry and one under water."

It was in a bay on the peninsula of Paria that Europeans first went ashore in South America. There was a native settlement from which the inhabitants had fled, leaving behind fish and unknown types of fruit, and everywhere in the bush the monkeys chattered and parrots screamed. Columbus coasted back south-westward along the peninsula – he was determined it was an island – and then doubled back on his tracks and sailed out through the Dragon's Mouth.

Hispaniola was his stumbling block. If only *Santa Maria* had not run aground on that quiet night and compelled him to plant a colony there he would have conclusively found out the truth of his great discovery. It was an easy sail back, for he had a strong current with him, something that added to his conviction that the world was shaped like a breast, that he had been very near the top of it, and was now, as it were, running downhill. He was sure that it was part of the mainland of China. As soon as the opportunity offered he must come back and find the strait which Marco Polo had described, the one that led through to the Spice Islands.

The astounding thing about Columbus is his almost uncanny skill as a dead-reckoning navigator. He may not have been much good at celestial observations, but the science was in its infancy in his day, as was the making of precision instruments. At pilotage and dead-reckoning he was a master. He had left the Cape Verde islands on July 4 and he had made a landfall at the then unknown island of Trinidad on July 31. He had been skirting the edge of an equally unknown continent. Yet, after leaving the Gulf of Paria and passing another island which he named Margarita (after the Austrian Princess who was married to the Infante Don Juan), he could still set the right course for his return to Hispaniola. It is difficult enough, even with modern charts, to get from one part of the globe to another solely on dead-reckoning. Columbus had no charts, he did not even have a log to estimate his speed. He had only a compass. But he had contained in that remarkable head of his – even if in other matters it was somewhat confused – a perfect memory-bank of the situation of the places he had discovered. The adulators of the Admiral have often carried their admiration to excessive lengths, the detractors likewise.

The only thing that any sailor would say of him is that he deserves to be called a seaman – and in capital letters.

He was without any information about the remarkably strong currents which flow along this part of the South American coast. But he observed them with his practised eye, commenting accurately on the marked westerly set. Even making due allowance for this he came out about 150 miles to the leeward of his destination, the new capital of Santo Domingo. Columbus, as Las Casas tells us, was very grieved at his error. Considering the circumstances it was a fantastically good landfall. It was irritating, though, for he had the prevailing winds and the strong westerly current setting against him, and he had found from previous experience how many days it took to beat back against them. The point where he made his landfall was a small island lying off the south-west coast of what is now the Dominican Republic. He named it after the Virgin, Beata, a name it bears to this day, as does the nearby headland. Anchoring between it and another islet, Alta Vela, High Sail, so-called because of its distinctive peaked shape, the Admiral sent a boat ashore to find some Indians to carry a message to Bartholomew at Santo Domingo.

Soon afterwards an Indian came aboard. Columbus observed with considerable disquiet that this native was carrying a crossbow. That certainly looked ominous. An arms trade with the local inhabitants had already begun. Or was it La Navidád all over again? He was relieved next day by the arrival of his brother, who had set out in a caravel to meet the three vessels which had formed the advance of the relief fleet. He had missed them but, hearing that ships had been sighted to the west, had

Map of the South American coast and West Indies. From Bordone's Isolario, *1534. It was in a bay on the peninsula of Paria that Columbus first went ashore in South America.*

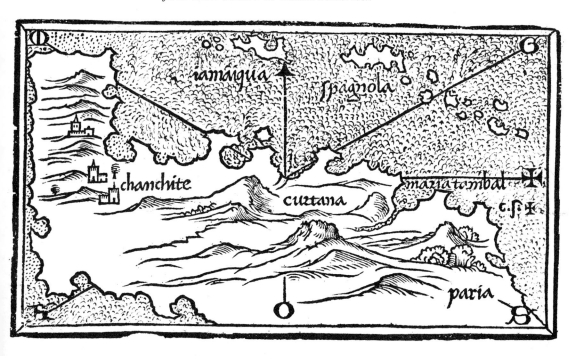

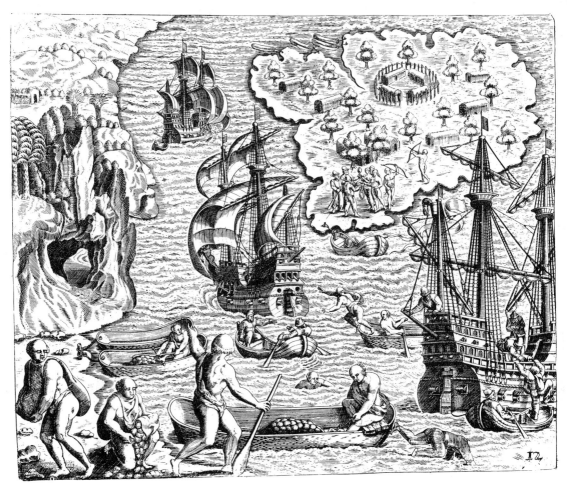

Pearl fishing, off the Golf de Paria. From Theodore de Bry, 1594.

come on down under easy sail before the Trades. The two brothers had much to talk about after their separation of nearly two and a half years. Columbus had another successful voyage to his credit. He had discovered more islands that could only prove to the greater glory and profit of the Sovereigns. The natives he had met with on this voyage had nearly all been friendly and, even when they were not, there had been no real conflict. It seemed that the people to the south were not cannibal Caribs. The world he had to tell about was very strange, with its monkeys and parrots, and curious fruits. But what was astounding was its freshwater seas. He was quite sure that back there, to the south and west, lay the Terrestrial Paradise. The story that Bartholomew had to tell sounded more like something out of Dante's Inferno.

Tribulations

After the pleasures of the trade-wind crossing and the excitement of discovering new lands Columbus was now faced with the hell of Hispaniola. While he had been away, Bartholomew as Adelantado had done as instructed and had started building the new capital of Santo Domingo. This in itself was on a good site, with a well-protected harbour at the mouth of a river, and hard by some of the richest parts of the island. At the same time, it was not far from the Mona Passage, Puerto Rico, the Lesser Antilles, and then the Great Ocean itself. It has remained the capital city to this day. The bad news was that a rebellion had broken out against the authority of Bartholomew, which amounted in effect against the Viceroy, Columbus. Francisco Roldán, whom Columbus had appointed as chief justice, had objected to taking orders from yet another foreigner and had set up what amounted to a separate independent kingdom in the south-western corner of Hispaniola, the area which the natives called Xaraguá. He had with him about seventy other dissident colonists. They could see no point in working at the Viceroy's projects. They had women, they had slaves, and they were enjoying a life of happy indolence. Columbus had been right when he had seen that crossbow in the hand of an Indian and suspected that things had gone wrong in his absence. The first American revolution had begun. A pattern had been set that was to continue – in parts of South America at least – right up to the 20th century.

Everything that Columbus heard was bound to increase his uneasiness. There had, inevitably, been trouble with the Indians over the payment of tribute. One of the reasons for Roldán's successful rebellion was that he not only promised his Spanish followers that they would not have to work if they joined him, but he also promised the Indians that he would not require tribute from them – provided always of course that food and women were freely available. In addition to all this there had been a great

247

deal of illness and a large number of men had died back at Isabella. Malaria and syphilis were almost certainly the root causes. Then, to make matters worse, the three caravels under Carvajal had made their landfall in the territory where Roldán and his men were living, and about forty of the new settlers had gone over to him, preferring quite naturally a life of lazy liberty to one of toil. Indeed it is surprising that they did not all opt for a lotus-eating existence. Carvajal, however, and the majority of the crews remained loyal to Columbus and the authority of the Sovereigns.

The Columbus brothers were not in a position of strength. Bartholomew's autocratic manner had never been likely to endear him to the caballeros, nor his harsh justice to the Spanish workers or the native Indians. Diego was weak and vacillating. Columbus himself, at any rate when he landed, was still suffering from his arthritis and his eyesight. Furthermore, in the colonists' eyes, they were all foreigners, Genoese, possibly Genoese Jews, and in any case everyone knew that a plain Genoese was more avaricious than any Jew. Despite the fact that Columbus's position and the Adelantado's were now reinforced by the declaration of the Sovereigns, they could only count on the loyalty of a limited number of the settlers. On October 25 Columbus wrote to Roldán in a manner that, far from being the stern rebuke of the Sovereign's Viceroy to a dissident subject, was more the voice of appeasement. He then went even further and promised a general amnesty for all the rebels and a guaranteed safe pass home to Spain, together with all necessary supplies. This bargaining with Roldán and his followers went on for months, Columbus displaying throughout a curious want of firmness which was very far from his behaviour in the old days in Isabella. A somewhat similar evasiveness is shown in a despatch to the Sovereigns sent at about the same time, in which he chronicles the situation in the colony but naturally enough does not say how bad conditions really were. Since the gold tribute had not come up to expectations he proposed to send back, as well as brazil-wood, "all the slaves that can be sold". He had been authorised to send as slaves to Spain any who were captured in warfare against the new state. As far as he could gather from Bartholomew, at one time or another practically every area of the island had been in revolt against the Spaniards. That was justification for him to enslave as many as he could.

The whole humiliating affair with Roldán finally ended with Columbus restoring him to his office of chief justice. His rebel followers were allowed, if they so wished, to settle down on the lands in Xaragua with their slaves and concubines. He had begun the Indian slave trade, he now proceeded to institute the system which was to become the prevailing one over the centuries throughout most of Spanish America. This was known as *repartimientos*, allotments or divisions. This was a system whereby the Spanish colonists were allocated plots of land, the cacique of each area being ordered to see that the natives who had formerly lived there worked for their new masters. Columbus was acting in the New World much as the Spartans had done many hundreds of years before when they had occupied Laconia in the Peloponnese and had enslaved the people of Helos, causing them and their descendants in perpetuity to work for them as Helots, or serfs.

He was not, one feels, essentially a bad man. He was trapped by circumstances. He had hoped originally to establish trading posts where he could exchange the manufactured goods of Europe for the riches of the Orient – to do in fact, although on a far larger scale, exactly what the Portuguese were doing in Africa. He had not found himself in the Orient. He had then hoped that this great island would yield plenty of gold, and that he could trade for it with the natives. The gold had been scarce. Instead of a trading post he had been forced by the wreck of *Santa Maria* to plant a colony. The site of the colony had also been forced upon him. It had been in an unsuitable position, and the simple men he had left behind had behaved just as thousands of others were later to do during the European colonisation of America, Africa and the East. He had then sensibly decided to make the main centre of the colony at Santo Domingo, a good site in all respects and nearer the area where the gold was said to come from. He had been away too long – again, not through his own fault but through the barrenness of the Spanish exchequer and the political preoccupations of Ferdinand and Isabella.

He had returned to find that the proud and factious Spanish nature, coupled with the poor quality of many of the colonists, had produced a state of anarchy. In any case, even if the report is true that some Spanish women had come out on a previous voyage, they were basically men without women – a situation that was bound to lead to trouble with the indigenous inhabitants. No, he had only made one grave error. It was one which he was paying for now: he had appointed his brother as governor in his absence. The peasant in Columbus's nature betrayed him. If, for instance, he had made Roldán or one of the other Spanish gentlemen Adelantado, it is possible that the colony would have developed without too much friction. On the other hand, knowing the nature of mankind, it is likely that under any circumstances something similar would have occurred. Whatever man or nation had first discovered America, the result would almost inevitably have been the same.

The subsequent history of the European expansion into North America does not make any more agreeable reading. The invasion of the Pacific lands and islands has rightly been called by Alan Moorehead "The Fatal Impact". The Admiral of the Ocean Sea, master of those blue driving acres where all was good and clean, was faced with the problem of Original Sin. Adam and Eve were no longer in Eden – and Columbus can hardly be blamed for that.

The news that filtered back to Ferdinand and Isabella about the state of things in their new lands was very disquieting. It had never been very good, and the returns from their investment were considerably poorer than they had hoped. This strange man had found for them some place on the far side of the Atlantic Ocean which, by all accounts, did not appear to be his promised Indies. He had involved them in great expense at a time when they could ill afford it. The people who had come back from Hispaniola all complained that Columbus and his brothers were usurping their position, behaving as if they alone were the real rulers of this land. It naturally seemed to the promoters of the whole 'Enterprise of the Indies' that their investment should be secured by the appointment of some thoroughly reliable man who would ensure that it was being properly administered. Returned sailors and colonists painted only a depressing picture of the new lands and, as Ferdinand Columbus records, when he and his brother were seen in any of the streets outside the court they were mocked and insulted by returned sailors and ex-colonists who cried out for the payment they had never got and shouted "There go the sons of the Admiral of the Mosquitoes!"

On March 21 1499, Ferdinand and Isabella decided that once again they should send someone out to investigate the affairs of the Indies. They chose, as Oviedo reports, "a gentleman, an old member of the royal household, a sincere religious man, Francisco de Bobadilla". Bernáldez says that he was "a great gentleman and loved by all", while Las Casas remarks that he had never heard him "accused of any dishonest action or anything like cupidity . . . On the contrary everyone spoke well of him". He was a Knight of one of the Spanish military Orders, and was clearly the kind of man who would not be deflected from his purpose by any considerations whatsoever. He was above the rank of caring whether Columbus was a Viceroy or whether Roldán was a chief justice. The old *nobleza* of Spain was coming out to take a look at the situation in this new and, as it seemed, very common world.

Bobadilla was granted complete power in the Indies. He was allowed to decide exactly who should, or should not, be returned to Spain, whether "gentlemen or other persons". The King and the Queen still seem to have hesitated about granting such powers even to a nobleman whom they trusted implicitly, so it was not until the midsummer of 1500 that Bobadilla left. One of the reasons that had most probably decided them to take this step of appointing someone over the head of their Viceroy and Governor was the return of some of the colonists bringing with them their private Indian slaves. Isabella had always hated the slave trade – it was bad enough when it was being used to assist the Treasury – but that common seamen and others should now have the effrontery to come back with slaves as personal booty was something that could not be tolerated. The order was given that all such Indians should be sent back to their native lands. There was something very wrong with the way these three Colón brothers, all those thousands of miles away, were administering property that belonged to the Crowns of Aragon and Castile.

It was not until August 23 that Bobadilla arrived off the harbour of Santo Domingo. Columbus himself was away at the time in the region of Vega Real, and the Adelantado, Bartholomew, was in Xaraguá putting down a further rebellion – but this time with the aid of his old adversary Roldán. The man left to meet the Sovereigns' royal commissioner was Diego, the irresolute youngest brother of the Admiral. Bobadilla was extremely incensed to find that one of the first things to confront him was the sight of a number of Spanish corpses hanging from a gallows. No doubt they had richly deserved it, but it did not give him any confidence in the way that this new possession was being administered. The powers that were allotted to Bobadilla were proclaimed by the Notary Public. It was seen at once that Columbus and his brothers were no longer at the head of affairs. This newcomer, so obviously a nobleman, was the Sovereigns' appointee. Now, as had happened before, people came freely to the Sovereigns' delegate, with all the stories of their complaints and wrongs. "The very stones," as Herrera says, "rose up against Columbus and his brothers."

Humiliation

The Admiral went home in chains.

Bobadilla swiftly decided after hearing the complaints, and receiving the depositions of the Sovereigns' subjects, that the Viceroy must be returned to Spain. It was the manner in which he did it that must excite disgust. The Sovereigns' instructions had been that an investigation into the affairs of the colony should be held and that, if necessary, the Viceroy and any others concerned in the administration should be sent back to Spain, where they would have to give a full account of their doings. There had been nothing in this about returning so distinguished a man as Columbus as if he was a common thief.

The fact of the matter was that Bobadilla as a Spanish aristocrat could not help disliking the Columbus brothers, even before he had left Spain for the Indies. They were common-bred upstarts and foreigners. It now appeared from all he had heard at court, as well as from returned colonists, that they were abusing true-born Spaniards and more probably than not were pocketing the gold that rightly belonged to their Majesties. Diego, who had refused to hand over some other prisoners due for execution, was the first to be clapped in irons. Bobadilla, who had the townsfolk of Santo Domingo solidly behind him, exerted not only his official authority but used the power of the mob. Columbus himself was then ordered to appear, and when he did so, as a dutiful servant of Ferdinand and Isabella, he too was ironed and put in the town jail. All this was without any formal trial. The Adelantado was still away with a comparatively large body of men and could almost certainly have re-sisted arrest, or even stormed Santo Domingo and released his brothers. It was solely on the Admiral's advice that he gave himself up peaceably. Bobadilla had certainly exceeded his authority. Physically he had triumphed, but morally it was Christopher Columbus who had won. Bobadilla now compounded his error by occupying the Admiral's house, taking possession of all his effects, including money and private papers, and by making a proclamation that the colonists need only pay one seventh of any gold they found to the Crown, rather than one third as had previously been the case. Las Casas, who never disguises his dislike of some of the actions of Columbus, nevertheless condemns Bobadilla for his behaviour. He dismisses nearly all the charges against the Admiral.

It was Columbus's own cook, Espinosa, says Las Casas, who rivetted the fetters on the Admiral's legs. No one else was prepared to do it. No man is a hero to his own valet, it has been said, and in this case clearly not to his cook either. In October 1500, just eight years since he had first sighted that outlying Bermudan island, Guanahaní, Columbus was embarked once more; this time in a caravel for Spain as a chained prisoner. With him went Diego, while Bartholomew was in another caravel. It was the anguish of total humiliation for a very proud spirit. As Columbus wrote in a letter which he later sent to a friend at court, Dona Juana, the governess of the Infante: "If I had stolen the Indies and given them to the Moors, I could not have met with more enmity in Spain." He went on to say – and with a great deal of justification – that he was being judged as if he had been a governor who had been sent to Sicily, "or to a city or town under regular government, where the laws have long been laid down and people are used to observing them". He pointed out that he should be judged as "a captain who sailed from Spain to the Indies and who had conquered a numerous and warlike [here he was not telling the truth] people, whose customs and religion are very different from ours, a people who live in mountains and who have no permanent townships. There by the will of God I have made the King and the Queen sovereigns of another world. . . ."

It is impossible not to feel the deepest sympathy for Columbus at this moment in his life. The Admiral of the Ocean Sea, one of the greatest sailors of all time, was being shipped back home like a criminal. Perhaps in one sense he deserved it. The sin of pride had overmastered him. He had all along maintained that he was going to hand the Indies to the Sovereigns. By now he must surely have known that he was not in Marco Polo's Cathay. Not a single thing that he had encountered had conformed to Polo's or Mandeville's descriptions of the Far East. But it was certainly not his fault that he had come up against a totally new colonial situation. Generations of people of Spanish or Portuguese blood were to fail in their administration of the vast sub-continent of South America.

So the Admiral went back in chains. When he reached Spain he was to keep his fetters ever after as a memento of his humiliation. "I remember," says his son Ferdinand, "that he always kept them in his room and that he gave orders that he was to be buried with them." Columbus was not going to allow anyone to forget what had been done to him. When Andrés Martin, the master of the caravel, and the hidalgo Alonso de Vallejo (who had been given the unwelcome task of being the Admiral's custodian) came to him, and suggested that they would like to remove his chains, he refused. They had been put there, as he understood it, by royal command, and only the authority of the Sovereigns could have them struck off. Columbus was going to make vast capital out of those chains. Bobadilla, quite apart from anything else, had committed a very stupid action. Had he returned the Admiral and Viceroy in full dignity it is possible that the sentiments running against him in Spain would have continued, or even been reinforced. As it was, the spectacle of the great discoverer treated in such a manner was to evoke a wave of popular sympathy.

The caravels had fair winds all the way home, and Columbus and his brothers arrived in Cadiz in October 1500. He went to lodge in the Carthusian monastery in Seville, still in chains and under escort. The popular reaction was an immediate one of sympathy and outrage. Here was a man who had given Spain a New World – for already the general impression had got about that these Indies were not the old Indies – and this was how the King and the Queen treated him! Even so, it was over a month before the Sovereigns gave the order for him to be released. They were in fact deeply engaged at that moment in concluding a treaty with Louis XII of France in connection with the partition of the Kingdom of Naples. Finally the order came for the Admiral to report to court. On December 17, at the Alhambra in Granada, Columbus fell on his knees before Ferdinand and Isabella. "With tears," say Oviedo, "he implored them to forgive him for his errors. When they heard him they extended their clemency and gave him words of consolation." Columbus always knew the way to Isabella's heart, "for the fact was that she more than the king always favoured and defended him . . ." The Queen herself is said to have burst into tears at the spectacle of her Admiral so dejected and debased. But, despite all their conciliatory words, it is quite clear that the Sovereigns had made up their minds that he was incapable of governing the lands which he had discovered for them. In this way they were quite right but, as the subsequent history of Spanish colonialism was to show, very few other men were either. Bobadilla did not, as some have made out, fall into disfavour, or lose the good opinion of the rulers. The Admiral might certainly keep his titles, but that of Viceroy was in future no more than nominal. As Admiral of the Ocean Sea he would once more sail along the coasts of this New World, but he would never again administer any part of it.

The Columbus brothers were pardoned for their mismanagement of affairs in Hispaniola, but there was never any intention of putting them back in positions of responsibility. The fact was that news was coming in thick and fast of the existence of this great continent. Other Spaniards, among them Hojeda and Peralonso Niño, as well as an ambitious Italian, Amerigo Vespucci (who was to give his name to America) were profiting by the Columbian discovery. Using copies of the charts he had sent back to Spain they were already scudding along the fringes of the mainland.

Ferdinand had repented more and more of the concessions he had made to Columbus – that he should be governor-general of all the new lands and receive an eighth of the profits. Had it been just a trading station, as he had at first envisaged, then it would have been more or less acceptable. But it was becoming clear that a continent was unfolding, some vast territory that would make Spain the richest and most powerful country in the world. Columbus and his brothers, by their maladmini-

Columbus and his brother arrested by Bobadilla to be sent home in chains.
From Theodore de Bry, 1594.

stration of Hispaniola, had given Ferdinand the opportunity to deprive them of effective financial control. He felt that in an honest nobleman like Bobadilla he had found the effective instrument to put Hispaniola on its feet and, in due course, he would find others of the same stamp to administer these territories – in the service of Spain and not of Genoese adventurers. The Admiral was clearly a remarkable seaman, and Ferdinand certainly conceded that he owed the discovery solely to this man. Well, he would make use of his services yet again – in the capacities of admiral, explorer, discoverer, but not of Viceroy. One cannot help suspecting that all along Bobadilla had secret instructions from the Sovereigns to return the Columbus brothers in disgrace if there was anything wrong in Hispaniola. They certainly knew that there was, from the many reports that had come back ever since the foundation of the colony. They had given Columbus, Bartholomew, and Diego, enough rope to hang themselves – which they had done.

The Sovereigns temporised. They had many political preoccupations, among them the marriage of their youngest daughter, Catherine of Aragon, who was fifteen-years-old, to Prince Arthur of England. (Arthur died within a year, and she subsequently became the first wife of Henry VIII. It was his divorce from her that caused Henry's break with the Papacy.) Columbus complained in a letter to an old friend Fra Gaspar Gorricio that "There is always something going on here that puts every-thing else in the background. The Princess left this morning, so perhaps now something will be done about the Indies." While he waited idle for many months, Columbus had the comfort of seeing his two sons con-stantly at court, Diego now twenty-one and Ferdinand aged twelve. Ferdinand would come with him on his next voyage. It was high time that he learned something about the trade of the sea. Meanwhile he busied himself with one of his old pre-occupations, the liberation of Jerusalem, and in compiling from the Bible a Book of Prophecies. He was concerned with the whole matter of faith. He had had faith, and he had been proved right when he had sailed due West. "St. Peter, when he jumped into the sea, walked on it as long as his faith was firm." The trouble was that, except as a seaman, the Sovereigns had lost their faith in Columbus.

In the meantime, as the months went by, others were opening up the world that he had found. Adventurers were taking advantage of his unique discovery. Worse was to come. On September 3, 1501, Don Nicolas de Ovando was appointed Governor of Hispaniola. He was to supersede Bobadilla, and it was quite clear from the instructions given to him by Ferdinand and Isabella that, although he was not being given the title, he was in effect the new Viceroy. One thing Columbus did manage to obtain from Ferdinand and Isabella was the concession that the moneys owing to him from Bobadilla were restored. It was now clear to the Admiral, that in the current circumstances the one thing that he must do was to get to sea again. If he had been deprived of Hispaniola, at least he was sure, from the experience of his last voyage, that there were other lands within his grasp.

The new Governor had sailed with a fleet of some thirty ships, and a complement of twenty-five hundred men. On March 14 1502, Columbus was also authorised by the Sovereigns to proceed to the Indies. It seems likely that they were both irritated by the continual presence of this man who had originally badgered them into this whole extraordinary enterprise, and who now hung around the court continually complaining that he was not being employed and that so many of his rights had been taken away from him. Very well, so he had proved his point several years ago, he had discovered new lands (though not the Orient, they were quite sure by now). It seemed likely from his account of his previous voyage that he might be on the edge of something considerably more profitable to the Crown. Unlike Ovando, Columbus sailed with a small fleet of four caravels, and something like one hundred and fifty men. The Admiral was going out not in the capacity of a Viceroy, but as a seaman who might possibly bring back the knowledge of unknown territory. He was a skilled chartmaker, and it was more than likely that he would manage to map some more areas to which the King and the Queen could in due course send efficient administrators.

Amerigo Vespucci after whom America was named. From Thevet's Portraits.

The High Voyage

One thing was made quite clear to Columbus before he left. He was to follow up his discoveries of the previous voyage, but he was on no account to put into Santo Domingo. The Sovereigns were quite adamant on that point. This meant that he was deprived at source of any chance of revictualling, or of the use of any shipyard. He and those with him were on their own in exactly the same way as he and the others had been on the momentous first voyage. Before he left, aware that he was aging and that he might never return, he remembered his native city and made arrangements for investments to be made in the bank of St. George in Genoa. Here, in Henry Harrisse's translation, is his letter of instructions to the bank. It gives something of the flavour of Columbus.

"High Noble Lords: Although the body walks about here, the heart is constantly over there. Our Lord has conferred on me the greatest favour to anyone since David. The results of my undertaking already appear, and would shine greatly were they not concealed by the blindness of the government. I am going again to the Indies under the auspices of the Holy Trinity, soon to return; and since I am mortal, I leave it with my son Diego that you receive every year, forever, one tenth of the entire revenue, such as it may be, for the purpose of reducing the tax upon corn, wine, and other provisions. If that tenth amounts to something, collect it. If not, take at least the will for the deed. I beg of you to entertain regard for the son I have recommended to you. Nicolo de Oderigo knows more about my own affairs than I do myself, and I have sent him the transcripts of any privileges and letters for safe-keeping. I should be glad if you could see them. My Lords, the King and Queen endeavour to honour me more than ever. May the Holy Trinity preserve your noble persons and increase your most magnificent House. Done in Sevilla, on the second day of April, 1502. The chief Admiral of the Ocean, Viceroy and Governor-General of the islands and continent of Asia and the

Indies, of my Lords, the King and Queen, their Captain-General of the sea, and of their Council."

There follows that curious signature of his which has been found on many other documents, and which, like the man himself, has provoked endless arguments among scholars.

$$.S.$$
$$.S. \quad A \quad .S.$$
$$X \quad M \quad Y$$
$$X \, \flat o \, FERENS$$

One of the most reasonable conjectures is that the first four letters stand for "Servus Sum Altissimi Salvatoris", "I am the servant of the Most High Saviour". The next may be an invocation to Christ, Mary, and Joseph; the last is clearly in Greco-Latin his own christian name "Christoferens", the Christ-Bearer. He had been sent into the world to bear Christ over the water, a conviction that had haunted him all his days.

On May 11 1502, the four caravels stood out to sea from Cadiz. They had been detained there for some days by the *vendaval*, the strong local south-wester. But, in Columbus's words, hearing that "the Moors were besieging Arcila" (a Portuguese port on the African coast) "I sailed there to its rescue". This was not only tactful of him, for the Spanish sovereigns and the King of Portugal were now on good terms, but also indicative of his character. The Moors were his eternal enemies, and his abiding dream was still that he would one day restore Jerusalem from the hands of the Moslem. They arrived at Arcila only to find that the siege had already been lifted. An exchange of courtesies took place, and Columbus was delighted to find among the Portuguese gentlemen some relations of his dead wife, Dona Felipa. They then sailed over to the Canaries, stayed there for five days, and took their departure on May 25. "The High Voyage" Columbus was to call it, though for what reasons it is difficult to say, for he took much the same route as before. He fetched up after a sparkling crossing of twenty-one days at the island of Martinique. Then, disregarding the Sovereigns' instructions, he made his way to Santo Domingo.

The Admiral's apologists have made much of the fact that one of his caravels was unseaworthy and that he wished to exchange her. They have also pointed out that he needed to send letters home, and he knew that the fleet was about ready to leave for Spain. What they have ignored – as Columbus did himself – was the explicit order of Ferdinand and Isabella that he should not touch at Santo Domingo on his outward voyage, but that he might, "if it appears necessary, stay there a little while upon your return". Bobadilla had been busy clearing up the mess that the Columbus brothers left behind them, Ovando was only recently installed as governor. The last thing that was wanted in Santo Domingo was the reappearance of the Viceroy, for such at any rate he nominally still was. Columbus could, in fact, have sent the caravel in question, *Santiago*, in which Bartholomew the former Adelantado was shipped, into the harbour alone. Letters could have been handed over, some transaction about an exchange of vessels could have been made, and he himself and his other three caravels could have anchored – as indeed they finally did – somewhere further down the coastline. But no, it was a natural curiosity and a desire perhaps to reassert that he was still, "Viceroy and Governor-General of the islands and continent of Asia and the Indies". Ovando's reaction was very natural. He knew the Sovereigns' instructions, and he refused permission for Columbus and his caravels to enter the port of Santo Domingo. Further humiliation. The Admiral had found the island, he had founded the township and the port, and now he was not even allowed to land.

The next act was like something out of a Greek tragedy. Columbus himself had already been punished for the sin of Hubris, pride, by Nemesis, retributive justice. Now it must be the turn of the men who had opposed him and had destroyed his authority. Columbus had already noted an uneasy swell making up from the south-east and renewed his request to be allowed to enter port. He was sure that a hurricane was on its way. He had been on the fringes of one before, and he had also experienced one when he was at La Navidád. He knew the signs. He sent messages ashore warning Ovando not to let the fleet sail for Spain. There was by far the richest cargo aboard that had ever come out of these new lands, for Bobadilla's efficient if somewhat tyrannical administration had wrung a great deal of gold out of his Indian labourers. One nugget in particular was said to be worth a fortune. Las Casas says it had been used as a dish for a roast pig (adding that the Indian woman who found it was lucky if she had even a slice of the meat). Perhaps what is meant by this story is that the nugget was big enough to have made a dish on which a roast pig could be carried. In any case, this was the first real Spanish treasure fleet of all the many that were to follow over the centuries.

September and October according to records compiled over the past century have the highest percentage of hurricanes in this area of the world, but these can still occur in June and July. The modern seaman has his barometer, whose sharp fall may give him forewarning of the advance of these tropical revolving storms. Columbus, as in everything else, had only his acquired knowledge – his seaman's instinct. Ovando paid no attention to his warning, continued to refuse the 'Viceroy' entrance to Santo Domingo, and went ahead with getting the treasure fleet ready for sea. Columbus prudently moved his vessels down the coast, keeping his eye on the high cirrus cloud overhead and noting, says Las Casas, the great number of dolphins that were leaping out of the water. Some writers have discredited this last observation as being part of medieval mythology. On the contrary, it is noticeable that considerable activity by dolphins or porpoises presages a storm, or at any rate heavy weather. Undoubtedly they feel the advance of a swell – the sea becoming more oxygenated – long before man with his simple (but so-called sophisticated) instruments. It is possible that the small fish upon which they feed come closer to the surface when they too feel the ocean beginning to stir in advance of great waves. At any rate, the old English sailors' adage, "When the sea-hog jumps, Stand by your pumps" has been proved right over and over again. Columbus was equally right.

Ovando foolishly disregarded the advice of the Admiral. He sailed the fleet. In it, among many others, went Bobadilla, who had enchained the Admiral, the unfortunate cacique of Vega Real, Guarionex, who was going to adorn a 'Roman Triumph', and the former chief justice Roldán, whose rebellion had been so largely responsible for the failure of the Columbus regime. All were drowned. On their way through the Mona passage the hurricane struck. Antonio de Torres, Columbus's friend, who was in command of the fleet, was among those who never saw home again. Only a few of the ships, disabled or dismasted, managed to creep back to the safety of Santo Domingo and the mouth of the Ozama river. Columbus, meanwhile, had moved his own four ships westward down the coast and come to anchor under the lee of the land. "The storm was terrible", as he later wrote to the King and Queen. "During that night it badly damaged my ships, dragging them all away so that each feared that the others were lost." He had a complaint to make and he was not going to fail to make it: "To think that I should be barred access to the harbour and the lands which I, by the will of God, won for Spain." Nevertheless, he and his ships – even the faulty *Santiago* – all survived the hurricane.

It was, he must surely have felt, the justice of God. The Sovereigns, who had displaced him from his Viceroyalty, had lost their fleet. Most of the men who had opposed him were dead. Strangely enough, the one ship that got through and carried on its way to Spain was a small caravel carrying Columbus's friend and agent Carvajal. He had been sent to Santo Domingo to ensure that the Admiral's share of the gold, which had been seized by Bobadilla, was restored to him. Carvajal and the Admiral's gold returned safely. It was hardly surprising that there were some who said that Columbus had raised this storm by sorcery.

Having made good their damage, the four caravels put out again, crossed the Windward Passage, and cruised along the southern shore of Jamaica. Then, taking advantage of a good north-easterly, they ran to the south and west, reaching the Bay Islands off the coast of Honduras in only three days. Here the Admiral obtained some evidence that the natives were of a more advanced culture than those he had hitherto met. A large canoe came out to meet them with twenty-five men in the crew, as well as a number of passengers and a cargo of cotton, copper hatchets and bells, and a crucible to melt copper. Both the men and the women aboard wore cotton clothing, colourful and well-cut. The Admiral was delighted by these evidences of civilization. He did a little brisk trading and took aboard one of the Indians to act as his local pilot. He also observed that these Indians had with them a type of nut which they appeared to treasure (they used them as currency). These were cacao beans, destined in due course to form a major industry and to give the western world a new drink. The ships now anchored off Cape Honduras and the Admiral had to make up his mind whether to go west or east. He was in search of that elusive strait which he knew would take him through to the Spice Islands.

Figuring that he was somewhere on the Malay peninsula, he reckoned that the Malacca Strait would accordingly lie to the south-east and he set course that way. Unfortunately he was bucking the prevailing wind and current. For the next month and more the ships were steadily working to windward under conditions which Columbus describes as "terrible . . . with never-ending rain, thunder and lightning". On an average they made good little more than six miles a day – depressing sailing, eternal tacking, and under their lee a dreary shoreline of mosquito-ridden swamps. On August 17 he and the Adelantado, Bartholomew, landed at the mouth of a river, where Columbus performed his formal possession ceremony. He was now, in the name of the Sovereigns, taking over the whole of South America. But still the strait could not be found. It was the most unhappy of any of Columbus's voyages in the Indies, and the most wearing on ships and crew. "I myself had fallen ill and often seemed to be at death's door. I conned the ship from a small cabin I had had built on deck. My brother was in the worst ship and the most unsound, and I felt very grieved because I had brought him to the Indies against his will." He was comforted, though, by young Ferdinand, who seems to have turned out to be a good little seaman, "and as for work he did as much as if he had been a sailor for eighty years".

On September 14 they finally rounded a cape which the Admiral named Gracias a Dios, "Thank God Cape", for here the land suddenly trended away almost due south. They also had a favourable wind and current, which meant that they could lay an easy course after the interminable tacking of the past weeks, which had driven the men to a state of almost mutinous despair. Anchoring at one point off the mouth of a great river (probably Rio Grande, Nicaragua) one of the ships' boats was overturned crossing the bar and the sailors in her were drowned. Columbus named it El Rio del Desastre. Every night, it would seem, following the normal Mediterranean practice when coasting, they closed the shore and dropped anchor. It was a sensible enough precaution when navigating along the shore of an unknown continent.

Still pressing on to the south, they finally reached an area which the natives seem to have called Cariay – another impetus to the Admiral's belief that Cathay was implied. They anchored behind an attractive islet which he named La Huerta, the Garden. It was possibly the island now called Uva, off Puerto Limón in Costa Rica. The natives here were eager to trade, but they had no gold – Columbus's eternal preoccupation. The trinkets that he offered them, and even gave freely as gifts, were all returned. They clearly felt that some magic was implicit in these hawks' bells, glass and jewellery. Finally, as a sign that they wished to be friends, they sent aboard the ships two young girls – virgins – as a present for the sailors. Columbus said that they behaved with "an immodesty scarcely credible in whores", but at the same time it appears that he did not let his sailors get their hands on them, and that he sent them back clothed and with presents. All these things were also returned. This particular tribe of Indians appears to have had a very distinct sense of the necessity of not being put under any form of obligation. When the Admiral himself went ashore next day, along with a notary, and took formal possession of the lands, the natives assumed that this was a kind of sorcery and returned with something like incense which they scattered in the air. What they were witnessing was indeed a kind of sorcery – and one which their descendants were to find out all about in generations to come.

The Deadly Worm

Disappointment followed disappointment. Several times Columbus thought that he had found the strait. He headed into great bays – one of them now commemorates his name as Bahia del Almirante – but none of them proved to be the passage that he was seeking. Persistently he sailed on down the coast of Veragua, trading with the natives here and there, and always hearing about mysterious places like "Ciguare" where there was an abundance of gold and the women all wore coral and pearls. How much of this was in his imagination, and how much was due to the faultiness of his interpreters, it is impossible to say. One must always remember that the ships were little, if anything, over 60 tons, no more than a large yacht by modern standards, and that the crews had no idea where they were. On November 2 they came into an excellent harbour which Columbus rightly named Puerto Bello. This was to become one of the principal Spanish colonial cities in later days, and it was off here that Sir Francis Drake was to be buried at sea in 1596. Columbus was now on the isthmus of Panama, a little east of the modern Panama canal. He kept on inquiring from the natives about the strait for which he was looking, and they made gestures to indicate that it lay not far away. It is possible that they were trying to tell him about the Pacific of which they must certainly have heard. Everything, as always, was very confusing: "In Ciguare . . . they also tell me that their ships have guns, and bows and arrows, and that there are horses in the land, and that the people are warlike. They wear rich clothes and are used to good living. They also say that the sea goes round Ciguare and that it is only ten days from there to the river Ganges."

Only in one place, a small harbour which Columbus named Retrete, Refuge, was there any real trouble with the natives, and this was certainly caused by the Spaniards. The sailors, in search of girls and gold, sneaked ashore at night into the local villages. Finally the Indians assembled in a threatening manner and Columbus was forced to put a shot among them, "so that after this they scarcely dared peep at us from over the hills". It was here also that they seem to have encountered their first alligators. Ferdinand mentions "great lizards", a natural enough comparison for a Mediterranean man, "which are so greedy and dangerous that if a man were asleep on the shore they would drag him into the water and eat him". Columbus by now was losing heart – as his crews had long since done – and the conditions of his caravels was worrying him. The teredo, or shipworm, so prevalent in those waters, had been rasping away in the planks for months, and all the vessels were in very poor condition.

On December 5 he decided to turn back westward. Even the elements now seemed to be against him. The wind, which had been heading them, whipped around and headed them once again. Provisions were growing short, the ships' biscuits were as invaded with weevils as the hulls with teredos, and it seemed as if they would never make home again. Columbus called this whole area The Coast of Contrasts, for whatever he did the wind and the weather was against him. The weather got even worse, continuous thunder and lightning, torrential rain, and "the people were so exhausted that they longed for death to put them out of their misery". There was little shelter in a caravel, their decks had opened up under the sun, their canvas was torn and frayed, the ropes were wearing threadbare, and they had continually to man the sails – dropping them for thunderstorms and then rehoisting for what seemed an eternal beat to windward. Besides all this, "on Tuesday December 13, a waterspout passed the ships". The crew, as Ferdinand tells it, recited the Gospel of St. John the Evangelist, while the Admiral made the sign of the Cross in the sky and, like some other Prospero, traced a protective circle around the small fleet with his sword.

The next hazard, and almost worse than the previous wind, was that they were becalmed. Their stores were so low that they were reduced to eating shark – not so bad as might be imagined, but sailors have always had an instinctive dislike to eating what may have been a maneater. They finally made harbour, probably Limón Bay, the day after Christmas Day. It was hardly the way they would have wished to spend the

Alligator seen on the fourth voyage. Watercolour by John White, c. 1590.

festival, "the biscuits being so maggoty that many men would not eat until after dark so that they could not see the worms in them". As they pressed on westward, determined to find the gold mines of Veragua about which they had heard, they were re-entering one of the rainy areas of the world. Everything stank of damp, and their worn-out clothes were permanently saturated. They were on what was subsequently called the Gulf of Mosquitoes. On January 6, they dropped anchor off a river which the Admiral named Belén, Bethlehem, the name which it bears to this day.

It was here that he decided he would set up his trading post and establish the Spanish presence on the mainland of what was clearly not China, even to the most simple of sailors. "The Lord," as Columbus reported to the Sovereigns, "granted me a river and a safe harbour, although it was no more than ten hands deep at the mouth. I entered with some difficulty, and the next day the bad weather began again. Had I been caught out in it at sea I would not have been able to get in owing to the shallows [the sea was roaring across the bar of Belén]. It never stopped raining until February 14 so that we were not able to land or see anything. On January 24 the river suddenly poured down very high and strong so that my anchors dragged and it looked as if I would lose all the ships. But Our Lord saw to it, as He always does. I do not know if any other man has suffered such martyrdom." The tragedy about Columbus is that he was always on the edge of things. The kernel always escaped him, and it was left to other men to harvest the vast riches of South America.

He goes on to detail his experiences in attempting to found yet another colony or trading post. "It was still raining on February 6 but I sent seventy men inland. Within five leagues they found many mines, and the Indians who went with them led them up to the top of a high hill and showed them from there that, as far as the eye could reach, there was gold. They named all the towns and villages and told them that towards the west the mines stretched for twenty days march. I later learned that the *Quibean* [the local cacique] who had produced these Indians had instructed them to indicate the mines that lay a long way away, and which belonged to an enemy of his . . ." But there was certainly plenty of gold in the area, and this determined Columbus to make a permanent settlement. On a hillock near the mouth of the river he set the men to work and named the place Santa Maria de Belén. Morison succinctly

Opposite: *Portolan chart by Grazioso Benincasa, 1476, showing the Atlantic before Columbus. It includes Antilia and other imaginary islands.*

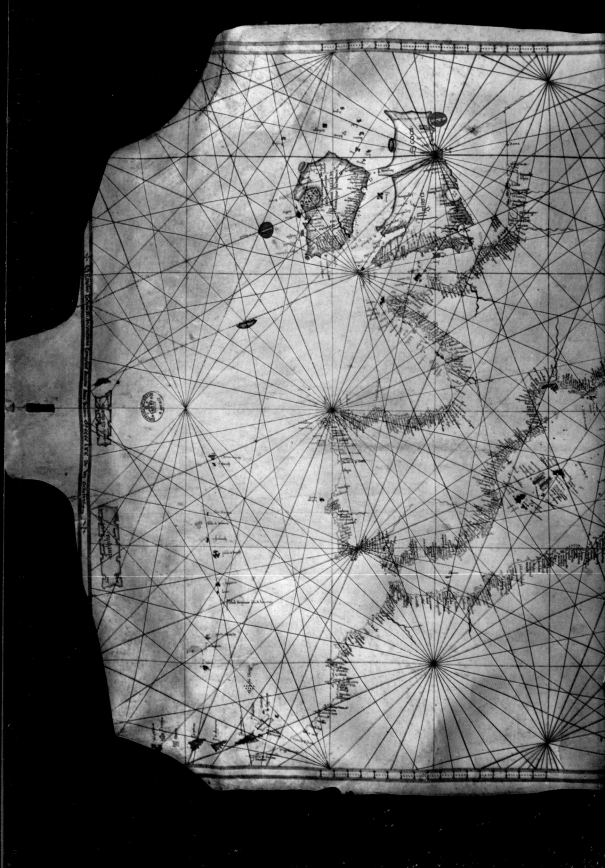

comments: "He had chosen just about the worst spot on the coast of South America to establish a beach-head."

Bartholomew led an expedition into the interior, met some of the local chieftains, and managed to do some brisk trading for gold. The natives and the neighbouring chief had at first been friendly, and the relationship between them and the Spaniards had been good. But when they saw that these strangers were building a township, and clearly intended to settle in their land, their mood changed. Meanwhile the rainy season was over, and the water at the bar of the river had dropped so much that the caravels could not get out. "In January the river mouth was closed. In April the ships were all eaten up with worm and I could hardly keep them afloat." Columbus in all his travels had never been in so bad a situation. One cannot help wondering why he had not by now hauled his caravels ashore, cleaned them off, caulked and pitched them. The only conceivable reason can be, that he had no pitch aboard; something which possibly he had hoped to collect at Santo Domingo. In any case, even the best pitch is little deterrent against the teredo or the gribble worm in those tropic waters. As the Spaniards were later to find out, the only real protection against worm was to plate the whole of the bottom with metal – an expensive procedure, and one that was only justifiable in the case of a vessel of some size and importance.

Diego Méndez, one of the gentlemen volunteers in the ships, having observed the growing concentration of natives, and the whole change in their attitude, now went on a bold reconnoitring expedition. He brought back word that the Quibean had assembled thousands of his followers and it was clear that an attack was impending. Columbus, stubborn as ever, went on with his project: the township where he intended to leave about 80 men behind with his brother, Bartholomew, as Adelantado in command. It was natural enough that having been, as it were, expelled from Hispaniola, and having found a territory where there was every evidence of gold to an amount that he had never before encountered in the Indies, he should determine to settle and trade. It was not to be. Everything was against him: climate, natives, the unpredictable conditions of the river, and the steady deterioration of his ships. In the end the whole project had to be abandoned. One of the caravels, which Columbus had intended to leave behind with the settlers, was also abandoned – to serve, no doubt, as a wonder to the Indians, until it finally sank under the onslaught of the deadly worm.

They were lucky to get away at all. Captain Diego Tristán of the

Opposite: *The open sea off San Salvador.*

Captain Diego Tristan and all but one of a boat's crew were ambushed and massacred by the Indians on the South American Coast. From Theodore de Bry, 1594.

caravel *Capitana*, along with all but one of a boat's crew, had been ambushed and massacred, and the boat itself destroyed. Columbus was suffering from a fever, probably malaria, and was seeing visions and hearing voices. He thought that God himself was talking to him, telling him how He had bestowed the Indies on Columbus and that he must "Fear not but be trustful. All these tribulations are written on marble tablets, and not without cause." Had the colonists stayed it is certain that, even without the hostility of the Indians, the hostility of nature in this part of the world would have overcome them. There has never been any successful European settlement in this area. Yet the Admiral was to write to the Sovereigns that "there is no country in the world whose inhabitants are more timid. Furthermore there is a good harbour, a beautiful river, and the whole place can easily be put in a state of defence." Columbus was a paranoiac.

On Easter night, 1503, the three remaining caravels set sail from Belén. The intention was to call at Santo Domingo – as he was permitted to do on his return voyage – and then head for Spain. Further disaster. Indeed, Columbus's fourth, or 'High Voyage' as he called it, might more truthfully be called 'The Voyage of Disasters'. The ships were riddled with worm and all hands were perpetually busy at the pumps or bailing with any utensil that came to hand. This was not the only reason for their discontent. The Admiral appeared to be going back east along the mainland again. Once more they put into Puerto Bello, and here another caravel had to be abandoned as totally unseaworthy. There were now, apart from those who had been killed at Belén, the crews of four ships packed into two. They fetched up finally on May 13 in Cuba, which the Admiral persisted in calling "a part of Cathay." The ships were literally sinking under their feet, and no one had anything to eat except weevilled biscuit, "and a little oil and vinegar".

Worse was to follow. A gale blew up, in the course of which the caravels dragged anchor and fouled one another, causing considerable damage and losing no less than three anchors in the course of the night. Shortly after this Columbus came to the conclusion that he would never make Hispaniola, through the buffeting of the Windward Passage, until he had made some repair to his ships. He decided to run down south on the port tack to Jamaica. Possibly he still had dreams about the bean-sized nuggets of gold he had heard about in that island. He had little to show for this voyage so far – two ships down, an abandoned settlement, and some breastplates of gold from Veragua. He was a sick man – arthritis and malaria – and he was suffering from the burdens of command, acute mental loneliness and physical exhaustion. The Admiral was drenched with despair.

On June 23 they put in at Puerto Bueno (Dry Harbour) in Jamaica. It is rightly named, for there is no water supply anywhere in the vicinity – a very good reason for moving on as soon as possible for the anchorage that Columbus had previously named Santa Gloria. Here they ran their sinking ships aground. The Spaniards now proceeded to establish the first European settlement in Jamaica. They had a good dry home after all those months of eternal damp, damp from the rain and from their fast-leaking ships. They arranged to trade with the natives, and they no longer had to toil all day at sails and running-tackle. The fact was, though, that they were – in that Spanish word *cimarron* – Marooned.

An Island Prison

The first concern of Columbus was to ensure that the usual trouble did not arise with the natives, upon whom they were all dependent for their food supply. There was one obvious answer to that – no shore leave. This was sensible, but hardly likely to be popular. The indefatigable Diego Méndez, who emerges as the true hero of the fourth voyage, now travelled to the eastern end of the island, made a contract with a friendly cacique for provisions, bought a canoe from him, and made his way back to the two beached caravels. A regular trade was established for fish, maize and cassava bread, in return for trading trinkets. But the main problem remained – how to get home? The ships seem to have been very inadequately equipped for a voyage into unknown waters. They appear to have had no axes, adzes or other tools for making major repairs, or for building another vessel out of the plentiful wood in Jamaica. On future voyages into the unknown areas of the world it was the sensible practice always to have all the equipment, as well as skilled craftsmen aboard, so that in the event of shipwreck another vessel could be built. Columbus had already had one wreck with *Santa Maria*, yet he appears to have come out on his fourth voyage totally unprovided for anything similar. This was a major fault in planning for which he was now to suffer.

There remained only one answer. Send a canoe to Hispaniola and ask the Governor to despatch a relief vessel. The reason why it had to be a native canoe was that the last of the ships' boats had been lost in the blow off Cuba. But who was going to volunteer for a voyage of some 500 sea miles, crossing the tricky Windward Passage, in an open canoe? Thinking of what men have endured in open boats in two World Wars, and what they have done purely for sport, the reluctance of these sailors seems rather curious. No volunteers were forthcoming – except, once again, Diego Méndez. He put a keel on the canoe that he had bought, rigged a mast and sail, and built up splashboards above the canoe's sides. Taking one other Spaniard (whose name we do not know) as crew, and six Indian paddlers, he set off from the harbour bearing with him a despatch from Columbus to the Sovereigns. This letter, parts of which have already been quoted, is a most extraordinary mixture of accurate fact, vivid description, and religious mania. It is indicative of the confused personality of this strange man. Even allowing for the medieval religious climate of his time, and for the natural colouring that this gave to his thinking, Columbus's words come out of a depth of confusion that make them painful to read. He gives an excellent description of a fight between a monkey and a wild pig, goes on to tell of the immense wealth that he is now conferring upon the Sovereigns in this mainland that he had discovered, and then goes wandering off about King Solomon, and how he is convinced that he has found the mines from which Solomon got the gold for the Temple of Jerusalem.

Salvador de Madariaga has made out a fairly convincing case that Columbus was a Jew, a *converso* or convert to the Catholic Faith, and Simon Wiesenthal has recently come up with the same theory. There is certainly plenty of evidence that he was familiar with the Jewish calendar and the Prophets, as well as with the work of the great Jewish historian Josephus – knowledge which one would hardly expect to find in a Genoese mariner of his time. The strange stumbling block in the character of Columbus, the disorder in his thought, might possibly be explained by the fact that he was, as it were, "thinking Jewish" (dangerous enough in the age of Ferdinand and Isabella), while on the surface acting as a very ardent Catholic. There is however absolutely no evidence for Columbus having had Jewish blood. The one thing that is important about him, which the theorists sometimes forget, is that he was a magnificent seaman.

The first expedition by Diego Méndez was a failure. He ran into some hostile Indians at the eastern end of Jamaica, and was very lucky to escape with his canoe and his life. The other Spaniard with him and his native crew seem to have been captured, while Diego managed to make his way back to Santa Gloria. His story alone would make an epic worthy of Homer. He now volunteered yet again to try and make the crossing to Hispaniola. This time, to ensure that he and his companions were safe until they had made their departure from Point Morant at the eastern end of the island, Bartholomew, the Adelantado, took an armed party along the shore. Diego Méndez, together with a Genoese, Bartolomeo Fieschi in another canoe, journeyed along the coast. There were six Spaniards and ten Indians in each of the canoes. With him Diego still had that historic document from the Admiral which concluded:

273

"Let those who have charity, truth and justice weep for me. I did not undertake this voyage for honour or wealth. This is true, for all hope of that is dead . . . I humbly entreat Your Highnesses, that, if God is pleased to allow me out of here, I may be allowed to go to Rome and make other pilgrimages . . . Done in the Indies, in the Island of Jamaica, on July 7th, 1503."

Month after month went by, and still the castaways at Santa Gloria waited for the caravel that would take them off, or for any news to come back that the two canoes had even reached Hispaniola. Nothing, It was almost inevitable that under such conditions some of the men should revolt against the discipline of the Columbus brothers and declare themselves for a free life away from the confines of the two ships. Under the leadership of Francisco de Porras, captain of one of the caravels, and his brother Diego, about half the remaining men opted "For Castile! For Castile!", and set off in some canoes that they had bought from the local Indians. Columbus was ill and weary. He was ageing badly and the climate of his Indies had reduced him even further. He had pointed out in moderate terms to Porras and his followers that they were unlikely to achieve their aim of reaching Hispaniola, but had been shouted down. He now lay in his bunk aboard his beached caravel and contemplated the ruin of his fourth voyage.

Meanwhile, unknown to the Admiral, Diego Méndez and Fieschi had made the crossing. It had not been an easy one and, owing to the Indians having drunk up most of the water supply on the first day, a number of them had died. They had first made the islet of Navassa not far from Cape Tiburon, the western point of Hispaniola, and then they had crossed to the main island itself. From here Diego Méndez made his way inland and ultimately managed to find Ovando, the Governor. The latter was not at all distressed to hear that Columbus was shipwrecked in Jamaica. So much the better. It had been a great mistake of the Sovereigns in the first place to have allowed this 'Admiral of the Ocean Sea and Viceroy of the Indies' to come back at all to a place where he and his brothers had made such a confusion. Bobadilla first, and he second, had managed to get some kind of order into this new territory. It appeared from the account he got from these returned Spaniards that Columbus had now lost four ships, and had nothing to show for it. Yes, Columbus was technically all that he claimed to be, but in fact he was no more than an adventurer who had entered the service of the Spanish Sovereigns for whatever loot he could obtain from an area called 'the Indies'.

Both Bobadilla and Ovando after him have been harshly criticised by those who would make a saint of Columbus, but the fact remains that they both appear to have been men who did their best to make something out of the extraordinary world that the explorer had accidentally discovered. They, no more than he, had an idea of how to cope with stone-age natives, an unfamiliar climate-pattern, an unknown sea, and fruit, fish and flesh of which Europeans had never had any previous experience. Ovando's reluctance to send help to the Admiral may be construed as very natural. He had no wish to have this ageing trouble-maker deposited on his territory. The result was that months passed by before Columbus was granted a ship to take him home.

The mutineers under the Porras brothers failed to manage the crossing to Hispaniola and began to live off the country of Jamaica – in much the same way as those who had first been left behind at La Navidád. There was little hope for the first Europeans in the new-found lands – and none at all in the long run for the indigenous inhabitants. But, for the moment, the real trouble for Columbus and the fifty or so men and youths who remained loyal to him was that the trade for food with the natives began to slacken and die. The Indians were not agri-culturalists, the Spaniards appear to have brought no seeds with them (Phoenicians had done better some 2000 years before, when they had sailed round Africa), and the demand for things like hawks' bells rapidly declined. At this moment in his star-crossed life Columbus was be-friended by the moon. He knew from his copy of Regiomantanus that an eclipse of the moon was due on February 29 of that year, 1504. With the aid of an interpreter he made clear to the caciques around and to the other natives that the God he worshipped was very displeased with the way that he and his people were being treated. The moon was going to die unless the Indians continued to supply them with food. Naturally enough, the locals – who no longer believed that the Spaniards were really superior to themselves – were cynical about this prognostication. But then the moon did exactly as the white-haired, white-bearded chieftain had said it would. The shadow began to draw over its face, and they began to believe once again that this man was a great sorcerer – even if those with him were no more than men like themselves. They raised great howls of protest and came and implored Columbus to stop the moon from dying. He said that he would think about it, retired to his cabin, sat down with his hour-glass and waited until he knew that the eclipse was due to end. Before it did he came out, announced that he had been talking with his God, and that the people had been pardoned.

In the spring of 1504, after Columbus and his men had been over eight months in their strange tenements on the shore of Jamaica, a small caravel suddenly announced itself on the horizon. It had been sent not to

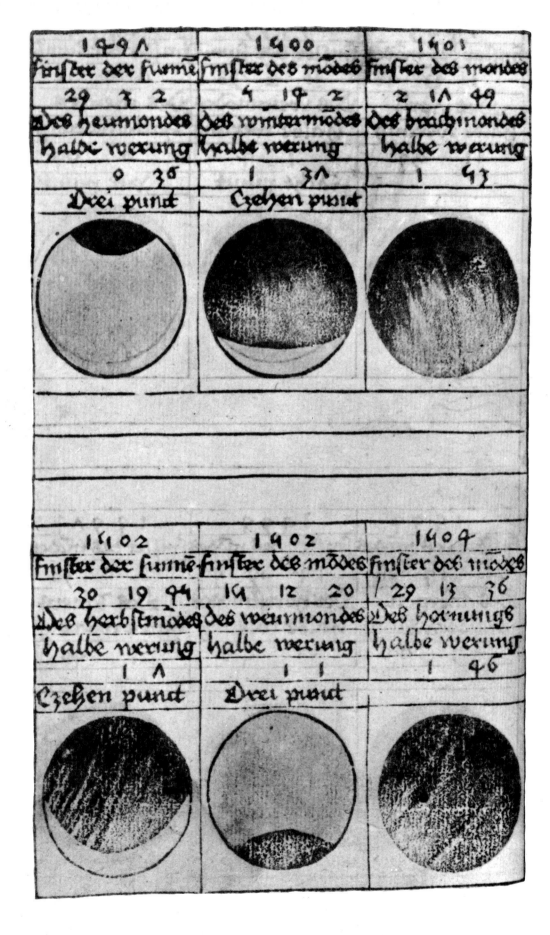

1398	1400	1401
finster der sunne	finster des mondes	finster des mondes
29 3 2	4 19 2	2 18 49
des heumondes	des wintermondes	des brachmondes
halbe werung	halbe werung	halbe werung
0 36	1 38	1 43
Drei punct	Czehen punct	

1402	1403	1404
finster der sunne	finster des mondes	finster des mondes
30 19 44	14 12 20	29 13 36
des herbstmondes	des weinmondes	des hornungs
halbe werung	halbe werung	halbe werung
1 8	1 1	1 46
Czehen punct	Drei punct	

Above: *Jamaica. Map from Bordone, 1534.*

Opposite: *Lunar eclipse. Page from the Ephemeris by Regiomantanus, a copy of which Columbus carried with him.*

take them off, but to report on their condition. Ovando had also carefully chosen its commander, Diego de Escobar, who had been one of Roldán's companions in the Hispaniola rebellion. The meeting of the Viceroy and the former rebel was cool but courteous. He presented Columbus with a side of bacon and a cask of wine, explained that Ovando very much regretted that he had no suitable vessel available at the moment to take the men away, and gave him a message from Diego Méndez that he was trying to obtain a ship. Columbus sent a courteous reply to Ovando saying that he fully understood the situation, and that he trusted that the governor would in due course send a vessel to their rescue. After this strange and somewhat inconclusive meeting the small caravel stood out to sea again. Ovando, one can be almost sure, had hoped to hear that Columbus was dead. The return of Diego de Escobar with the news that the Viceroy and his brother the Adelantado were both alive was depressing.

On May 19 the final showdown came with the mutineers. Columbus had offered them honourable terms of peace which had been refused. Porras and his followers now marched against Santa Gloria and were conclusively defeated by the loyalists commanded by Bartholomew. Porras was captured and the others who survived submitted, and were pardoned by the Admiral. An interesting feature of this first small-scale war between Europeans in the island of Jamaica was that the whole scene was watched by the local natives, who were no doubt delighted to see these one-time god-men hacking each other to pieces.

Rescue came finally on June 28 1504, when two caravels arrived from Santo Domingo. They had been ashore in their unhappy colony for a year and five days. Diego Méndez was to write: "As Columbus told me later in Spain he had never in his life known so joyful a day, for he had never expected to leave that place alive." The voyage back against the prevailing wind and current was slow and tedious – over six weeks to Santo Domingo – but at least they knew that they were going home. They were released from the green prison of Jamaica.

Columbus was received civilly enough by Ovando, although one must suspect that this was mere formality. One of the Governor's first actions was to release the two Porras brothers from confinement. He was thereby, as it were, asserting that Columbus had no power in the Indies to sentence or condemn anybody. Columbus, although he disputed his rights and authority to the very end of the End Game, finally resigned and conceded the match. His chess board was the Ocean. It was only on those dappled squares that he was a Grand Master.

The battle between Porras and his mutineers and the loyalists commanded by Bartholomew Columbus on the island of Jamaica. From Theodore de Bry, 1594.

"Home is the Sailor . . ."

On September 12 1504, Christopher Columbus embarked from Santo Domingo in the same caravel that had brought him from Jamaica. One cannot help wondering what he felt as he looked back at the shoreline of Hispaniola – *his* Hispaniola – as the ship beat eastward against the trade-winds. It was there, all of it, the island, and beyond it the mainland of Cathay, and the edges of the land-mass along which he had stumbled in such misery. He had unlocked for Europeans a vast new continent that he was never to see again.

The passage home was hardly any better than his experience off the shores of Veragua. They set off in two caravels, one was dismasted, and the Admiral, his brother and his son, finally ended up in Spain on November 7 after the worst ocean-crossing of his career. "It is a sure thing," as he was to write to his son Diego. "that I have served Their Majesties with as much diligence and love as I might have used to win the gates of Paradise and more. If I have failed in other matters it was beyond my knowledge and my strength . . ."

Their Majesties were not very disposed to give a favourable reception to this returned Admiral, who had lost them four caravels, who had brought a little gold back with him, and who had only tales to tell of some extravagant land which it seemed – at least to judge from his experience – was impossible to colonise. Columbus was not invited to court. The King had always mistrusted him, and Queen Isabella was dying. Her death on November 26 1504 removed the final hope for Columbus's reinstatement as active Viceroy or even, in a real sense, as Admiral. He was in any case a very sick man himself. Even his brother, much younger and stronger than he, was suffering from ill-health due to his privations in the Indies. Columbus lived in Seville. He had brought back enough gold to maintain a fair station of life, and he also had his tenth share of the revenue from Hispaniola. His elder son, Diego, was now employed as one of the royal bodyguards, and young Ferdinand, now sixteen years old, had been taken back as a page after his strange and exciting time in the new world that his father had found. It appears that, with the simple arrogance of youth, he greatly bored his elder brother, as well as the other courtiers, with his tales of the Indies, the natives, the hurricanes, and the wild world of the sailor.

The last two years of Columbus's life, bedevilled by illness and with the usual preoccupations of the aged – wills and testaments, disputes about his rights, and concern about the privileges that should be accorded to his sons – are sad indeed. His great English peer, Sir Francis Drake, although his life too ended in gloom and failure (off the very coast that Columbus had discovered), was at least permitted to die at sea. Christopher Columbus, ocean navigator, explorer, and one-time Viceroy of all the Indies, was to die ashore. In May 1506 he made his last will, confirming Diego as his heir, and requiring him to look after Ferdinand as well as Beatriz. It had already been agreed with the King that Diego should have the title of Admiral after his father's death. He was, in fact, ultimately to be appointed Governor of Hispaniola. Diego and Ferdinand, together with those friends, Diego Méndez and the Genoese Fieschi, were at Columbus's deathbed. He went out on the tide of May 20 1506, in the city of Valladolid. He had discovered a new continent and never knew it – or never permitted himself to know it. His last words were very typical, for he constantly thought of his trials and tribulations as not so dissimilar from those of Christ "O Lord, into Thy hands I commend my spirit."

Columbus should be forgiven his failures. He should be remembered always for that wonderful first, sparkling voyage – Westward, ever Westward! – across the Atlantic Ocean. He deserves to be called its Admiral for ever.

REQUIESCAT IN PACE

Opposite: *The replica of the Santa Maria in the port of Barcelona, today.*

Short Bibliography

Alba. Autógrafos de Cristóbal Colón. Madrid, 1892.

Bacon Sir Francis. The Historie of the Raigne of King Henry the Seventh. London, 1622.

Barros, J. de. Da Asia. Lisbon, 1552.

Beltrán, R. Cristóbal Colón y Cristoforo Colombo. Madrid, 1921.

Bernáldez, A. Historia de los Reyes Católicos. Seville, 1870.

Buron, E. Pierre d'Ailly: Ymago Mundi. Edit. Paris, 1930.

Colón, Don F. Historia del Almirante Don Cristóbal Colón. The history of his father's life in the Madrid edition of 1892.

David, M. Who was Columbus? New York, 1933.

Documents. The second edition of documents relating to the discovery, conquest and colonisation of the Spanish possessions in America. Madrid, 1885–1900.

Duro, C. F. Colón y Pinzón. Madrid, 1896.

Gómara, F. L. de. La Historia General de las Indias. Antwerp, 1554.

Harrisse, H. Christophe Colomb, son origine, sa vie. Paris, 1884.

Humboldt, F. H. A. von. Examen critique de l'Histoire de la Geographie. Paris, 1836.

Las Casas, B. de. Historia de las Indias. Madrid ed., 1875.

Madariaga, Salvador de. Christopher Columbus. Hodder and Stoughton, 1939.

Morison, S. E. Admiral of the Ocean Sea (2 vols). Oxford University Press, 1940

Morison, S. E. Christopher Columbus Mariner. Faber and Faber, 1956.

Navarrete, M. F. de. Colleción de los viajes y Descubrimentos que hicieron por mar los Españoles. Madrid ed., 1825.

Oviedo, G. F. de. Crónica de las Indias. Madrid ed., 1851–5.

Pulgar, H. de. Crónica de los Señores Reyes Católicos. Valencia, 1780.

Spotorno, G. B. Memorials of Columbus. London, 1823.

Stefansson, V. Edit. Great Adventures and Explorations. New York, 1952.

Taylor E. G. R. The Haven – Finding Art. London, 1958.

Vignaud, H. Toscanelli and Columbus. London, 1902.

Winsor, J. Christopher Columbus. London, 1892.

Index

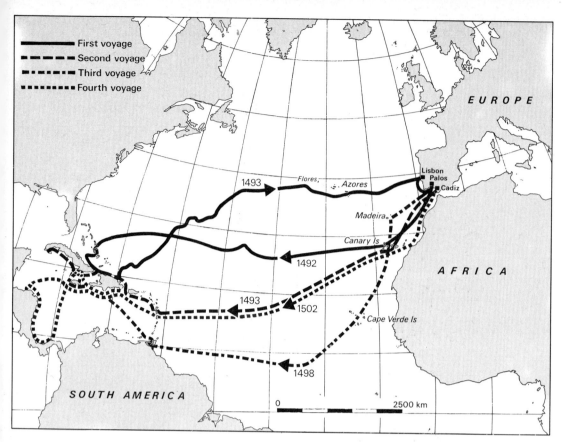

Map of the Atlantic showing the voyages of Columbus, by C. Fisher.

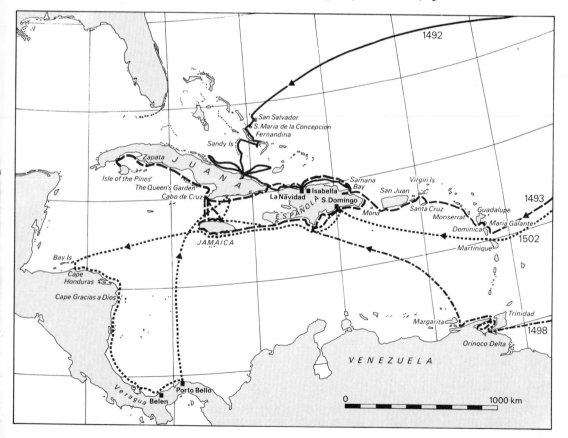

Acknowledgments

The Publishers wish to express their thanks to the following museums, libraries, and other institutions from whose collections works have been reproduced:

Accademia, Venice: 30–31; Addison Gallery of American Art, Andover, Massachusetts: 87; Biblioteca Capitular Colombina, Seville: 39, 79; Biblioteca Marciana, Venice: 57, 58; Biblioteca Nazionale, Florence: 134–135; Biblioteca Universitaria, Bologna: 133; Bibliothèque Nationale, Paris: endpaper, 44, 98, 136, 240–241; The British Museum, London: 18–19, 20, 25, 26, 34, 38, 41, 46, 47, 49, 53, 54, 65, 75, 91, 95, 100–101, 108, 118, 121, 124, 127, 130, 138, 146, 155, 158–159, 165, 175, 181, 183, 185, 188, 190, 195, 204, 206, 210, 213, 219–220, 221, 223, 227, 232–233, 236, 245, 257, 259, 265, 267, 276–277; Collection of the Duke of Alba, Madrid: 139; Kunsthistorisches Museum, Vienna: 150–151, 169; Mansell Collection, London: 23 *left*, 37; Metropolitan Museum of Art, New York: 10; Musée de la Marine, Paris: 1; Museo de America, Madrid: 29, 166; Museo Naval, Madrid: 16, 97; Museo Navale, Pegli-Genoa: 13, 214; Museo del Prado, Madrid: 67, 197; Museu Nacional de Arte Antiga, Lisbon: 32, 37; The National Maritime Museum, Greenwich, London: 2–3, 5, 42–43, 83, 111, 145, 201, 208, 225, 246, 251, 255, 270, 278; Pinacota, Siena: 14–15; Topkapi Museum, Istanbul: 173; Villa Hermosa Collection, Madrid: 23.

All photographs reproduced, with the exception of those listed below, are from the Park and Roche Establishment archives.

Bahamas Tourist News Bureau: 115, 123, 148, 268; Giraudon, Paris: 44, 98, 136; Michael Holford, London: 188; MAS, Barcelona: 65, 68, 139; Stephen Harrison, London: 239, 242; Anne Bolt, London: 187; Radio Times Hulton Picture Library, London: 72; Scala, Florence: 13, 15, 30–31, 57, 133, 134–135, 170, 214; Spanish National Tourist Office: 60–61, 81, 163, 281.

Books and documents referred to in captions of illustrations

Pierre d'Ailly *Imago Mundi*
Girolamo Benzoni *La Historia del Mondo Nuovo*, 1572
Benedetto Bordone *Isolario*, 1534
Braun and Hogenburg *Civitates Orbis Terrarum*, 1572
von Breydenbach *Journey to the Holy Land*, 1486
Theodore de Bry *America*, Part 4: 1594; Part 5: 1595
Aliprando Capriolo *Ritratti di Cento Capitani Illustri*, 1596
Diego Garcia de Palacio *Instrucion Nauthica*, 1587
Fernando Gonzalez de Oviedo y Valdes *Historia General de las Indias*, 1547
Antonio de Herrera *Historia General de los Hechos de los Castellanos en las Islas I Tierra Firme del Mar Oceano*, 1601
Pedro de Medina *Arte de Navegar*, 1545
    — *Regimiento de Navigacio*, 1563.
H. Philopono *Nova Typis Transacta Navigatio*, 1621
André Thevet *Cosmographie Universelle*, 1575
    — *Portraits et Vies des Hommes Illustres*, 1584
    — *Singularitez de la France Antartique, autrement nommée Amerique et de Plusieurs Terres et Isles Découvertes de Notre Temps*, 1558
The Nuremberg Chronicle, 1493